BIOGRAPHIES OF
CREATIVE ARTISTS

GARLAND REFERENCE LIBRARY
OF THE HUMANITIES
(VOL. 1185)

BIOGRAPHIES OF
CREATIVE ARTISTS
An Annotated Bibliography

compiled by
Susan M. Stievater

GARLAND PUBLISHING, INC. • NEW YORK & LONDON
1991

Library of Congress Cataloging-in-Publication Data

Stievater, Susan M., 1939–
    Biographies of creative artists : an annotated bibliography /
compiled by Susan M. Stievater.
        p.   cm. — (Garland reference library of the humanities ; vol.
1185)
    Includes bibliographical references and indexes.
    ISBN 0-8240-4948-9
    1. Artists—Biography—Bibliography. 2. Arts—Bibliography.
I. Title. II. Series.
Z5938.S75 1991
[NX90]
016.7'0092'2—dc20
[B]   91-6744
                                                                                              CIP

Printed on acid-free, 250-year-life paper
Manufactured in the United States of America

DEDICATION

This book is dedicated to my mother and my late father, avid readers.

CONTENTS

PREFACE

This annotated bibliography of significant book-length
biographies of creative artists in English is highly selective.
Some very significant artists are not listed because their
biographies did not meet my criteria for inclusion. Some minor
artists are included as they did have a biography that met these
criteria. This work evaluates the biographies of this most
interesting group of people.

My criteria for inclusion were: the major emphasis of the
book is biographical as opposed to a study of the artist and/or
his or her work; the work covers the creative life of the
individual; it is a significant biography of the individual; the
book is readable. If not all of these criteria were met, that
fact is noted in the annotation.

I define a creative artist as someone who has contributed to
the fields of literature, the visual arts, music, theater and
dance. A narrower definition of the creative artist is one who
created the art as opposed to one who interpreted the art. In
reality I found few significant biographies of the latter. So
this book is primarily about the creative writer, composer,
visual artist and choreographer.

The creative artists are entered in alphabetical order and
are briefly identified. Then the biography or biographies are
listed with brief annotations. There are four indexes at the end
of the listing of the subjects: Art Form Index, a list by kind of
artistic activity; Country of Origin Index, a list by nationality
and chronologically within that nationality; Women Creative
Artists Index, a list of the women artists selected for this
book; Author Index, a list of the authors of the biographies
included in the book.

All of the names are listed according to the Library of
Congress, which may or may not correspond to your library's
entries. The present method is that, generally, if an author is
better known under his or her pseudonym, then the pseudonym is
used. The date(s) of the artist are those listed by the Library
of Congress. More recently the Library of Congress has not added
a death date in some cases, so this was verified in other
sources. The nationality of the individual is established by
general consensus. Not all sources agree with either the
nationality or some or all of the fields of activity. A few
individuals spent a significant part of their lives in two
countries and these few are listed under both in the index by
nationality.

Each book citation was verified using the Library of Congress cataloging and classification scheme whenever possible.

This bibliography was compiled from a preliminary list of about 3,000 titles taken from bibliographies given in general, subject and biographical references. Book reviews were used to evaluate the biographies. The artist is briefly identified using the general and subject encyclopedias as well as information from the books listed. The annotations of the books are compiled from book reviews and from the examining of the book. There were discrepancies in the information about the artists. The compiler takes the responsibility for the choice of facts and opinions used.

Susan M. Stievater

ACKNOWLEDGMENTS

The compiler wishes to thank the many individuals who
assisted either directly or indirectly with this work. The
inspiration for this book is from the book

Gedo, John E. **Portraits of the Artists: Psychoanalysis of
Creativity and Its Vicissitudes.** New York: The Guilford Press,
1983.

as well as the many people I have met who love to read
biographies and whose interest in the area spurred me on as a
librarian to fill the need for a book to evaluate biographies.
   I am especially grateful to the Information Services
Department at E. H. Butler Library, Buffalo State College for so
graciously filling in for me during the sabbatical leave
that I took to research and write this book. I also wish to
thank the librarians at Butler Library who assisted and supported
me. Of special note are Carol Richards, Head of the
Information Services Department, Marjorie Lord, and Elizabeth
Plewniak of the Interlibrary Loan Department of Butler Library
and Dr. Morris I. Stein, New York University. I am grateful for
a research grant from the United University Professionals.
   I appreciate the help of my mother, my nephew, Katherine
Hill and Carol Richards with the manuscript.

Biographies of
Creative Artists

ADAMS, Ansel (1902-84), American photographer

Although trained as a pianist, Ansel Adams at the age of
twenty-eight, through the inspiration of the photographer Paul
Strand, decided to concentrate fully on photography. He was one
of this century's most important photographers. His black and
white photographs of the pristine landscapes of the American
West, especially of its national parks, show an incredible use of
masses of light. He was a founder, with Imogen Cunningham,
Edward Weston and others, of the influential Group F/64. His
love for the beauty of nature urged him to work for the
preservation of this Western environment.

Newhall, Nancy. **Ansel Adams: The Eloquent Light, His
Photographs and the Classic Biography.** rev. ed. Millerton, N.Y.:
Aperture, 1980. 175 p.
TR140.A55.N48 1980

Written by a close friend of the photographer, this
biographical tribute, exquisitely illustrated, reveals the
photographer as artist, as he speaks in his own words of some of
the fundamental issues of art: realism, abstraction, and
communication. A creative personality is brought to life in the
art of photography.

Adams, Ansel. **Ansel Adams, an Autobiography.** with Mary
Street Alinder. Boston: Little, Brown, 1985. 400 p.
TR140.A3.A33 1985

This autobiography, warmly written, shows the genius of the
artist and the compassion of the man. It is strikingly
illustrated by more than 250 photographs, some seen here for the
first time, and printed with a laser technology so refined as to
make the photographs vividly alive. Not only is the
incorporation of his work into this book exceptional, this is an
outstanding documentary of an American photographer and
photography finished by Mary Street Alinder after his death in
1984.

AGEE, James (1909-55), American writer

An American writer who wrote distinctively in a variety of
literary forms, James Agee used his creative writing as
autobiography. His 1934 volume of poetry, **Permit Me Voyage,** was
published by the Yale Series of Younger Poets. His novel,
recalling the loss of his father at the age of seven, **A Death in
the Family,** won the 1958 Pulitzer Prize. A friendship with a
priest from his days at a boarding school resulted in an exchange
of letters that extended until Agee's death and have been

3

published. He worked at various times in his life for the magazines **Time, The Nation** and **Fortune.**

Bergreen, Laurence. **James Agee: A Life.** New York: Dutton, 1984. 476 p.
PS3501.G35.Z59 1984

This seminal biography of James Agee, based on previously unpublished letters, memoirs and interviews, presents candidly his painful existence with his writer's blocks, bouts with alcoholism and stormy marital life. Despite the potentially exploitive nature of such an undertaking, Laurence Bergreen writes dispassionately of his subject.

AIKEN, Conrad (1889-1973), American poet

As a youngster Conrad Aiken found his mother murdered by his father, who took his own life. This experience haunted his eighty-four years and resulted in his writing poetry as a kind of therapy. To live was pain, to write release. Some critics feel he had more published than was publishable. Nevertheless he is known as a poet. His best poetry was written in his forties. He tried to "rewrite" those years unsuccessfully later. He did, however, hold the chair in poetry at the Library of Congress from 1950 until 1952 and won the National Medal for Literature in 1969.

Butscher, Edward. **Conrad Aiken, Poet of White Horse Vale.**
Vol. 1- Athens: University of Georgia Press, 1988- 498 p.
PS3501.I5.Z59 1988

This is the first of two volumes on Conrad Aiken and chronicles his life through his late thirties. Despite the mixed reviews as to his real creativity, his life is interesting. Two volumes may be more than we need to know of Conrad Aiken, but then Aiken had published more than we needed to read of him. So far Edward Butscher has written a thoroughly researched work of a creative personality.

ALAIN-FOURNIER (1886-1914), French writer

The author, killed in World War I, wrote the masterful novel, **The Wanderer,** based on his obsession with a woman. After working on it for six years, he published it the year before his untimely death. It is autobiographical in its references to his childhood lived in the idyllic landscapes of France. It influenced writers dissatisfied with the realism and naturalism of contemporary literature at that time. He also was a poet and journalist.

4

Gibson, Robert Donald Davidson. **The Land without a Name: Alain-Fournier and His World.** New York: St. Martin's Press, 1975. 328 p. (Published in 1953 and 1954 under title: **The Quest of Alain-Fournier.**)
PQ2611.O85.Z65 1975b

Gibson's specialty is Alain-Fournier. This is the second study of the man that he has done. This is a fresh translation of the private writings of a man who lived amidst the rich culture of Paris and corresponded with several prominent writers of the period. The author of only one well known work is the subject of this absorbing biography.

ALCOTT, Louisa May (1832-88), American novelist

Author of more than 270 works, Louisa May Alcott is known primarily for her children's novels. The autobiographical novel, **Little Women,** a portrayal of four sisters, written for adolescents, is also popular with adults. Her father was the noted educator and transcendentalist, Bronson Alcott. He was involved in a number of financially disastrous experimental communities. When the family moved to Concord, Massachusetts, they were neighbors of Thoreau, Hawthorne, Margaret Fuller and Emerson. The latter befriended her and helped her launch her writing career. The money earned from her writings salvaged her family's financial situation. She worked for the abolition of slavery, the Temperance movement and women's suffrage. Ironically, she died a few days after her father who wielded power over her life despite her success as an author and in movements which showed an independent spirit.

Saxton, Martha. **Louisa May; a Modern Biography of Louisa May Alcott.** Boston: Houghton Mifflin, 1977. 428 p.
PS1081.S2

Although she has been the subject of numerous biographies and included in biographies of her father, this book breaks new ground in portraying Louisa May's excessive devotion to her parents, her self-destructiveness, thwarted sexuality, her occasional use of morphine. It is a valuable insight into a woman of the Victorian age who lived many contradictions, both a successful writer and involved in the issues of the day and a dutiful daughter whose devotion to her father stifled a possibly greater contribution to society.

Worthington, Marjorie Muir. **Miss Alcott of Concord; a Biography.** Garden City, N.Y.: Doubleday, 1958. 330 p.
PS1018.W6

This biography received mixed reviews when it came out. It
is well researched and presents a true picture of Louisa May
Alcott most of the time. Unfortunately, because her rather
restricted life was not overly dramatic, the biographer
conjectures about parts of her life. However, it is worthy of
being read as a portrait of this widely read transcendentalist
children's writer.

ANDERSON, Maxwell (1888-1959), American playwright

Maxwell Anderson's reputation as a dramatist has been in a
decline, but it reached its peak in the 1930's. He wrote mostly
verse plays, which critics now consider to be clumsy with
unrealistic plots. His best known play, in prose, is **What Price
Glory?** (1924). He won the Pulitzer Prize for the 1933 comedy
Both Your Houses. His life was as dramatic as his works as he
struggled for elusive love and gave generously of his money at
great cost to himself.

Shivers, Alfred S. **The Life of Maxwell Anderson.** New York:
Stein & Day, 1983. 397 p.
PS3501.N256.Z89 1983

Alfred Shivers shows the drama in the life of Maxwell
Anderson in this in-depth biography. Despite his present
reputation as a dramatist, he was a powerful influence during a
most important period of the American theater. Shivers, in this
first substantial biography, brings Anderson to life in an
exceptional way.

ANDERSON, Sherwood (1876-1941), American author

Ultimately known as a short-story writer and critic as well
as a novelist, Sherwood Anderson successfully managed a paint plant
in Ohio before launching his literary career at the age of
thirty-seven. His contribution to the short story genre was his
concentration on the psychological aspect rather than the story
line. Among his best known works is **Winesburg, Ohio,** a group of
related stories of midwesterners with such shattered lives as to be
called "grotesques" by its author.

Townsend, Kim. **Sherwood Anderson.** Boston: Houghton Mifflin,
1987. 370 p.
PS3501.N4.Z87 1987

There have been attempts to write the life of Sherwood
Anderson previous to Mr. Townsend, but none penetrated the inner
journey of Anderson through his stint in the military, his
business careers, writings, restless wanderings and marriages.

Mr. Townsend chronicles his leaving the creative writing scene to become a newspaper publisher and journalist. Sherwood Anderson's writings have been the subject of many critics but until this book, he lacked a good major biography.

ANTHEIL, George (1900-59), American composer

Musical composition that incorporated other than standard instruments caused Antheil to be nicknamed the "bad boy" of music. He wrote a number of film scores, operas and ballets. He also was a writer of a mystery, containing a prophetic warning of World War II, and his autobiography.

Whitesitt, Linda. **The Life and Music of George Antheil, 1900-1959.** Ann Arbor, Mich.: UMI Research Press, 1983. 351 p. ML410.A638.W5 1983

This revised doctoral dissertation on Antheil received mixed reviews. At times fascinating and readable is its account of a man who, some felt, wrote music with seemingly no knowledge of its basic elements.

APOLLINAIRE, Guillaume (1880-1918), French poet

Better known for his contributions to the history of art, Apollinaire was a poet of some renown. Considered his masterpiece was his 1913 "Alcools," translated into English nearly fifty years later. In this work, a collection of poems, the poet radically combined traditional rhyming with free verse. The son of a Polish aristocrat, he was raised in Monte Carlo and then was associated with the Parisian art scene of the 1910's. He also wrote some fiction and surrealistic drama. He died two years after suffering a head wound in World War I.

Steegmuller, Francis. **Apollinaire, Poet among the Painters.** New York: Farrar, Straus, 1963. 365 p. PQ2601.P6.Z83

Considered more of an introduction than a full-scale biography, Francis Steegmuller's book intertwines the poetry and prose with the narrative of Apollinaire's life. Several interesting photographs are in the book as well as reproductions of some of the works of art he critiqued.

Adéma, Pierre-Marcel. **Apollinaire.** Translated by Denise Folliot. New York: Grove Press, 1955. 298 p. PQ2601.P6.Z5383 1955

This is not the smoothest of translations but nevertheless very absorbing. It tries successfully to cut through the rather confusing existence of its subject. There are few areas of writing in which Apollinaire did not venture. He is considered a very minor poet by some, an important one by others.

Davies, Margaret. **Apollinaire**. London: Oliver & Boyd, 1964. 312 p.
PQ2601.P6.Z6

Ms. Davies, drawing on interviews and unpublished sources, emphasizes the colorful life of Apollinaire. She places him in the middle of the artistic ferment of pre-war Paris. Again, although a significant poet, it is his connections with the visual art world that is the theme of this book.

ARNOLD, Matthew (1822-88), English poet

Matthew Arnold, a major Victorian poet, had a relatively small, but significant, body of work. His most characteristic works were "Dover Beach" and "The Scholar Gipsy," which embodied his themes of the loss of the authority of conventional ideas and institutions. He was also a professor of poetry at Oxford and for thirty-five years an inspector of teacher training schools. He wrote little poetry after he began publishing literary criticism in 1857.

Honan, Park. **Matthew Arnold, a Life**. New York: McGraw-Hill, 1981. 492 p.
PR4023.H6

This book is exemplary as a literary biography. Ten years in process, nearly three-quarters of the information is new, filling in the details of his childhood and the role of women in his life. Despite the many roles he lived, Honan shows how they flowed naturally from the circumstances of Arnold's life.

ASHTON-WARNER, Sylvia (1908-84), New Zealand novelist

Sylvia Ashton-Warner's first novel, **Spinster**, written in 1958, was warmly received. Her other novels about the problems of women and her nonfiction about education have made her an important writer in women's and educational circles. Her personal life was punctuated by periods of mental illness and tempestuous relationships with both men and women.

Hood, Lynley. **Sylvia! The Biography of Sylvia Ashton-Warner**. New York: Viking, 1988. 264 p.
PR9639.3.A8.Z66 1988

This lively account of Sylvia Ashton-Warner looks at her feeling of being "a rampaging male artist," who left the child care and housekeeping responsibilities to her husband. This book both clarifies and heightens the enigma of Sylvia.

AUDEN, W.H. (Wystan Hugh) (1907-73), Anglo-American poet

Educated at Oxford, Auden immigrated to the United States at the age of thirty-two. Some critics feel his best poetry was written in his twenties. He broke new ground with his unusual meters and images, for example, juxtaposing the industrial theme with nature. He received several distinguished prizes for his poetry and influenced a new generation of poets by his lecturing in the United States and England. The years before his death he was considered the outstanding living poet writing in English.

Carpenter, Humphrey. **W.H. Auden, a Biography.** Boston: Houghton Mifflin, 1981. 495 p. PR6001.U4.Z636 1981.

Carpenter draws a sensitive portrait of Auden in this scholarly biography. Auden is seen as an intellectual whose later poetry, also considered his best in terms of poetic style, reflects his intellectualism. His striving for personal relationships and his eccentricities are also explored.

Osborne, Charles. **W.H. Auden; the Life of a Poet.** New York: Harcourt Brace Jovanovich, 1979. 318 p. PR6001.U4.Z764 1979

The strength of this well researched and readable book is in its first half, which describes Auden's upbringing. The second half of the book seems to be a report of his life and does not delve as deeply as the first half does.

AUSTEN, Jane (1775-1817), English novelist

Jane Austen's six novels are considered among the greatest in English literature, yet she had to publish her first, **Sense and Sensibility,** herself. Despite her rather reclusive lifestyle, this daughter of a clergyman was most perceptive. **Pride and Prejudice,** Austen's best known work, displays her psychological probings about middle-class society at that time. She had a select group of admirers in her lifetime, among them Sir Walter Scott. Austen is said to have influenced Henry James and other later writers.

Halperin, John. **The Life of Jane Austen.** Baltimore, Md.:
Johns Hopkins University Press, 1984. 399 p.
PR4036.H24 1984b

This is a fairly balanced biography of Jane Austen
considering most of the sources were her own letters. Halperin
tries to penetrate her life through her novels as her lifestyle
does not lend itself to interpretation. The minutiae of the
Austen household were her life. Halperin is criticized for
manipulating his sources as well as exhibiting a love-hate
relationship with Jane Austen.

AVERY, Milton (1885-1965), American painter

Although considered an influence for the abstract
expressionist movement after World War II, Avery, in his oils and
watercolors, employed a vanguard figurative style. He was
influenced by the art of Matisse and left a substantial number of
works.

Haskell, Barbara. **Milton Avery.** New York: Whitney Museum of
American Art in Association with Harper & Row, 1982. 223 p.
ND237.A85.H37 1982

This is primarily a catalog of the Avery exhibit at the
Whitney Museum of American Art. It does, in its biographical
section, integrate in a sensitive, scholarly way his life from a
working-class background and his strong marriage, which supported
his artistic independence.

BACH, Johann Christian (1735-82), German composer

The youngest son of Johann Sebastian Bach, Johann Christian
studied in Berlin and Bologna. At the age of 27 he moved to
England and was master of music to King George III. He had a
profound influence on English musical life and his symphonies
influenced those of Mozart and Haydn.

Terry, Charles Stanford. **Johann Christian Bach.** 2d ed.
New York: Oxford University Press, 1967. 373 p.
ML410.B15.T3 1967

The first edition of this book appeared in 1929 and was
considered the most important study of the "English" Bach. The
first part of the book is biographical; the second part, a
thematic catalog of his works.

BALANCHINE, George (1904-83), Russian-American choreographer

At the age of seventeen George Balanchine joined the corps de ballet of what is now the Kirov Ballet. Three years later he joined the Ballets Russes of Diaghilev and became the company's chief choreographer at twenty-one. After the death of Diaghilev he worked with other ballet groups. He came to the United States in 1934 and worked with a number of unsuccessful forerunners of the New York City Ballet. From 1948 until his death he choreographed, almost exclusively for the New York City Ballet, some 200 works. His was a neoclassical, nonnarrative, mostly nonrepresentational style. He is considered the most prolific and influential ballet choreographer of the twentieth century.

Taper, Bernard. **Balanchine, a Biography.** New York: Times Books, 1984. 438 p.
GV1785.B32.T3 1984

This book is not as comprehensive as one would wish but it is well written. However, Balanchine is, as many geniuses are, an enigma and a man of contradictions.

BALZAC, Honoré de (1799-1850), French novelist

Author of the monumental "La Comédie humaine," consisting of nearly 100 novels and 50 fragments of novels, he used his bourgeois upbringing as the core of the theme of this opus. In boarding school during his early adolescent years he read so voraciously that he had to return home because of nervous exhaustion to attend a local lycée. When the family moved to Paris he reluctantly studied law but was able to persuade his family to support his literary career. He wrote sixteen hours a day. As successful as his literary career was, his debts always exceeded his income. This most energetic genius lived the life of a celebrity, courting women of great beauty and position. He is said to have been the first male novelist to portray women so compassionately. His life has fascinated a number of biographers.

Maurois, André. **Prometheus: The Life of Balzac.** Translated by Norman Denny. New York: Harper & Row, 1966, c1965. 573 p.
PQ2178.M333 1966

A captivating look at the life of Balzac by one of the greatest French biographers. It is very detailed and refers, at times, to sources available only in French.

Pritchett, V.S. (Victor Sawdon). **Balzac.** New York: Knopf, 1973. 272 p.
PQ2178.P74 1973

A penetrating biography of this extraordinary genius of a writer. Of great interest are the numerous illustrations inserted at appropriate places in the text, many in color. Pritchett is a great storyteller with a great story to tell.

Zweig, Stefan. **Balzac.** Translated by William and Dorothy Rose. New York: Viking Press, 1946. 404 p.
PQ2178.Z9 1947

Although the biographies mentioned above supersede Zweig in terms of modern scholarship, his understanding of Balzac's early struggles as a writer is unsurpassed.

BARRIE, J.M. (James Matthew) (1860-1937), Scottish playwright; novelist

Best known as the author of "Peter Pan," James Barrie's greater play was "Dear Brutus," also a mixture of the fairy tale and realism. He wrote a biography of his mother, to whom he was very attached and is said to have never grown up; the theme of the eternal childhood appears in "Peter Pan." He loved children but his childless marriage failed.

Dunbar, Janet. **J.M. Barrie; the Man behind the Image.** Boston: Houghton Mifflin, 1970. 413 p.
PR4076.D8

Janet Dunbar had access to documents of the literary estate not available to earlier biographers. She presents a neurotic personality who was driven by the need to possess and be possessed. It is nevertheless a fine biography of this novelist and playwright.

BARTOK, Béla (1881-1945), Hungarian composer

One of the great composers of the twentieth century, Bartók and fellow Hungarian composer Zoltán Kodály searched the folk roots of his country incorporating them into his music. His most prolific period was following World War I. His music is dissonant with irregular chords and tone clusters. Some of his string quartets are considered to be the most important contribution of a twentieth century composer to that genre. Five years before his death he immigrated to the United States. These were years of illness and financial difficulties.

Lesznai, Lajos. **Béla Bartók.** Translated by Percy M. Young. New York: Octagon Books, 1973. 219 p.
ML410.B26.L53 1973b

Lesznai writes a readable life of Bartók with emphasis on his pioneering efforts to incorporate folksongs of his region into his music. He also discusses his creativity despite his poor health and financial problems.

Milne, Hamish. **Bartók, His Life and Times.** New York: Hippocrene Books, 1982. 112 p.
ML410.B26.M54

Milne's book is primarily an introduction to Bartók, written clearly and succinctly and containing many excellent illustrations.

Ujfalussy, Jozsef. **Béla Bartók.** Translated by Ruth Pataki. Boston: Crescendo Pub. Co., 1972, c1971. 459 p.
ML410.B26.U383

Ujfalussy gives details of the social conditions surrounding his life. The translation is very readable.

BAUDELAIRE, Charles (1821-67), French poet

Charles Baudelaire was able to live a life of leisure because of an inheritance. He was a successful art critic but is best known for his poetry. He established himself as a poet after **The Flowers of Evil** was condemned as immoral. Despite his theme of the dark side of humanity, Baudelaire's poetry extracted a beauty from this. His emphasis on the role of imagery had a great influence on modern poetry.

Hemmings, F.W.J. (Frederick William John). **Baudelaire the Damned: A Biography.** New York: Scribner, 1982. 251 p.
PQ2191.Z5.H4 1982

This book details the emotional sufferings that led to his painful demise. His life is uninspiring but Hemmings' approach is sensitively done with an emphasis on the role of Baudelaire's mother in her son's "damnation."

Starkie, Enid. **Baudelaire.** Norfolk, Conn.: New Directions, 1958. 622 p.
PQ2191.Z5.S8 1958

The reader may wish to have a copy of **The Flowers of Evil** when they read this book as Enid Starkie makes numerous references without translating them from the French. At the time the book came out it was considered the most definitive biography of Baudelaire.

BEAUMARCHAIS, Pierre Augustin Caron de (1732-99), French playwright

Beaumarchais is known primarily as the author of **The Barber of Seville** and **The Marriage of Figaro**. He was involved in numerous other activities as a watchmaker, court official, secret envoy and businessman. The playwright was an active supporter of the American Revolution and was imprisoned and then lauded during the French Revolution. He established the first society to protect the rights of playwrights and edited the works of Voltaire.

Cox, Cynthia. **The Real Figaro; the Extraordinary Career of Caron de Beaumarchais.** New York: Coward-McCann, 1963, c1962. 212 p.
PQ1956.C6 1963

Written in a readable style and making good use of primary sources, Cynthia Cox's work delves into the many political intricacies in which Beaumarchais was involved.

BECKETT, Samuel (1906-89), Irish-French novelist; playwright

Samuel Beckett began his working life as a lecturer. In 1932, two years after living in Paris and meeting James Joyce, he returned to Ireland to be a free-lance writer, ultimately returning to Paris to live. He is of the "theater of the absurd" movement and is best known for his play **Waiting for Godot**, written in 1952 and still challenging contemporary audiences.

Bair, Deirdre. **Samuel Beckett: A Biography.** New York: Harcourt Brace Jovanovich, 1978. 736 p.
PR6003.E282.Z534 1978

In a powerful biography written with Beckett's permission, Deidre Bair probes the psychological anguish of this genius whose works are yet to be comprehended by contemporary theatergoers. This book was widely reviewed and, some feel, has altered the way Beckett is approached so influential is this biographical study.

BEETHOVEN, Ludwig van (1770-1827), German composer

One of the greatest instrumental composers of all times, Beethoven was born in Bonn, Germany, but spent most of his life in Vienna. He studied with Haydn and Mozart. He had the patronage of the Viennese aristocracy but also supported himself by concerts, teaching piano and increasingly through his composing. As early as the age of thirty Beethoven was exhibiting symptoms of deafness. He was no longer able to

perform in public. His early music was in the classical style of
Mozart and Haydn. Highly dramatic compositions mark his middle
period. His late period contains his more introspective, more
complex works as his deafness totally enveloped him. His is a
particularly significant musical genius despite his inability to
hear.

Marek, George Richard. **Beethoven: Biography of a Genius.**
New York: Funk & Wagnalls, 1969. 696 p.
ML410.B4.M227 1970

Marek's aim in this biography is to illuminate the music of
Beethoven through greater knowledge of his personality. It
discounts many of the legends surrounding Beethoven.

Solomon, Maynard. **Beethoven.** New York: Schirmer Books, 1977.
400 p.
ML410.B4.S64

Considered at the time of its publication to be the epitome
of Beethoven scholarship, Solomon probes the relationship of his
life to his creativity. The book is based on authentic documents
and reminiscences and places Beethoven within his family and
cultural milieu.

Thayer, Alexander Wheelock. **Life of Beethoven.** Revised and
edited by Elliot Forbes. 2 vols. Princeton, N. J.: Princeton
University Press, 1964.
ML410.B4.T33 1964

Originally written in the second half of the nineteenth
century and revised by three other editors before Elliot Forbes,
this continues to be the classic biography of Beethoven, recent
scholarship not withstanding. Despite these various reworkings
of the original, the basic conclusion of Thayer remains intact.

BEHN, Aphra Amis (1640-89), English playwright; novelist

Aphra Behn's claim to fame is her being the first woman to
be a professional playwright. Details of her life are wanting,
but they do include a friendship with John Dryden.

Goreau, Angeline. **Reconstructing Aphra: A Social Biography
of Aphra Behn.** New York: Dial Press, 1980. 339 p.
PR3317.Z5.G6

Angeline Goreau has thoroughly researched not only the
primary documents of Aphra Behn's life but also the social forces
affecting her life and work.

Woodcock, George. **The Incomparable Aphra**. New York: T.V.
Boardman, 1948. 248 p.
PR3317.Z5.W6

Less thoroughly researched than the Goreau book, Woodcock's
work remains the best introduction to her life. His conclusions
about her and her work are based on clues to her life, not always
considered to be contemporary scholarship but still favorably
reviewed.

BELL, Vanessa (1879-1961), English painter

Less illustrious than her sister, Virginia Woolf, Vanessa
Bell was a part of the Bloomsbury Group. She began her working
life as a designer. She moved on to painting, where her style is
considered a mixture of fauvism and impressionism. She was also
a portrait painter of famous people.

Spaulding, Frances. **Vanessa Bell**. New Haven: Ticknor &
Fields, 1983. 399 p.
ND497.B44.S62 1983

This chronicles the Bloomsbury Group much as most books
about its members do. It takes a sympathetic look at the demands
of Bell's life as wife and mother and her creative output.
Frances Spaulding looks at Vanessa Bell as an artist in her own
right rather than just a support figure in the Bloomsbury Group.

BELLOC, Hilaire (1870-1953), English poet; writer

Primarily noted as a major figure in the English Catholic
literary tradition, Belloc is hardly acknowledged today for that
contribution. Rather it is his light poetry and novels that are
sometimes recalled. Although his literary and other
contributions are nearly forgotten, his controversial life is the
subject of two excellent biographies. He was also an historian
and essayist.

Wilson, A.N. **Hilaire Belloc**. New York: Atheneum, 1984.
398 p.
PR6003.E45.Z893 1984

Wilson makes the character of Hilaire Belloc very much
alive, discussing his various roles in Roman Catholicism at that
time. Wilson, a novelist, writes of the story of a man as a
creative artist with numerous other interests.

Speaight, Robert. **The Life of Hilaire Belloc.** New York:
Farrar, Straus & Cudahy, 1957. 552 p.
PR6003.E45.Z85 1957a

Although the Wilson book, noted above, has superseded this
biography in a number of ways, this was the official biography of
Belloc as requested by his literary executors. Speaight lays
bare the complexities of his controversial life. The book is
possibly better than is the subject.

BELLOWS, George (1882-1925), American painter

George Bellows is considered the best known member of the
"Ashcan School" of painting with its emphasis on the vivid
portrayal of urban life. His background as an athlete influenced
the many pictures of sports events, particularly those of boxing.
In his later years he worked in the medium of lithography and
greatly enhanced its stature to an art form in this country.

Morgan, Charles Hill. **George Bellows, Painter of America.**
New York: Reynal, 1965. 381 p.
ND273.B45.M6

Written almost in the form of a diary, Charles Morgan gives
a detailed and exciting account of the emotional and aesthetic
life of Bellows as seen in the era in which he worked. The book
contains a number of illustrations of his work. Unfortunately
the numerous black and white reproductions are lacking in
contrast.

BENET, Stephen Vincent (1898-1943), American poet; short story
writer

Stephen Vincent Benét won the Pulitzer Prize for Poetry in
1929 for "John Brown's Body," a long epic narrative. He also
wrote some lesser known short stories, novels and the librettos
for two operas, **The Headless Horseman** in 1937 and **The Devil and
Daniel Webster** in 1939. He posthumously received another
Pulitzer Prize for his unfinished epic poem "Western Star."

Fenton, Charles A. **Stephen Vincent Benét; the Life and Times
of an American Man of Letters, 1898-1943.** New Haven: Yale
University Press, 1958. 436 p.
PS3503.E5325.Z62

Charles Fenton based this biography on the Benét papers at
Yale as well as the cooperation of his family. The flow of the
biography is a bit stiff but it is considered the only
authoritative biography of Benét and is successful in portraying

his precocity as a student at Yale as well as his struggles in supporting a family during the Depression.

BENNETT, Arnold (1867-1931), English novelist; playwright

Arnold Bennett was a prolific portrayer of Edwardian provincial life. He used his upbringing in the industrial area of Staffordshire for the settings of much of his work. His highly successful work is a series of five novels, "Five Towns." A disciplined writer, he also authored numerous short stories and some successful plays. He was also a reviewer and wrote nonfiction.

Barker, Dudley. **Writer by Trade; a Portrait of Arnold Bennett.** New York: Atheneum, 1966. 260 p.
PR6003.E3.Z556 1966a

This readable biography emphasizes Bennett as a commercial writer and literary entrepreneur.

Drabble, Margaret. **Arnold Bennett: A Biography.** New York: Knopf, 1974. 396 p.
PR6003.E6.Z715 1974b

Margaret Drabble is a sympathetic biographer, sharing the same lower-class background and Wesley Methodism.

Pound, Reginald. **Arnold Bennett, a Biography.** New York: Harcourt Brace, 1953. 385 p.
PR6003.E6.Z784 1953

This is still the standard biography of Bennett despite the more recent biographies noted above. He challenges Bennett's reputation as the disciplined writer and sees him as a harried man of psychological complexity.

BENTON, Thomas Hart (1889-1975), American painter

Benton is a powerful figure in American art. His so firmly established approaches and convictions alienated even his supporters. He championed the rugged, rural America in his murals. His notorious sexism was flaunted in his approach to his art.

Adams, Henry. **Thomas Hart Benton: An American Original.** New York: Knopf, 1989. 357 p.
ND237.B47.A84 1989

A very objective biography shows an obstinate, opinionated artist whose colorful personality seems to be out of a Twain work. He shows Benton's willingness to depart from the accepted form. The last half of his life is, unfortunately, compressed into a single chapter, which makes for an uneven understanding of the whole man.

BERNANOS, Georges (1888-1948), French novelist

Today Bernanos is best known for his novel, **The Diary of a Country Priest,** and the libretto of the opera, **The Dialogues of the Carmelites** with music by Francis Poulenc. Despite the very Catholic content of these two works, these artistic expressions have universal themes, the frightening experience of the world ungrounded in a spiritual life.

Speaight, Robert. **Georges Bernanos; a Study of the Man and the Writer.** New York: Liveright, 1974. 285 p.
PQ2603.E5875.Z8 1974

Robert Speaight writes a clear, nonpolemic biography relating Bernanos' life to the creation of his literary works as well as to the social and political milieu in which they were written.

BERNSTEIN, Leonard (1918-90), American composer; musician

Leonard Bernstein was known as a contemporary musical Renaissance man. He was primarily known for his conducting and was considered among the best of the present generation. He was the conductor laureate for life of the prestigious New York Philharmonic Orchestra. He conducted worldwide both orchestral and operatic music. A serious composer of both classical and popular music he had symphonies, ballets, choral works and Broadway musicals to his credit.

Peyser, Joan. **Bernstein, a Biography.** New York: Beech Tree Books, 1987. 481 p.
ML410.B566.P5 1987

Joan Peyser's book will appeal to a wide range of readers as it looks at Bernstein in his various musical capacities. It is a well researched, readable biography of a multi-talented composer and musician.

BIERCE, Ambrose (1842-1914?), American short story writer; novelist

"Bitter Bierce" was an author of macabre works about horror, wars and death. He fought and was wounded in the Civil War and after the army became an editor of a San Francisco publication. He then went to England where he had three works published. He returned to San Francisco in the capacity of an editor and brought out his best known collections of short stories, **In the Midst of Life** and **Can Such Things Be?**. His **The Devil's Dictionary** contained sardonic definitions. His restlessness took him to Mexico where he is thought to have died during the Villa Revolution of 1914.

Fatout, Paul. **Ambrose Bierce, the Devil's Lexicographer.** Norman: University of Oklahoma Press, 1951. 349 p. PS1097.Z5.F3

Fatout's theory as to Bierce's kind of writings is more from an inner conflict of his childhood Calvinism, man's imperfections and his lack of desire to improve himself.

BINGHAM, George Caleb (1811-79), American painter

George Caleb Bingham was a regional painter of Missouri. The themes of his paintings were of the riverboatmen and rural life. Among his most famous is "Fur Traders Descending the Missouri" from 1845. In 1856 he studied in Germany and this experience caused him to lose the strength of his older style.

Bloch, E. Maurice. **George Caleb Bingham.** Vol. 1. California Studies in the History of Art, vol. 7. Berkeley: University of California Press, 1967. ND237.B59.B4

This is part of a two-volume set. The first is biographical; the second a catalog of his works. Bloch's emphasis is upon the influences of his art and its style.

BLAKE, William (1757-1827), English poet; artist

A literary genius as well as an exceptional visual artist, William Blake spent a rather subdued life in London. His early education was at home. At the age of ten he went to a drawing school and then was an apprentice to an engraver. He exhibited his first work at the age of twenty-three. His first poems were published three years later. Rather than continuing to exhibit, he produced his watercolors and engravings in book form. His most significant poetry had biblical themes. "The Marriage of Heaven and Hell" is most representative of him. After 1818 he concentrated on his engraving, woodcuts and other visual expressions. Some of his work was destroyed shortly after his death.

Wilson, Mona. **The Life of William Blake.** 3rd ed. Edited by Geoffrey Keynes. New York: Oxford University Press, 1971. 415 p. PR4146.W5 1971

The first edition of this biography was published in 1927. With scholarly updates it has yet to be superseded as the definite biography of the poet-artist. Mona Wilson's research is based upon detailed reflections of Blake's friends and associates. Because of his exceptional creativity, Mona Wilson reflects the need of Blake scholars at the time to defend this exceptionality.

BLOK, Aleksandr Aleksandrovich (1880-1921), Russian poet

Blok is considered the foremost prerevolutionary symbolist poet of Russia and the greatest lyric poet since Pushkin. He riveted his generation with his poetry, a reflection of the fascination of his rich, inner life. His intellectual pursuit in his poetry was to escape isolationism through the feminine.

Pyman, Avril. **The Life of Aleksandr Blok.** 2 vols. New York: Oxford University Press, 1979-1980. PG3453.B6.Z6958

This is truly a masterpiece. Avril Pyman uncovers layer upon layer of the inner life of this remarkable poet. The volumes are heavily footnoted but have significant photographs and gracefully translated verses of his poetry.

Mochulskii, K. (Konstantin). **Aleksandr Blok.** Translated by Doris V. Johnson. Detroit: Wayne State University Press, 1983. 451 p. PG3453.B6.Z6813 1983

The Pyman book has access to more current material, but this book written many years earlier (the author died in 1948) is still important in understanding both the feminine and the mystical in the life of Blok. The translation is, in general, quite smooth.

BOGAN, Louise (1897-1970), American poet

Louise Bogan was the poetry critic for the **New Yorker** magazine in 1931 and for the next thirty-seven years. Her **Collected Poems, 1923-53** won the Bollingen Prize in Poetry, which Bogan's poetry is noted for its lyrical style. Her themes were of the consolations of art and love's limitations.

Frank, Elizabeth. **Louise Bogan: A Portrait**. New York: A.A. Knopf, 1985. 460 p.
PS3503.O195.Z66 1985

Elizabeth Frank's biography had mixed reviews when it was published. She shows the intertwining of her life and poetry but with unevenness. It is sympathetic, at times too wordy and without direction, but a worthwhile look at a woman who was an important influence in the lives of poets of her generation.

BONINGTON, Richard Parkes (1801-28), English painter

Bonington spent much of his time in France where he was an important influence on the emerging school of romanticism. He was both a watercolorist and an oil painter. To both media he brought new interpretations of color, light and atmosphere. His landscapes influenced the Barbizon School.

Peacock, Carlos. **Richard Parkes Bonington**. New York: Taplinger, 1980. 109 p.
N6796.B65.P4 1980

This too brief study, incorporating biographical information, does cover Bonington's whole career as painter and printmaker. The color plates are of quite good quality but the thirty-five black and white reproductions are poor.

BRADSTREET, Anne (1612?-72), American poet

Anne Bradstreet's book of poems **The Tenth Muse Lately Sprung Up in America** (1650), published in England, was the first written in America. Her background was that of a Puritan who came from England at the age of eighteen with her husband. Her subject matter went from historical to domestic. Her later more reflective poems speak of the many deaths in her family, especially those of her grandchildren.

White, Elizabeth Wade. **Anne Bradstreet, "The Tenth Muse."** New York: Oxford University Press, 1971. 410 p.
PS712.W54

The definitive biography of Anne Bradstreet describes her beginning to write poetry as she settled in America and started a family. It looks at her Puritan upbringing and influences of English poetry upon her work.

BRAHMS, Johannes (1833-97), German composer

One of the major composers of all times, Brahms wrote in all major musical mediums but opera. He studied music with his father and at the age of fourteen gave his first public piano recital. His first songs and piano sonatas were published with the help of Robert Schumann, who hailed him as a musical genius. At thirty-five he moved to Vienna where his major works were written, including the "German Requiem" and chamber music. Some of his best works were written at the end of his life, such as his shorter piano works and chamber music for the clarinet. His music is known for its refined craftsmanship. He was his own severest critic allowing only his best to be published. His music is abstract but of the romantic period.

Geiringer, Karl. **Brahms, His Life and Work.** 3rd ed. New York: Da Capo, 1947. 397 p.
ML410.B8.G42 1947

This is the best book available on Brahms. Geiringer is a well-known writer about music. Half of the book is devoted to an analysis and criticism of his music. Geiringer thoroughly researched his life using letters by and to Brahms in a well-organized and readable way.

BRECHT, Bertolt (1898-1956), German playwright; poet

At the age of twenty-four he won the chief German literary award, the Kleist Prize, for his play, **Drums in the Night.** Primarily he was a poet who expressed the "dark times" in which he lived. He began his working life after some education as a medical student as a hospital orderly but moved into writing plays following the "epic theater" movement among other expressions in drama. He collaborated with the composer Kurt Weill on **The Threepenny Opera** and **The Rise and Fall of the City of Mahagonny.** When the Nazis took over in 1933 he went into exile in Scandinavia. He then settled in California where he worked rather unsuccessfully in Hollywood. He also wrote political songs. In 1947 he returned to Europe after being interrogated by the U.S. Un-American Activities Committee.

Hayman, Ronald. **Brecht: A Biography.** New York: Oxford University Press, 1983. 423 p.
PT2603.R397.Z6668 1983

This is not the definitive biography but certainly a readable one using the available previously unpublished sources. Brecht is a very complex artist. He wrote plays and some prose but he is most importantly a poet. However, the other literary efforts are easier to trace. Not only was his creativity seen in his psychological approach but also the political reality was there. He was a phenomenon to whom a biographer may never do justice.

Ewen, Frederic. **Bertolt Brecht; His Life, His Art, and His Times.** New York: Citadel Press, 1967. 573 p.
PT2603.R397.Z617 1967

This is the first biography of Brecht in English. Brecht's involvement in the tumult of the Weimar Republic is well told in this absorbing work. There is more emphasis on his drama whereas it is commonly held that he was primarily a poet.

BRETON, André (1896-1966), French writer

Breton is noted more for his being a theorist of an artistic movement than as a poet, which is one of his literary genres. Nevertheless his prose writings exhibit a great deal of creativity and for this he is acknowledged as a creative writer in the broad sense of the term. He laid the foundation for the surrealism, a multidisciplinary artistic movement.

Balakian, Anna Elizabeth. **André Breton, Magus of Surrealism.** New York: Oxford University Press, 1971. 289 p.
PQ2603.R35.Z59

When this biography came out in 1971 it had mixed reviews. Anna Balakian is criticized for being too agreeable in her assessment of this very controversial Frenchman. However, it is a clear, informative, intellectual work. She was able to interview Breton himself for this biography as well as his family and close associates.

BRITTEN, Benjamin (1913-76), English composer

Benjamin Britten helped revitalize English opera, which had languished since the time of Henry Purcell of the seventeenth century. His early compositions were incidental music. He was not influenced by the avant-garde. Of particular importance was his first opera **Peter Grimes** (1945) and his later **War Requiem** (1962). He had unique ability to wed his music to the text.

Headington, Christopher. **Britten. The Composer as Contemporary.** New York: Holmes & Meier, 1982, c1981. 166 p.
ML410.B853.H4 1982

This is a clear, concise life of Britten, breaking no new ground but well written. Headington exhibits a real comprehension of Britten and his music.

White, Eric Walter. **Benjamin Britten, His Life and Operas.**
2d ed. Edited by John Evans. Berkeley: University of California
Press, 1983. 322 p.
ML410.B853.W4 1983

This biography of Britten approaches him not only from his
vocal works but all his creative activity in the context of music
of the twentieth century and especially his role in the revival
of English opera. The first edition of this book came out in
1948 and was updated to include his last years. It is written by
a devotee of Britten and is criticized for being somewhat too
laudatory. The second part of the book treats his operas.

BRONTE, Charlotte (1816-55), English novelist; poet
BRONTE, Emily (1818-48), English novelist; poet

Charlotte Brontë's life is that of her sister Emily's except
that Charlotte outlived Emily and eventually married a year
before her death. They were raised with five other children by
their father, an Anglican minister, and their mother, who died
when the children were very young. An aunt took over their
upbringing. The five girls were sent to a boarding school during
which time two of the sisters died, possibly because of the
harshness of the school's regime. Charlotte and Emily returned
home to live among the moors and graves of Yorkshire. They left
again for further education and some teaching only to return home
to take care of their ailing father and unstable brother. They
wrote a number of novels and some poetry but it is Charlotte's
Jane Eyre and Emily's **Wuthering Heights,** with autobiographical
references, that are their claim to fame. They are the subjects
of numerous biographers.

Gaskell, Elizabeth Cleghorn. **The Life of Charlotte Brontë.**
2 vols. London: Smith, Elder, 1857.
PR4168.G3

This biography was written at the request of Charlotte's
father. Some of the material to which Gaskell had access was
later suppressed. It portrays her as a heroine, a silent
sufferer.

Gérin, Winifred. **Charlotte Brontë: The Evolution of Genius.**
Oxford: Clarendon Press, 1967. 617 p.
PR4168.G4

This is the most thorough of the biographies, written by a
woman who lived in the same area of England as the Brontës. She
probes Charlotte's genius and corrects the flaws in the Gaskell
work.

Gérin, Winifred. **Emily Brontë: A Biography**. Oxford:
Clarendon Press, 1971. 290 p.
PR4173.G4

This book, published four years after Gérin's one on
Charlotte, distinguishes between fact and fiction in the life of
Emily Brontë. She works through her development as a person and
a writer.

Simpson, Charles Walter. **Emily Brontë**. New York:
C. Scribner's, 1929. 205 p.
PR4173.S5

This book is superseded by the Gérin book but nevertheless
presents a scholarly approach to her life and creativity.

Chitham, Edward. **A Life of Emily Brontë**. New York:
B. Blackwell, 1987. 284 p.
PR4173.C45 1987

This is a refreshing biography which leaves unanswered
questions unanswered and does not try to speculate. Chitham's
biography may appear at times to be about being a biographer with
insufficient material with which to construct the complete life.
A painful life is nevertheless portrayed with full documentation
when possible.

BROOKE, Rupert (1887-1915), English poet

Rupert Brooke's life was cut short at the age of twenty-
eight during World War I. His poetry is considered sentimental
now but at the time it seemed to portray an optimism not seen in
his contemporaries. His best known book is **1914 and Other Poems**.
He was educated at Cambridge and is said to have incorporated the
Gregorian style in his first volume, **Poems,** of 1911.

Hassell, Christopher. **Rupert Brooke; a Biography**. New
York: Harcourt, Brace & World, 1964. 556 p.
PR6003.R4.Z67 1964

This is one of the examples of an exceptional biography, a
biography greater than its subject. Hassell captures the
symbolism in Brooke and nearly every detail of his brief life.
He also gives us a real feel for the history of the time and some
of the poet's notable acquaintances.

BROOKS, Gwendolyn (1917-   ), African-American poet

Gwendolyn Brooks won a Pulitzer Prize for **Annie Allen** in 1950. She continues to write poetry which reflects the African-American struggle in America and is a critic, teacher and philanthropist.

Kent, George E. **A Life of Gwendolyn Brooks.** Lexington: University Press of Kentucky, 1989. 288 p.
PS3503.R7244.Z73 1989

George Kent writes a carefully constructed book looking at the familial and political influences in the life and writing of Gwendolyn Brooks. Brooks' anecdotes add to the enjoyment of this biography.

BROWNING, Elizabeth Barrett (1806-61), English poet

Elizabeth Barrett's reputation as a poet was established before that of her husband-to-be, Robert Browning. She was an invalid at the age of fifteen after a riding accident. She published her first poetry at the age of twenty. Perhaps her finest poetic expression is found in **Sonnets from the Portuguese,** a collection of love poems dedicated to her husband.

Taplin, Gardner B. **The Life of Elizabeth Barrett Browning.** New Haven: Yale University Press, 1957. 482 p.
PR4193.T3

Elizabeth Barrett Browning is the subject of many biographies herself and with her husband. Possibly the best of these is Gardner Taplin's. It was many years in process and used previously unavailable material which added some new insights to her life at the time of its publication.

BROWNING, Robert (1812-89), English poet

Robert Browning ranks among the greatest Victorian poets according to some. His childhood was steeped in culture. His first attempt was not as successful as his **Bells and Pomegranates** covering the writing years of 1841 through 1846 when he married Elizabeth Barrett, at that time a more established poet. They lived in Florence until her death. He returned to England where he wrote **The Ring and the Book,** considered by some to be the most important Victorian poem. He also returned to preserving a more private life continuing to write; his last volume was published the day of his death.

Irvine, William, and Park Honan. **The Book, the Ring, and the Poet; a Biography of Robert Browning.** New York: McGraw-Hill, 1974. 607 p.
PR4231.I7

An excellent example of a serious work employing current biographical scholarship. This detailed work intertwines the poetry and the artist and approaches the delicate relationship of the influence of his mother's religiosity. It also examines Shelley as the influence in Browning's poetry.

Miller, Betty Bergson Spiro. **Robert Browning, a Portrait.** New York: Scribner, 1953. 302 p.
PR4231.M5

This book is a psychological interpretation and should be approached with this in mind. Her thesis is Browning's need to be dominated by women beginning with his mother. Enjoyable to read but written in a very definite psychological vein.

Thomas, Donald Serrell. **Robert Browning, a Life within Life.** New York: Viking Press, 1983, c1982. 334 p.
PR4231.T48 1983

For years Robert Browning seemed to be in the shadow of his wife. After her death he became part of the social whirl but then found it necessary to withdraw from a frenzied existence to preserve his creativity. This is a strong biography that sends the reader to the poems.

BRUCKNER, Anton (1824–96), Austrian composer

This Austrian is more widely acclaimed today than when he was composing. His nine significant symphonies are considered a link between the Viennese classical school of Haydn and Beethoven and Mahler and Schoenberg of the late nineteenth and early twentieth centuries. His early years were influenced by his training and later teaching in the monastery of St. Florian. In Linz two teachers broadened his musical maturity, culminating in the "Mass in D minor" of 1864. In 1868 he returned to Vienna where he taught and established a reputation as a virtuoso organist. His critics attacked his greatest works, his symphonies. He allowed them to revise them but kept the original manuscripts, which are the ones used today.

Schönzeler, Hans Hubert. **Bruckner.** Library of Composers, vol. 3. New York: Grossman Publishers, 1970. 190 p.
ML410.B88.S24

Schönzeler has written a credible but rather brief biography of this complex man. The issue of his own revisions and his allowing others to revise his works takes a predominant place in this book.

BRYANT, William Cullen (1794-1878), American poet

William Cullen Bryant is known better as a literary critic and journalist. He is, however, the first significant poet of the nineteenth century in America. His theme was primarily of the love of nature in the romantic style. His poem, "Thanatopsis" (1815) is his best known with its theme of death in the classic American romantic style. That same year he was admitted to the Massachusetts bar but ten years later left law for a writing career in New York City, where he edited the **New York Evening Post** for fifty years. He was very active in politics and helped form the Republican Party.

Brown, Charles Henry. **William Cullen Bryant**. New York: Scribner, 1971. 576 p.
PS1181.B74

William Cullen Bryant has been the subject of previous biographies. This readable narrative corrects the errors of those earlier attempts at his life. There is more emphasis on his activities than his thought but the forcefulness of Bryant comes through.

BUCK, Pearl S. (Pearl Sydenstricker) (1892-1973), American novelist

Pearl Buck lived with her missionary parents in China and is best known for her novels set in that country, especially **The Good Earth,** for which she won the Pulitzer Prize of 1932. Some critics feel her strength is her humanitarian concern rather than originality as her characters in her novels are stereotypical. She also wrote fiction for women's magazines.

Stirling, Nora B. **Pearl Buck, a Woman in Conflict**. Piscataway, N. J.: New Century Publishers, 1983. 357 p.
PS3503.U198.Z85 1983

Nora Stirling looks at Buck's unhappy marriage and her separation from her institutionalized daughter and the impact these had upon her life and her literary output.

BULGAKOV, Mikhail Afanasevich (1891-1940), Russian novelist; playwright

This Russian novelist and playwright is considered one of Russia's finest twentieth century satirists and fantasy writers. **The Master and Margarita**, a novel published in a censored edition twenty-six years after his death, is considered his masterpiece. He wrote numerous plays, **The Days of the Turbins** being his best known.

Proffer, Ellendea. **Bulgakov: Life and Work**. Ann Arbor, Mich.: Ardis, 1984. 670 p.
PG3476.B78.Z8 1984

Ellendea Proffer has carefully researched the political and intellectual climate. She also interviewed a number of his associates. The results are a significant literary biography and a contribution to the understanding of the broader Russian literary heritage.

BURCHFIELD, Charles Ephraim (1893-1967), American painter

Charles Burchfield's paintings do not belong to a particular school of American painting but reflect the distorted inner life he sensed. He figuratively anthropomorphizes buildings and even the wind. "Church Bells Ringing, Rainy Winter Night" (1917) and "Night Wind" (1918) are among his better known works. He was a watercolorist who alternated the lyrical with the bold.

Baur, John I.H. **The Inlander: Life and Work of Charles Burchfield, 1893-1967**. Newark: University of Delaware Press, 1982. 280 p.
N6537.B86.B38 1982

This book is based on the lengthy diaries of the artist. As with most biographies of visual artists the reproductions of works add to the life of the artist.

BURNE-JONES, Edward Coley (1833-98), English painter; designer

Burne-Jones was an important pre-Raphaelite painter. He used medieval mythology and Arthurian legends as themes. Among his best known paintings is his "King Cophetua and the Beggar Maid" of 1884. He was also a designer of some note of stained glass windows and tapestries. His highly acclaimed woodcuts for the book for **Chaucer** was published in 1896. His work fell into disfavor after his death. However, it is being looked at in a new light with a revival of interest in that period of English decorative and fine arts.

Burne-Jones, Georgiana (Macdonald). **Memorials of Edward Burne-Jones.** 2 vols. in 1. New York: The Macmillan Co., 1906, c1904.
ND497.B8.B85 1906

This widely acclaimed book at the time of its publication is by his wife. This clear portrait of a charming man is based on his letters and sketches which exhibit significant wit. It is an exceptionally well done biography.

Fitzgerald, Penelope. **Edward Burne-Jones: A Biography.** London: Joseph, 1975. 320 p.
ND497.B8.F58

An interesting biography which at the time of publication had reviews that saw very different things in the same book. It is factual and the conclusions are based on this aspect. Burne-Jones does not appear to be the person his wife saw in her biography listed above. Rather Burne-Jones appears to be elusive and his wife, a more important player in his life than she was aware of.

BURNEY, Fanny (1752-1840), English novelist

Not a particularly significant novelist, Fanny Burney is noted more for her diary and letters, which gave a vivid picture of English life during that time. Her father's circle of friends included the most brilliant individuals of the day. Possibly her most successful novel was her first, written when she was twenty-six, **Evelina.** Her works did influence the future of the English novel. She spent five unhappy years in the Queen's court and married a French exile when she was forty-one and wrote a potboiler, **Camilla,** in 1796.

Hemlow, Joyce. **The History of Fanny Burney.** Oxford: Clarendon Press, 1958. 528 p.
PR3316.A4.Z647

This is a biography based not only on the diary and letters of Fanny Burney but also those of her correspondents. Joyce Hemlow highlights the novelist's life during her writing of her novels as well as other aspects of her rather painful existence into old age.

Kilpatrick, Sarah. **Fanny Burney.** Newton Abbot, Eng.: David & Charles, 1980. 232 p.
PR3316.A4.Z664 1981

Sarah Kilpatrick does not break any new ground with her biography but offers a readable, sympathetic account of a woman of a rich cultural background.

BURNS, Robert (1759-96), Scottish poet

A rural background is the setting for this best known of all Scottish poets. After an unsuccessful attempt at continuing the farming tradition of his family, Robert Burns began to have his poetry published. The literary circles of Edinburgh were impressed by his poetic approach to the simple things in life. He became a celebrity of sorts for a while but was disgusted with that life and returned to the hard farming that may have contributed to his premature death. He became a national hero as a result of a sentimentalizing of his poetry, but his real poetic stature was recognized a century later by literary scholars. Most of his poems are short lyrics. He has many themes, uses satire and concise emotion, ranging from the bawdy to the tender. "Tam o'Shanter" is his only narrative poem. He wrote hundreds of songs, among them, "Auld Lang Syne" and "Comin' thro' the Rye."

Snyder, Franklyn Bliss. **The Life of Robert Burns.** New York: Macmillan, 1932. 542 p.
PR4331.S6

Snyder, in his scholarly biography, clears away the myths and conjectures about the cult surrounding Robert Burns. His biography is considered the first to be truly impartial.

Daiches, David. **Robert Burns and His World.** New York: Viking Press, 1972, c1971. 127 p.
PR4331.D28 1972

This is a brief biography but nevertheless erudite. It has many illustrations that give us visual impressions of his times.

Fitzhugh, Robert Tyson. **Robert Burns: The Man and the Poet; a Round, Unvarnished Account.** Boston: Houghton Mifflin, 1970. 508 p.
PR4331.F57

Fitzhugh's biography is similar to the one by Snyder in its accuracy and completeness.

BUTLER, Samuel (1835-1902), English novelist

Samuel Butler went to New Zealand as a sheep farmer for five years after graduating from Cambridge rather than being ordained a minister as expected by his family. He returned to England and started to paint but preferred writing. His first novel was **Erewhon,** a utopian romance. His best known work is the autobiographical **The Way of All Flesh,** a bitter but realistic study of English middle class and an indictment of their sanctimoniousness. This book greatly influenced English society and literature by its intergenerational conflict theme.

Stillman, Clara Gruening. **Samuel Butler, a Mid-Victorian Modern.** New York: Viking Press, 1932. 319 p.
PR4349.B7.Z94

Despite the continuing popularity of **The Way of All Flesh,** Butler has not been the subject of recent significant biographies. This one is quite old but is well written and is based on good documentation.

BYRON, George Gordon Byron, Baron (1788-1824), English poet

Lord Byron's life was plagued with family problems and illicit love affairs. He traveled through the Middle East after leaving Cambridge. When the first cantos of his **Childe Harold's Pilgrimage,** written during the years 1812 through 1818, appeared he became famous. He wrote other successful verse-tales during that time also based on his Middle East experience. After a year-long marriage his wife left him. He went into exile, continuing his tumultuous love life. **Don Juan,** a satire, is considered his masterpiece and he was a profound influence, not only on English literature, but also on other European literature with his emphasis on individualism and fighting against the oppression of monarchical regimes.

Marchand, Leslie Alexis. **Byron; a Biography.** 3 vols. New York: Knopf, 1957.
PR4381.M33

Marchand edited twelve volumes of Byron's letters before writing this definitive biography. However, it is limited by the distorted views of Byron's admirers and critics.

CABLE, George Washington (1844-1925), American fiction writer

George Washington Cable was a regionalist American writer of novels and short stories which took place in nineteenth century Louisiana society. His most important novels are **Dr. Sevier** (1885) and an earlier work in 1880, **The Grandissimes.** His theme was the lowly position of the Southern blacks. He was heavily criticized by the Creoles and felt it necessary to leave Louisiana, moving to Massachusetts where he continued to write but produced less significant work.

Rubin, Louis Decimus. **George W. Cable: The Life and Times of a Southern Heretic.** Pegasus American Authors. New York: Pegasus, 1969. 304 p.
PS1246.R8

This very readable biography emphasizes the social aspects of the writings and life of Cable. Rubin had access to his correspondence and other writings. Rubin feels his social concerns impinged upon his artistic expression.

Turner, Arlin. **George W. Cable, a Biography.** Durham, N.C.: Duke University Press, 1956. 391 p.
PS1246.T8

This is the definitive, scholarly biography of Cable despite more recent ones. It is very detailed and written in a rather uninspiring style, but the documentation makes for a full profile of Cable.

CAIN, James M. (James Mallahan) (1892-1977), American novelist

James Cain was a suspense novelist, setting a standard for the tough psychological thriller. Three of his novels were made into films, **The Postman Always Rings Twice**, written in 1934, **Mildred Pierce** (1941) and **Double Indemnity** two years later.

Hoopes, Roy. **Cain.** New York: Holt, Rinehart and Winston, 1982. 684 p.
PS3505.A3113.Z69 1982

Hoopes writes an exceptional biography of a writer of suspense novels. His exhaustive research and interviewing have produced a readable work about an interesting personality and provided an insightful look at American cultural history of his time.

CAMUS, Albert (1913-60), French novelist; playwright

Albert Camus was born in extreme poverty in Algeria. His years at the university were cut short by tuberculosis, which plagued him periodically throughout life. He began his writing career as a journalist in Algeria, establishing a sufficient reputation to edit a resistance daily showing his deep desire for political action based on moral values. During World War II his finest work of fiction, **The Stranger**, contained his thoughts on the philosophy of the absurd—human life is meaningless and irrational. He worked through his philosophical development in his writings. **The Plague** (1947) explores his rebellion against nihilism. He wrote two plays with strong political themes. His last important novel, **The Fall**, illustrates some of his Christian ideas.

Lottman, Herbert. **Albert Camus: A Biography.** Garden City, N.Y.: Doubleday, 1979. 753 p.
PQ2605.A3734.Z698

This is as close to a definitive biography available on this very complex thinker and writer. It deals primarily with the detailed externals of his life, more than most may wish at times.

McCarthy, Patrick. **Camus.** New York: Random House, 1982. 359 p.
PQ2605.A3734.Z72135 1982

This biography of Camus complements the Lottman book. It is a gracefully written but penetrating look at the emotional complexity of Camus, exploring the public view of a writer and the real man.

CARPEAUX, Jean-Baptiste (1827-75), French sculptor; painter

Carpeaux's sculpture is noted for its spontaneity, originality and gracefulness. His preferred media were clay and plaster. He was a favored sculptor of Napoleon III and was commissioned to do some of the decoration at the Louvre. His best-known work is "The Dance." His most complex is the bronze "Ugolino and His Sons" finished in 1863.

Wagner, Anne Middleton. **Jean-Baptiste Carpeaux: Sculptor of the Second Empire.** New Haven: Yale University Press, 1986. 328 p.
NB553.C3.W33 1986

There is more emphasis in this book on other than the biographical but it contains his life interwoven with a study of his work and the period in which he sculpted.

CARY, Joyce (1888-1957), Anglo-Irish fiction writer

Joyce Cary studied art, then was in the colonial service in Nigeria. The latter formed the basis for one of his earliest and best novels, **Mister Johnson,** written in 1939. As with much Irish literature there is wit with an underlying seriousness in his works.

Foster, Malcolm. **Joyce Cary, a Biography.** Boston: Houghton
Mifflin, 1968. 555p.
PR6005.A77.Z66

This is the present standard biography of Joyce Cary. It is
a readable, well documented book.

CASSATT, Mary (1844-1926), American painter

Mary Cassatt was the first American impressionist. She
studied in the United States but then settled in France, where
she came under the influence of Degas. Not only did she paint in
the style of Degas but she also used many of his subjects. She
was primarily a figure painter and from the end of the 1880's
devoted herself to the theme of mother and child in several
media. Her artistic activities were severely diminished after
cataract surgery.

Sweet, Frederick Arnold. **Miss Mary Cassatt, Impressionist
from Pennsylvania.** Norman: University of Oklahoma Press, 1966.
242 p.
ND237.C3.S9

This is a well researched but uncritical biography of the
only American to exhibit with the French impressionists. Sweet
had access to many unpublished letters of Mary Cassatt's to her
family in Philadelphia, giving them the details of her unique
existence as an expatriate in Parisian artistic circles.

Hale, Nancy. **Mary Cassatt.** Garden City, N. Y.: Doubleday,
1975. 333 p.
ND237.C3.H3

Nancy Hale looks at the influences that shaped the artistic
career of Mary Cassatt, her moving away from the United States
and being accepted by the French impressionists.

CATHER, Willa (1873-1947), American novelist

Willa Cather came from a rural Nebraska background, the
pioneering atmosphere of which was the setting of her writings.
After graduating from the University of Nebraska she moved east
where she worked in journalism and taught high school. During
those years she also published short story and poetry
collections. Her first novel, **O Pioneers,** came out in 1913 after
she decided to make writing her life's work. Her finest work may
be **Death Comes for the Archbishop** (1927), where she blended
history and religion. Her fiction, considered among the best in
twentieth century American literature, was acclaimed at the time

of its publication, went briefly out of favor and since her death, is considered exceptional, probing universal themes.

O'Brien, Sharon. **Willa Cather: The Emerging Voice.** New York: Oxford University Press, 1987. 464 p.
PS3505.A87.Z746 1987

This first of two volumes poses the hypothesis that once Willa Cather accepted her lesbian orientation she felt able to do her best writing.

Woodress, James Leslie. **Willa Cather: A Literary Life.** Lincoln: University of Nebraska Press, 1987. 583p.
PS3505.A87.Z939 1987

This biography is considered the most accurate because of Woodress' access to sources and method of research. It is scholarly in tone, the prose is graceful. He does dispute Sharon O'Brien's theory of Willa Cather's sexual orientation and claims, also just as speculatively, Cather's desire to devote herself more single mindedly to her art.

CELLINI, Benvenuto (1500-71), Italian sculptor

Cellini was trained as a goldsmith and employed that technique in his early works. He was a very spirited individual, noted for his rivalry and violent impulses, which forced him to move around quite frequently. However, his art was so significant that his patrons were the aristocracy and the papacy. His best known work, "Perseus," in Florence, was also a technological triumph. His autobiography is one of the most important documents of the sixteenth century.

Pope-Hennessy, John Wyndham. **Cellini.** New York: Abbeville Press, 1985. 324 p.
NB623.C4.P66 1985

This biography is based on Cellini's dramatic autobiography. Pope-Hennessy incorporates photographs of his sculptures that illustrate the hectic emotional content of his life.

CERVANTES SAAVEDRA, Miguel de (1547-1616), Spanish novelist

Cervantes was born of a poor family and had little education. He lost his left hand in battle and after his return was kidnapped by pirates who held him for several years until his family could afford to pay his ransom. He wrote little in his early life. Toward the end of his life he found a literary patron and could spend his time on his writing. His claim to fame in world literature lies in **Don Quixote**, a parody of the knight-errant who meets some very amusing people in his travels. The book is considered the first modern novel.

McKendrick, Melveena. **Cervantes**. The Library of World Biography. Boston: Little, Brown, 1980. 310 p.
PQ6337.M134

Melveena McKendrick uses every scrap of evidence and finds much that is autobiographical in his works to present a remarkable portrait of a complex but deeply human personality. She emphasizes accidents in his life as that served as vehicles for bringing forth his creative genius.

CEZANNE, Paul (1839-1906), French painter

Cézanne, a contemporary of the impressionists, developed a bolder style with heavy brushwork. He exhibited very little in his life and worked in isolation. He is considered to be one of the major influences of contemporary art, particularly of cubism, in its unique treatment of space, color and mass. He studied law and drawing at the same time. Against his father's wishes he pursued the latter and joined his friend from school days, Emile Zola, in Paris, where with his father's financial support and later a significant inheritance was able to pursue his style of art. Among his most well known works are a series entitled "Card Players" from 1890-1892, which show a kind of architectural approach. "Bathers," which was painted over several years from 1898 until 1905, contains several aspects of his visualization.

Rewald, John. **Cézanne: A Biography**. New York: H.N. Abrams, 1986. 288 p.
ND553.C33.R37 1986

This is a reworking of John Rewald's dissertation of 1936 at the Sorbonne. Rewald is one of the foremost authorities on nineteenth century French painting and presents a readable life based on the artist's own words and that of his eloquent friend, Emile Zola. Although he might have gone into greater depth in searching for the creative person, Rewald does bring Cézanne to life with insightful analysis of his artistic methods and aims.

Lindsay, Jack. **Cézanne; His Life and Art**. Greenwich, Conn.: New York Graphic Society, 1969. 360 p.
ND553.C33.L5 1969b

This book also successfully penetrates Cézanne's complex personality. Recent scholarship is incorporated, and this could be considered as definite a life as possible considering the complexity of the subject.

CHAGALL, Marc (1889-1985), Russian painter

Chagall incorporated his Russian village background and Yiddish folklore to create his own style of painting. During his second stay in Paris he was a graphic artist of note doing engravings for LaFontaine's **Fables** and the Bible. He moved to the United States during World War II and designed ballet scenery for Stravinsky's "Firebird," stained glass windows, mosaics and tapestries with religious themes. He was the first living artist to exhibit at the Louvre.

Venturi, Lionello. **Chagall: Biographical and Critical Study.** Translated by S.J.C. Harrison and James Emmons. The Taste of Our Time, vol. 18. New York: Skira, 1956. 122 p. ND699.C5.V42

This introduction to Chagall is not the most lively volume but the wonderful plates add to the biography of this visual artist, written many years before his death.

CHEEVER, John (1912-82), American fiction writer

The theme of his novels are the lives of upper middle class suburbia with a surrealistic and humorous moral tone. His **Wapshot Chronicle** of 1957 won the National Book Award. A collection of his short stories of 1978 won both a Pulitzer and the National Book Critics Circle for fiction. He is considered a master of satire.

Cheever, Susan. **Home Before Dark.** Boston: Houghton Mifflin, 1984. 243 p. PS3505.H6428.Z59 1984

Less chronological than thematic, this book by the author's daughter offers an intimate portrait of their family in clear prose. She also reveals the tortured alcoholic, the secret homosexual and her own struggles with him. Despite this sensitive material and the closeness of their relationship, Susan Cheever writes a remarkable memoir.

Donaldson, Scott. **John Cheever.** New York: Random House, 1988. 416 p. PS3505.H6428.Z64 1988

This is more of a chronology than a biography, but is well researched as it moves through his youth to the more painful years of middle age and beyond when his alcoholism and homosexual promiscuity tore him open. Cheever remained unknown to himself and to others.

CHEKHOV, Anton Pavlovich (1860-1904), Russian playwright; short story writer

Chekhov is considered one of the major playwrights in world literature. The themes of his plays are love and work, and the drama is built upon a lack of movement in the plot and mood, which develops into an internal tension for the characters. His contributions to the short story are the some sixty works published between 1880 and 1904. His most mature dramas are **Uncle Vanya, The Three Sisters** and **The Cherry Orchard** written between 1899 and 1904. He studied medicine and practiced it sporadically in a free clinic for peasants and in disaster relief. He was renowned in his native Russia in his lifetime.

Pritchett, V.S. (Victor Sawdon). **Chekhov: A Spirit Set Free.** New York: Random House, 1988. 235 p. PG3459.P57 1988

This life by a master storyteller in his own right could be called a chronology of an imagination. He outlines and then fleshes in the life and works of Chekhov, quoting from the interesting letters of Chekhov and from his published works.

Troyat, Henri. **Chekhov.** Translated by Michael Henry Heim. New York: Dutton, 1986. 364 p. PG3458.T7613 1986

Chekhov's life seems to be rather commonplace in comparison to other artists. His artistry flourished, despite a demanding family and a life as a doctor. It is nuanced as are his plays and Troyat, a well known biographer, skillfully and sympathetically picks up this subtleness.

CHESTERTON, G.K. (Gilbert Keith) (1874-1936), English novelist

G.K. Chesterton was a novelist, poet and best known as the author of the series of short stories in which Father Brown was the main character. These superbly written stories have unlikely plots and intriguing paradoxes. He was also noted as an essayist, a biographer and illustrator of some of his writings.

Barker, Dudley. **G.K. Chesterton; a Biography.** New York: Stein & Day, 1973. 304 p. PR4453.C4.Z529

This is a solid book on a solid man. But Chesterton was also the "Jolly Journalist" of Fleet Street who wrote in many unconventional places, such as wine shops.

Ward, Maisie. **Gilbert Keith Chesterton.** New York: Sheed & Ward, 1943. 685 p.
PR4453.C4.Z84

Maisie Ward of the same conservative English Catholic stance as her subject writes a sympathetic portrait of the friendly opponent of Bernard Shaw and H.G. Wells.

Ffinch, Michael. **G.K. Chesterton.** San Francisco: Harper & Row, 1986. 369 p.
PR4453.C4.Z63 1986b

Ffinch offers a delightful look at Chesterton and his travels.

Dale, Alzina Stone. **The Outline of Sanity: A Biography of G.K. Chesterton.** Grand Rapids, Mich.: Eerdmans, 1982. 354 p.
PR4453.C4.Z588 1982

Alzina Dale portrays a man of many interests, a writer without a significant masterpiece but still worthy of a biography. She looks at the milieu in which he wrote and the philosophical bent of his mind.

CHESTNUTT, Charles Waddell (1858-1932), African-American novelist

Charles Chestnutt is considered the first African-American novelist to have been successful in penetrating the white publishing establishment with works that had a serious social message and popular appeal. He was born before the Civil War into a middle-class free Negro society that also counted whites among its milieu.

Chestnutt, Helen M. **Charles Waddell Chestnutt, Pioneer of the Color Line.** Chapel Hill: University of North Carolina Press, 1952. 324 p.
PS1292.C6.Z68

Helen Chestnutt offers a very fine biography of her father and the influences on his writings from his personal papers.

Keller, Frances Richardson. **An American Crusade: The Life of Charles Waddell Chestnutt.** Provo, Utah: Brigham Young University, 1978. 304 p.
PS1292.C6.Z75

This is based on the biography of Chestnutt's daughter's and puts forth no new data. However, it is still a contribution to an understanding of the life and times of Charles Chestnutt as its

narrative and organization put Charles Chestnutt's life and
writings in a different, somewhat clearer perspective.

CHOPIN, Frédéric (1810-49), Franco-Polish composer

Considered one of the greatest composers of piano music of
all times, Chopin was also acclaimed as concert pianist and a
piano teacher. He was born near Warsaw, Poland, but spent most
of his life in Paris, where he died of consumption. His liaison
with the writer George Sand is a significant aspect of his life.
His shorter works consisted of dance pieces and preludes as well
as his two books of études that raised that level of technical
development to works of musical merit and beauty. His two
piano concertos are among his large scale but early works. Among
his mature compositions are the sonatas and his "Fantasy in
F minor."

Marek, George Richard, and Maria Gordon-Smith. **Chopin**. New
York: Harper & Row, 1978. 289 p.
ML410.C54.M37

This is a major piece of Chopin scholarship that attempts to
demythologize the composer. Chopin was a very complex man and
Marek and Gordon-Smith handle the intricacies of his life
sensitively. It is rewarding reading.

CHOPIN, Kate (1851-1904), American novelist

Kate Chopin did not begin to write until she was in her
early forties and widowed. Her most significant work is her
novel **The Awakening** (1899), which because of its statement
of a woman's need for sexual and artistic expression, was not
fully appreciated until the 1960's. She also wrote some regional
sketches of Louisiana.

Seyersted, Per. **Kate Chopin. A Critical Biography.** Baton
Rouge: Louisiana State University Press, 1969. 246 p.
PS1294.C63.S4

This Norwegian scholar has edited all the works of Kate
Chopin and has written the standard biography to date. It is
primarily biographical but does detail her style and her novel
The Awakening.

CHRISTIE, Agatha (1891-1976), English novelist

Who has not read or seen a dramatization of an Agatha
Christie mystery? She was the foremost British writer of

mysteries having written over 100 in the more than half-century-long span of her writing career. The stories of her Belgian detective Hercule Poirot and Miss Jane Marple continue to be dramatized on television. Her mysteries have been translated into all major languages, and her play The Mousetrap of 1952 ran in London almost continuously for more than thirty years. In 1971, in recognition of her stature in this genre, she was made a Dame Commander of the British Empire. She was educated at home. She married Archibald Christie and retained his name for professional reasons after their divorce, although she did most of her writing as the wife of Max Mallowan.

Morgan, Janet P. **Agatha Christie: A Biography.** New York: Knopf, 1985, c1984. 393 p.
PR6005.H66.Z75 1985

This recent book is by the first authorized biographer of Dame Christie. She had access to her personal papers and met more than 200 of Agatha Christie's associates to prepare this biography. It is a very well written, readable biography of a most popular mystery writer.

CLARE, John (1763-1864), English poet

John Clare may not be a household name to most. He was a poorly educated farm laborer who became the "Northampton peasant poet" with his **Poems Descriptive of Rural Life and Scenery** of 1820. He spent the last twenty-six years of his life in a mental asylum but continued to write poetry. An appreciation of his later poetry had to wait until the twentieth century, and he is studied as one of the British romantics. His unfinished autobiography has also been published.

Storey, Edward. **A Right to Song: The Life of John Clare.** London: Methuen, 1982. 330 p.
PR4453.C6.Z89 1982

Edward Storey is himself a poet from the same regional roots as John Clare. He is most sympathetic with the plight of John Clare in his life of great insecurity and poverty. He gives us an insight into Clare's years in a mental asylum that exhibited unusual character despite this confinement.

CLAUDEL, Paul (1868-1955), French playwright; poet

Paul Claudel led a full life as an ambassador to numerous countries for France, yet he was a significant dramatist and poet whose work deeply reflected his religious and sensuous fervor. Claudel specifically uses the theme of the spiritual necessity of renunciation of the physical world. This is best expressed in his drama **The Satin Slipper**. He also used ballet, music and pantomime and collaborated with composers Darius Milhaud and Arthur Honegger. His plays as well as his poetry were characterized by irregular meter and rhyme and powerful images.

Chaigne, Louis. **Paul Claudel: The Man and the Mystic.** Translated by Pierre de Fontnouvelle. New York: Appleton-Century-Crofts, 1961. 280 p.
PQ2605.L2.Z6123

This is written by a fellow Frenchman who understood Claudel and his need for solitude as well as the active life of an ambassador. It presents the man in a very favorable light and seems at times to be written by the subject.

CLOUGH, Arthur Hugh (1819-61), English poet

Arthur Hugh Clough was a Victorian whose works reflected the skepticism of the day. He was influenced by Ralph Waldo Emerson and Thomas Carlyle. He wrote longer works but he is best known for his short poetry. He is an example of an "Oedipus complex" in his relationship with his possessive mother, which has been the subject of much post-mortem Freudianism by his biographers.

Biswas, Robindra Kumar. **Arthur Hugh Clough; Towards a Reconsideration.** Oxford: Clarendon Press, 1972. 489 p.
PR4458.B5

This is the most thorough and recent of psychoanalytical biographies.

COCTEAU, Jean (1889-1963), French poet; fiction writer

Jean Cocteau, "enfant terrible," was a multi-talented and prolific artist in the visual arts, writing, theater and dance. He influenced a whole generation of the French art scene. His works are influenced by dreamlike visions. He was often the center of literary scandals. He wrote more than twenty plays and his prose masterpiece of 1929 is **Les enfants terribles.** His most lasting success is in his films. In 1955, after years of being dismissed as a literary impostor, he was elected to the prestigious French Academy.

Steegmuller, Francis. **Cocteau, a Biography.** Boston: Little, Brown, 1970. 583 p.
PQ2605.O15.Z86

This exceptional biography received the National Book Award.
It is based on unpublished letters and interviews of his
associates. Despite Cocteau's difficult personality, Steegmuller
sees him as a creative genius. In this substantial book his
activities are noted as well as his personality probed.

Sprigge, Elizabeth and Jean-Jacques Kihm. **Jean Cocteau: The
Man and the Mirror.** New York: Coward-McCann, 1968. 286 p.
PQ2605.O15.Z85 1968b

This biography is written by two people who knew Cocteau
well. It is an objective biography, accurate in its detail. It
has been superseded by the Steegmuller book as being more
definitive, but it is necessary reading to get a more complete
picture of this very colorful artist.

COLERIDGE, Samuel (1772-1834), English poet

Coleridge was a major romantic poet very closely associated
with William Wordsworth. Together they wrote in 1798 **Lyrical
Ballads** in which he contributed "Rime of the Ancient Mariner."
His poetry spoke of the more mysterious, demonic side of English
romanticism. He had many other interests including trying
unsuccessfully to establish a utopian community in the United
States. He was a major philosopher and literary critic.
Wordsworth and he spent time in Germany studying Kant and other
philosophers. In addition to his marital difficulties, he was a
drug addict, and this problem impacted negatively upon his
remaining years as a poet and literary critic although he did
produce some successful works during this period. One of his
last major works was **Biographia Literaria,** an analysis of the
poetry and his theory of primary and secondary imagination.

Doughty, Oswald. **Perturbed Spirit: The Life and Personality
of Samuel Taylor Coleridge.** Rutherford, N. J.: Fairleigh
Dickinson University Press, 1981. 565 p.
PR4483.D6 1981

This book was carefully researched but the author died
before the book was finished, leaving much of the documentation
unknown. It is considered the most comprehensive biography to
date but not a definitive one. Some critics felt the book dwelt
too much on the negative aspects of his personality at the
expense of his creativity. Nevertheless, it is a sympathetic
portrayal of Coleridge as a poet, critic and thinker.

COLETTE (1873–1954), French novelist

Colette was one of the most famous French women of her day. Her novels are marked by a keen insight into human psychology and her ability to enter into the sensuous. Her first novels were in collaboration with her first husband and are known as the Claudine novels. She established her reputation with **Cheri** written in 1920. She has been compared to Proust for her subtleness of mind. One of her last novels was **Gigi**, which was made into a musical in 1958. She is a favorite subject of biographers.

Mitchell, Yvonne. **Colette: A Taste for Life.** New York: Harcourt Brace Jovanovich, 1975. 240 p.
PQ2605.O28.Z74 1975b

Yvonne Mitchell, also a writer in her own right, enters into the life of Colette, capturing the dynamism of Colette's long and illustrious existence. Eighty-five photographs add much to understanding the personality of Colette and the milieu in which she lived and worked.

Cottrell, Robert D. **Colette.** New York: F. Ungar Pub. Co., 1974. 150 p.
PQ2605.O28.Z73

This is a gracefully written biography of the long life of Colette with insights into the psychological and philosophical backgrounds in her novels. Cottrell finds her writings among the best of French literature.

Goudeket, Maurice. **Close to Colette; an Intimate Portrait of a Woman of Genius.** Translated by Enid McLeod. New York: Farrar, Straus & Cudahy, 1957. 245 p.
PQ2605.O28.Z673

This biography is written by her third husband to whom she was married her last thirty years. It is essentially the reminiscences of their life together, written in a touching unpretentious way.

Massie, Allan. **Colette.** Lives of Modern Women. New York: Penguin Books, 1986. 152 p.
PQ2605.O28.Z734 1986

This is a brief but brilliant assessment of the many aspects of the colorful life of Colette.

Richardson, Joanna. **Colette.** New York: Watts, 1984. 276 p.
PQ2605.O28.Z825 1984

Joanna Richardson has access to new sources about Colette, most significantly from her two stepsons who saw her in very different lights. Her research is thorough and the uniqueness of the personality of Colette comes through, but at times the book seems to be little more than a spewing of facts with little shaping of the narrative.

COMPTON-BURNETT, I. (Ivy) (1884-1969), English novelist

The settings of Compton-Burnett's nineteen novels were all no later than 1910 and concerned the middle class of Edwardian and Victorian times. Conversation rather than narrative was her style. Some critics felt she was a humorous storyteller, but others felt a cruelty in her characters that predominated her writings.

Spurling, Hilary. **Ivy, the Life of I. Compton-Burnett.** New York: Knopf, 1984. 621 p.
PR6005.O3895.Z93 1984

This is a biography full of lively detail and witty prose. A wonderfully definite biography of an elusive modern novelist, this is especially engaging in the second half.

CONNELL, Clyde (1901-   ), American sculptor

This woman sculptor began her career as an artist at the age of fifty-nine after a full life managing the household of her cotton plantation and her various involvements in religious and social causes.

Moser, Charlotte. **Clyde Connell: The Life and Art of a Louisiana Woman.** Austin: University of Texas Press, 1988. 94 p.
NB237.C614.M67 1988

This copiously illustrated book brings to life a most interesting artist, who is not very well known. As with many books of biographies of visual artists there is not much text but nevertheless one finds a fine portrait of Clyde Connell.

CONRAD, Joseph (1857-1924), English novelist

Joseph Conrad was born in Poland. His family was exiled because of his father's political activity and his mother died in exile. His father returned to Poland to die, so his uncle raised him. The first part of Conrad's life was spent as a seaman. He was nearly forty when he seriously began his career as a writer.

47

In 1913 his novel **Chance** received critical acclaim. An earlier and now well known novel, **Lord Jim** (1900), was based on his experiences at sea. His masterful short story is "Heart of Darkness." Conrad's characters live in an amoral world, reflecting his fatalistic attitude. He is considered one of the greatest writers of the English language.

Baines, Jocelyn. **Joseph Conrad, a Critical Biography.** New York: McGraw-Hill, 1960. 523p.
PR6005.O4.Z554

This biography is based on Conrad's correspondence and the impressions of some of his literary friends, H.G. Wells, John Galsworthy, Arthur Symon and Ford Madox Ford. Jocelyn Baines examines the political atmosphere against which he wrote in clear, readable prose.

Karl, Frederick Robert. **Joseph Conrad: The Three Lives—a Biography.** New York: Farrar, Straus, & Giroux, 1979. 1008 p.
PR6005.O4.Z759

This massive work looks at the interplay of the three segments of the life of Joseph Conrad as a youth in Poland, a global seaman and a writer. Criticism of Conrad's fiction is incorporated in this biographical study.

Tennant, Roger. **Joseph Conrad.** New York: Atheneum, 1981. 276 p.
PR6005.O4.Z882 1981

This modest book looks at Conrad, the man, and presents a believable portrait in a readable style.

Najder, Zdzislaw. **Joseph Conrad, a Chronicle.** New Brunswick, N. J.: Rutgers University Press, 1983. 647 p.
PR6005.O4.Z844313 1983

This is a very detailed year by year account of a writer of very complex works. Despite this seemingly rather tedious approach, a full, rich portrait comes through. This is certainly a book scholars will continue to use for its insights into the minutiae of Conrad's life.

COURBET, Gustave (1819-77), French painter

Courbet was the foremost French realist painter of the mid-nineteenth century. He did not appreciate his critics and so constructed his own pavilions to show his works during two world's fairs. He painted in the genre style on a grand scale, but his smaller works were more popular. He was imprisoned for his political leanings and then exiled.

Mack, Gerstle. **Gustave Courbet**. New York: Knopf, 1951. 406 p.
ND553.C9.M3

This biography is copiously illustrated, not only with reproductions of Courbet's works, but also of those of his contemporaries. Courbet's complex views both in the art world and in politics are discussed. It is a thoroughly researched book.

COWPER, William (1731-1800), English poet

William Cowper's poetry foreshadowed the nineteenth century romantic style with its emphasis on descriptions of country everyday life. His life was haunted by bouts of insanity and religious despair that influenced the tone of his writings. His very long poem "The Task" established him as a major poet. His letters are considered exceptional.

King, James. **William Cowper: A Biography**. Durham, N. C.: Duke University Press, 1986. 340 p.
PR3383.K5 1986

This biography shows how Cowper channeled his spiritual and emotional anguish into art. King, the editor of the Oxford edition of Cowper's works, handles exceptionally well the delicate issue of his insanity with the seemingly contradictory strength of the man as manifested in his poetry.

COZZENS, John Gould (1903-78), American novelist

John Cozzens' theme in his well-crafted novels was the professional man's crises and compromises. He won the 1949 Pulitzer Prize for **Guard of Honor.**

Bruccoli, Matthew Joseph. **James Gould Cozzens: A Life Apart.** San Diego: Harcourt Brace Jovanovich, 1983. 343 p.
PS3505.O99.Z59 1983

This is not a definitive but rather an informative biography of a man who seemed to undervalue his contribution to American literature. The goal of Bruccoli in this book is to bring Cozzens and his work into the public eye. It is a biography of a man whose sole occupation was writing.

CRANE, Hart (1899-1932), American poet

Although he only published two books of poetry, Hart Crane
is a most original poet. He used New York City and the Brooklyn
Bridge as inspirations for these two volumes. Plagued by
alcoholism, sexual and personal problems he ended his own life by
drowning.

Unterecker, John Eugene. **Voyager; a Life of Hart Crane.** New
York: Farrar, Straus & Giroux, 1969. 787 p.
PS3505.R272.Z797

This biography is the result of Unterecker going through
voluminous materials on the poet. Despite all the research, an
unclear picture of the poet emerges, but then maybe no complete
portrait can ever emerge of this very troubled artist.

Weber, Brom. **Hart Crane, a Biographical and Critical Study.**
New York: Bodley Press, 1948. 452 p.
PS3505.R272.Z8

More than a third of the book is devoted to an analysis of
Crane's volume of poetry **The Bridge.** Weber gives a picture of
the artistic personality and the poet at work.

CRANE, Stephen (1871-1900), American novelist

Stephen Crane is considered the first modern American
writer. His means of support was journalism. His **Red Badge of
Courage,** an American literature classic (1895), is his
masterpiece. However, he was also a very good short story writer
toward the end of his life. He was a war correspondent for the
Spanish-American War. He moved to England and died at a German
spa while seeking a cure for his tuberculosis.

Stallman, R.W. (Robert Wooster) **Stephen Crane; a Biography.**
New York: G. Braziller, 1968. 664 p.
PS1449.C85.Z9

This biography is a very factual account of Stephan Crane.
It gives a picture of the life and times of Crane as seen through
his experiences. Stallman does not probe his artistry very
deeply and gives a rather poor account of Crane's best known
works. However, despite these flaws it is definitive because of
its detail.

Beer, Thomas. **Stephen Crane; a Study in American Letters.** New
York: A.A. Knopf, 1923. 248 p.
PS1449.C85.Z55

Beer bases his biography upon first-hand sources and interviews of contemporaries of Stephen Crane. More recent scholarship has shown some of Beer's dates and quotes to be inaccurate, but the book is insightful of Crane and his era.

Berryman, John. **Stephen Crane.** The American Men of Letters Series. New York: Sloane, 1950. 347 p.
PS1449.C85.Z56

This is a literary biography in the true sense of the word. It is not without controversy in Berryman's interpretation of Crane as a naturalist writer rather than the generally accepted realist. His rather Freudian interpretation of Crane's relationship with his mother may be too original.

Colvert, James. **Stephen Crane.** San Diego: Harcourt Brace Jovanovich, 1984. 186 p.
PS1449.C85.Z579 1984

This is a straightforward account of Stephen Crane. James Colvert uses Crane's art to show us the man. It is not as probing as the other biographies listed but is useful for an introduction to Crane and his work. Colvert is a noted Crane scholar.

CRANKO, John (1927-73), English choreographer

John Cranko was born and trained in ballet in South Africa. He choreographed his first ballet there at the age of fifteen. He then moved to England. He choreographed a number of works for the internationally known Sadler's Wells Ballet. In 1961 he was invited to become the artistic director of the German Stuttgart Ballet, where he attracted international attention and developed a large repertoire.

Percival, John. **Theatre in My Blood: A Biography of John Cranko.** New York: F. Watts, 1983. 248 p.
GV1785.G7.P47 1983

Biographies of choreographers are scarce. John Percival has written a fine biography of this enormously talented man and expressed the humor and pathos of his career and life.

CUMMINGS, E.E. (Edward Estlin) (1894-1962), American poet

e.e. cummings was a multi-talented man not only as a poet but also as a playwright, novelist and painter. This lower case writing of his name was originally a printer's error. However, this lower-case designation transferred itself to his poetry,

which took a unique form of typography and punctuation. He also
created new words. These were the surface features of some frank
language. His autobiographical prose work **The Enormous Room**,
based on his war experience, is considered one of the best books
on World War I.

Kennedy, Richard S. **Dreams in the Mirror: A Biography of E.
E. Cummings**. New York: Liveright Pub. Corp., 1980. 529 p.
PS3505.U334.Z7 1980

This is considered the definitive biography of e.e.
cummings. It is carefully researched and details the significant
events of his life with insightful attention to the development
of his style.

DALI, Salvador (1904-89), Spanish painter

Dali, the leader of the surrealist school, studied art in
Madrid. Although influenced by the futurist school and Spanish
modernists, Dali claims it was his Catalan sense of fantasy and
his megalomania that were the motivational forces of his art. He
moved to Paris in 1929 and exhibited with the French surrealists.
Among his best known works are "Soft Watches" (1931) and "The
Sacrament of the Last Supper" (1955). His life was as colorful
as his appearance.

Secrest, Meryle. **Salvador Dali**. New York: Dutton, 1986.
307 p.
N7113.D3.S43 1986

Meryle Secrest gets caught up in the surrealist atmosphere
of Dali in this biography based on the stories of some rather
uncooperative associates of the then-living artist. She tries to
probe, not always too successfully, into the artistry and the
persona of Dali.

D'ANNUNZIO, Gabriele (1863-1938), Italian poet; novelist; playwright

D'Annunzio dominated the Italian cultural scene for more
than forty years with not only his artistry but also his
political and personal exploits. He wrote his first poetry at
the age of sixteen and soon afterward was recognized as a lyric
poet who plumbed the depths of the beauty of the Italian
language. Paralleling his writing were numerous romantic
liaisons with the aristocracy and celebrities. His most powerful
poetry came at the age of forty with "Alcyone" in 1904 and "La
nave" in 1908. During World War I he was a flier and naval
commander. He was a dictator-mayor of Fiume. Then he retired to
his villa after many controversial political activities.

Rhodes, Anthony Richard Ewart. **The Poet as Superman; a Life of Gabriele D'Annunzio.** London: Weidenfeld & Nicolson, 1959. 251 p.
PQ4804.R5 1959

D'Annunzio is portrayed objectively as a Renaissance man who was swayed from his art into a life of excessiveness in a number of areas.

DAUMIER, Honoré (1808-79), French painter; sculptor; caricaturist

Honoré Daumier is best known as a satirical cartoonist whose main subjects were the corruption of the French régime, law and society. In the mid-1840's he turned to sculpture and painting but his more than 5000 lithographs, which exhibit exceptional fine line and refined tonalities, are his most significant contribution to art.

Larkin, Oliver W. **Daumier, Man of His Time.** New York: McGraw-Hill, 1966. 245 p.
ND553.D24.L37

This book is less a biography than a significant intertwining of the times of Daumier and his contributions to the world of art and satire. It is copiously illustrated and documented.

Vincent, Howard Paton. **Daumier and His World.** Evanston, Ill.: Northwestern University Press, 1968. 267 p.
ND553.D24.V5

The emphasis in this book is on Daumier the lithographer. Howard Vincent reads the artistic clues to bring forth the life of the man. The book is well written and informative; the reproductions, for the most part, well executed.

DEBUSSY, Claude (1862-1918), French composer

Debussy studied piano and composition at the Paris Conservatory. He performed little and associated more with the leading impressionist poets and painters than the musicians of his day. His main compositions were orchestral suites, piano music and some vocal music. Among the titles of his best known works of the impressionist style of which he was the creator and leading exponent in France are "Prelude to an Afternoon of a Faun" (1892-94) and two books of "Preludes" for the piano from 1910 to 1913. Considered the most important impressionist opera is his **Pelléas and Mélisande.** His piano music is considered the most significant since Chopin. Cancer sapped his strength as did the overall depressive atmosphere of World War I. He died during the German bombardment of Paris.

Lockspeiser, Edward. **Debussy; His Life and Mind.** 2 vols. London: Cassell, 1962-65.
ML410.D28.L85

Although he fails to to bring his subject to life, Lockspeiser writes a most important biography. It does bring the age of Debussy into focus. It is not chronological in the strict sense, but looks at the man and his thinking. It is full of material not available to the author in the earlier shorter biography he did of Debussy. Debussy's spur to creativity, claims Lockspeiser, was his emotional state when he had to obtain money under duress.

DEFOE, Daniel (1661-1731), English novelist; poet

Robinson Crusoe (1719) is considered the first successful English novel and marks Defoe as one of the originators of realist fiction of the eighteenth century. He was a journalist and prolific pamphleteer before turning to fiction writing in his late fifties. Among his other important works was **Moll Flanders** (1722), which firmly established him as a writer of adventure fiction of a style that is straightforward, vivid and detailed. He also continued to write nonfiction.

Moore, John Robert. **Daniel Defoe, Citizen of the Modern World.** Chicago: University of Chicago Press, 1958. 408 p.
PR3406.M58

Moore's Defoe appears as a hero. This biography is probably the most ambitious available but overlooks the flaws of Defoe to prove his thesis and therefore the reader misses the more complex, contradictory man.

Sutherland, James Runcieman. **Defoe.** 2d ed. London: Methuen, 1950. 300 p.
PR3406.S78

This is a well-rounded portrait of a fascinating personage with much detail on his political career. However, it is not a full treatment of the man as a literary artist.

DEGAS, Edgar (1834-1917), French painter

Degas' best known subject is the ballet dancer. He painted, used pastels, and, as his eyesight began to fail at the end of

his life, he turned to sculpting dancers and other human and
animal figures. He was a part of the impressionist movement, but
his special contribution was his concern for movement and
contour. He started to study at the Ecole des Beaux Arts but
left to spend five years studying the Italian Renaissance art.

Sutton, Denys. **Edgar Degas, Life and Work.** New York:
Rizzoli, 1986. 343 p.
ND553.D33.S88 1986

Denys Sutton has access to previously unpublished
correspondence and with these documents seeks to develop the
personality of Degas. His professional life comes through, his
personal life may always remain unclear. This book with its
lavish illustrations places Degas in his social milieu.

McMullen, Roy. **Degas: His Life, Times, and Work.** Boston:
Houghton Mifflin, 1984. 517 p.
ND553.D3.M38 1984

This is a biography of the man rather than of the artist.
Degas is a complex man and an interesting one and, although this
book has been criticized for being too psychological in thrust,
it is a penetrating portrait based on his diaries and letters.

DELACROIX, Eugène (1798-1863), French painter

Delacroix lived a very full life. He is considered the
foremost painter of the romantic movement in France. His themes
were influenced by his knowledge of mythology, politics, religion
and literature focusing on the unresolved tension of human
mortality. "Lion Hunt" is filled with figures reflecting much of
his intellectual background. He was acclaimed as a painter in
his lifetime and given the medal of the Legion of Honor in 1831
and elected to the Institut de France in 1857.

Huyghe, René. **Delacroix.** Translated by Jonathan Griffin. New
York: H.N. Abrams, 1963. 564 p.
ND553.D33.H793

This biography brings to life a very vital man whose self-
realization had to come through art. He lived in a time of great
cultural richness and creative opportunity. The book is both
objective and very personal. More than 400 plates enhance the
text.

DEMUTH, Charles (1883-1935), American painter

Charles Demuth began as a watercolorist of exquisite

character, painting many still lifes. In his later years he moved into the precisionist style, somewhat like cubism. He also did watercolor illustrations for the works of Emile Zola and Henry James, among others.

Farnham, Emily. **Charles Demuth; Behind a Laughing Mask.** Norman: University of Oklahoma Press, 1971. 238 p. ND237.D36.F3

This is an absorbing book, informative as well as entertaining. His influence in pop art is in the last chapter of this very good biography which also deals with a criticism of him and his works.

DICKENS, Charles (1812-70), English novelist

Charles Dickens is considered one of the greatest English novelists. His works are autobiographical, reflecting the difficulties of his childhood and his unhappy work experience as a clerk in a law firm. He wrote much of his work in serial form for a monthly magazine. His **Pickwick Papers** of 1836-1837 went from 400 copies in the first part of its serialized version to 40,000 by the fourth. He soon became an international success, reading his own works and being involved in their dramatic interpretations. He traveled a great deal and always needed to be with friends. His marriage was unhappy. He had to support seven of his ten children until his death. Among his best known works are **A Christmas Carol** (1843), **A Tale of Two Cities** (1859) and **Great Expectations** (1860). His novels are noted for their rich portrayal of all aspects of society and the abuses against that society and his characters such as Ebenezer Scrooge, Uriah Heep, and Mr. Micawber. Despite his success as a writer he died an embittered man.

Kaplan, Fred. **Dickens: A Biography.** New York: Morrow, 1988. 607 p. PR4581.K28 1988

This is a most absorbing biography of a man of extraordinary talent and energy who seemed to live a very rich existence despite his unhappy family life. Kaplan's life, despite its length and at times the anguish of its subject, moves at a very lively pace.

Johnson, Edgar. **Charles Dickens, His Tragedy and Triumph.** rev. ed. New York: Viking, 1977. 601 p. PR4581.J6 1977

This is a revised and abridged edition of Johnson's two-volume work of 1952 which, until the Kaplan book, had been the standard biography. The abridged version lacks the excellent criticism of the original work though.

MacKenzie, Norman Ian, and Jeanne MacKenzie. **Dickens, A Life.** New York: Oxford University Press, 1979. 434 p. PR4581.M18

This is a good biography for the general reader. Its focus is on Dickens as a man of paradoxes and is based on his letters. It contains no new material but because of the exceptionality of the man it is worthwhile looking at him through many eyes.

Allen, Michael. **Charles Dickens' Childhood.** New York: St. Martin's Press, 1988. 148 p. PR4582.A44 1988

The childhood of Dickens is so significant to his life and works that Michael Allen devotes a book to this period of time in which Dickens moved more than fifteen times. He also corrects some errors and fills in the gaps of the Johnson and Mackenzies biographies.

Maurois, André. **Dickens.** Translated by Hamish Miles. New York: Harper & Brothers, 1935. 206 p. PR4581.M46 1935

André Maurois was a noted biographer of several literary lives. His approach is that of sympathy toward the mixture of genius and the ordinary mortal of the man and should be read in the light of the period in which it was written.

DICKINSON, Emily (1830-86), American poet

Emily Dickinson was one of the foremost nineteenth century American poets and possibly one of the greatest women poets of all times, whose works continue to be explored for their unusual power and impact. Her life story is a very popular subject with biographers and readers. She lived her entire life in her birthplace, becoming a virtual recluse. There is much conjecture as to every aspect of this life and its stimulus except for the fact that she was steeped in Emersonian thought and that it was her choice to preserve her vocation as a poetess. She allowed only a few of her more than 1,000 poems to be published in her lifetime, poems of a uniquely lyrical quality, aphoristic style, imagery and an exceptional command of metrical variations.

Wolff, Cynthia Griffin. **Emily Dickinson.** Radcliffe Biography Series. Reading, Mass.: Addison-Wesley, 1988. 635 p. PS1541.Z5.W58 1988

This book is not to be read by itself but is to be considered one of many interpretations of her life. It is a kind of psychobiography which may have missed the mark in some of its conclusions but it does intertwine her life with her poetry.

Sewall, Richard Benson. **The Life of Emily Dickinson.** 2 vols. New York: Farrar, Straus & Giroux, 1974. PS1541.Z5.S42

An exceptional and objective biography which looks at Emily Dickinson in the context of her life, drawing upon all available resources available to the biographer at the time. It is a scholarly but readable insight.

Johnson, Thomas Herbert. **Emily Dickinson: An Interpretive Biography.** Cambridge, Mass.: Belknap Press, 1955. 276 p. PS1541.Z5.J6

Johnson is considered to be one of the foremost scholars of the life and works of Emily Dickinson. He edited her work. This blends her life, her poetry and criticism.

Mossberg, Barbara Antonina Clarke. **Emily Dickinson: When a Writer Is a Daughter.** Bloomington: Indiana University Press, 1982. 214 p. PS1541.Z5.M67 1982

This is a feminist approach to Dickinson, particularly her relationships with her cold, authoritative father and elusive mother. Barbara Mossberg draws her conclusions from an analysis of her poetry.

DINESEN, Isak (1885-1962), Danish fiction writer

Isak Dinesen is the pseudonym of Baroness Karen Blixen-Finecke, a Danish author who is noted for her Gothic short stories, based on the stylistic tradition of the eighteenth century Gothic novel and her full-length work **Out of Africa,** from her experiences on a plantation in British East Africa, now Kenya. She returned to Denmark where her writing career flourished.

Thurman, Judith. **Isak Dinesen: The Life of a Storyteller.** New York: St. Martin's Press, 1982. 495 p. PT8175.B545.Z73

This is a brilliant biography of a woman which looks at her enigmatic personality and rich stories. Judith Thurman learned Danish and traveled to Africa to research her subject and had access to drafts of her writings and other personal papers. She is portrayed as an aristocrat and is seen in her fall from this stature at the end of her life.

DONNE, John (1572-1631), English poet

John Donne is the greatest of the poets of the metaphysical school, a style which combined the use of language for its own sake and striking imagery from philosophy, law, psychology and mathematics. He was also an outstanding preacher and at his death was dean of St. Paul's in London. His poetry was very secular in the early part of his life and turned more religious and philosophical after his being ordained in the Anglican Church and the death of his wife shortly thereafter. He and his poetry were rediscovered in the twentieth century and greatly influenced such poets as W.B. Yeats, T.S. Eliot and W.H. Auden.

Bald, R.C. (Robert Cecil). **John Donne, a Life.** New York: Oxford University Press, 1970. 627 p.
PR2248.B35 1970b

This is a carefully written biography which, in its almost too reliable account, may be criticized for not bringing life to its subject. But it is an important chronology, although a more definitive biography is still needed.

DOS PASSOS, John (1896-1970), American novelist

His epic trilogy **U.S.A.** is a contender in the "great American novel" category. In this work he developed the technique of combining stream of consciousness, biography, narration and quotations from newspapers and magazines. He was the spokesman for the "lost generation," those who lived through the upheaval of a first world war. As a social commentator his views went from radical liberalism to a more conservative position with a body of work during that period that was much less favorably received.

Carr, Virginia Spencer. **Dos Passos: A Life.** Garden City, N. Y.: Doubleday, 1984. 624 p.
PS3507.O743.Z548 1984

This clearly written, well researched biography is not focused on a particular facet of his personality or work but rather allows the well organized documentation to draw the portrait.

Ludington, Townsend. **John Dos Passos; A Twentieth Century Odyssey.** New York: Dutton, 1980. 568 p.
PS3507.O743.Z74 1980

Ludington pursues Dos Passos' journey both ideologically and physically. This readable book penetrates the complexities of his life and as a major interpreter of the United States in the twentieth century.

DOSTOYEVSKY, Fyodor (1821-81), Russian novelist

One of the giants of world literature, Dostoyevsky wrote his first novel **Poor Folk** (1846) after being trained in engineering. He was exiled to Siberia and hard labor after his membership in a secret political group was detected. His harsh experiences were recorded in **The House of the Dead** (1862). His youthful liberalism turned to religious orthodoxy. His most fruitful period of creativity included **Crime and Punishment** (1866) and **The Idiot** (1868), the latter written in Germany. Other successful novels followed. **The Brothers Karamazov**, a novel of incisive psychological insight into the depth of the human soul, is one of the greatest works of fiction ever written. His incredible output has drawn many biographers to his life, which showed its philosophical evolution in his works. The following are some of the important biographies about Dostoyevsky. Besides those annotated here Henri Troyat's **Firebrand: The Life of Dostoevsky** (1946), Leonard Grossman's **Dostoevsky: A Biography** (1974), and K. (Konstantin) Mochulskii's **Dostoevsky: His Life and Work** published in English in 1967 are recommended.

Frank, Joseph. **Dostoevsky: The Seeds of Revolt, 1821-1849.** Princeton, N. J.: Princeton University Press, 1976. 401 p. PG3328.F7

Frank, Joseph. **Dostoevsky: The Years of Ordeal, 1850-1859.** Princeton, N. J.: Princeton University Press, 1983. 320 p. PG3328.F74 1983

Frank, Joseph. **Dostoevsky: The Stir of Liberation, 1860-1865.** Princeton, N. J.: Princeton University Press, 1986. 395 p. PG3328.F73 1986

These are three volumes of a projected five, chronicling the significant periods of the life of Dostoevsky. Despite its erudition, it is of a readable style but very detailed.

Kjetsaa, Geir. **Fyodor Dostoyevsky, a Writer's Life.** Translated by Siri Hustvedt and David McDuff. New York: Viking, 1987. 437 p. PG3328.K5513 1987

This is a lively biography by a Norwegian scholar in a very well done translation. It brings fresh insights into existing information about this literary genius.

Hingley, Ronald. **Dostoyevsky, His Life and Work.** New York: Charles Scribner's Sons, 1978. 222 p.
PG3328.H54 1978b

Ronald Hingley's contribution to the biographical insights of Dostoyevsky in this comparatively short work cuts through the excess by its incisive organization. Hingley is an experienced biographer.

Yarmolinsky, Avrahm. **Dostoevsky; Works and Days.** New York: Funk & Wagnalls, 1971. 438 p.
PG3328.Y34

This is a more popular but not unscholarly view of the Dostoyevsky legend. It is based upon meticulous examination and interpretation of his works and personal papers to describe this uniquely creative but complex literary artist.

DOYLE, Arthur Conan, Sir (1859-1930), English novelist

Arthur Conan Doyle was a medical doctor-novelist, then full-time creator of the famous Sherlock Holmes. However, Doyle would preferred to have been remembered for his historical novels. An interest in spiritualism produced a two-volume history of this parapsychological phenomenon toward the end of his life.

Higham, Charles. **The Adventures of Conan Doyle: The Life of the Creator of Sherlock Holmes.** New York; Norton, 1976. 368 p.
PR4623.H5 1976

This is a popular biography in which Higham gets some of his clues for his subject by looking at the personalities of both his Sherlock Holmes and his Dr. Watson.

Edwards, Owen Dudley. **The Quest for Sherlock Holmes: A Biographical Study of Arthur Conan Doyle.** Totowa, N. J.: Barnes & Noble Books, 1983. 380 p.
PR4623.E38 1983

This enthusiastic book covers the first twenty-three years of Conan Doyle's life with a great deal of psychological and cultural probing. An epilogue adds five years. It has the atmosphere of a Sherlock Holmes story, searching for the clues. He gets caught up in the biographical process as Doyle does in his fiction and offers possibly too much conjecture.

Carr, John Dickson. **The Life of Sir Arthur Conan Doyle.** New York: Harper, 1949. 304 p.
PR4623.C3

This is the first general biography of Conan Doyle done with the cooperation of his family and based on unpublished personal papers. Conan Doyle comes out as a heroic Victorian knight. Doyle's interest in spiritualism is cursorily addressed in this book.

Nordon, Pierre. **Conan Doyle**. Translated by Frances Partridge. London: Murray, 1966. 370 p.
PR4623.N613 1966

This scholarly biography looks at the public face of Conan Doyle and its influence on his writings. Nordon, a French scholar of English literature, discusses his preoccupation with spiritualism and his devotion, you might say, to chivalric virtue.

DREISER, Theodore (1871-1945), American novelist

Theodore Dreiser began as a journalist but became known as the pioneer of naturalism. **Sister Carrie** (1900), his first novel, an initial failure, and **Jennie Gerhardt** (1911) caused an outcry by their portrayal of "fallen women." His greatest work, **An American Tragedy,** written in 1925, is the story of a poor man's attempt at success. A strong theme of his was the mechanistic view of life. He also wrote short stories and some nonfiction.

Lingeman, Richard R. **Theodore Dreiser**. Vol. 1- New York: Putnam, 1986-
PS3507.R55.Z664 1986

This first of a two-volume work moves from his childhood to his despair at the initial failure of **Sister Carrie**. Mr. Lingeman is a social historian and brings to this biographical writing a great deal of the cultural milieu in which Dreiser lived and wrote. The projected enterprise has the potential of being the definitive biography of Dreiser.

Elias, Robert Henry. **Theodore Dreiser, Apostle of Nature.** rev. ed. Ithaca: Cornell University Press, 1970. 435 p.
PS3507.R55.Z63 1970

Lingeman's biography supersedes Elias' now, but Elias is worthwhile reading as he takes a thorough look at the influence of Dreiser's life upon his work. A sensitive chronicle of Dreiser's life.

DRYDEN, John (1631-1700), English poet; playwright

Foremost a poet and then a playwright, Dryden also
distinguished himself as a satirist, critic and translator.   His
blank verse masterpiece drama, **All for Love**, was written in 1677.
His works fell into disfavor but there has been a revival of
interest in them in the twentieth century.

Ward, Charles Eugene. **The Life of John Dryden**. Chapel Hill:
University of North Carolina Press, 1961. 380 p.
PR3423.W3

This book presupposes some knowledge of Dryden and his
writings.   He addresses himself to the distortions in
interpretation of previous biographies and criticisms of the man.
We really do not have an interpretation of the man but rather
details about him.   Nevertheless, this is the standard biography.

DUCHAMP, Marcel (1887-1968), French painter

Marcel Duchamp emerges as the prominent theorist and most
influential artist of dadaism.   Looking at his works and their
titles one might conclude that this art is a performance or a
display and seems not to be related to the classic definition of
art.   His famous or infamous "Nude Descending a Staircase, No. 2"
caused a stir at the 1913 Armory Show.   He moved to New York and
from 1915 until 1923 worked on his major creation "The Large
Glass" or "The Bride Stripped Bare by Her Bachelors, Even."   He
stopped painting for about twenty years and mostly played chess.

Marquis, Alice Goldfarb. **Marcel Duchamp = Eros, C'est la
Vie: A Biography**. Troy, N. Y.: Whitston Pub. Co., 1981, c1980.
475 p.
N6853.D8.M368 1981

Alice Marquis has succeeded in portraying this very
different man, Duchamp.   His contradictory attitude toward
materialism which resulted in his taking up chess is
interestingly addressed.

DUMAS, Alexandre (1802-70), French playwright; novelist

Dumas was the master of historical melodrama.   His plays
were so dramatic in form that the audiences could barely follow
the plot.   He then wrote novels, also of an historical bent, upon
which his reputation in French literature lies.   He wrote
prolifically, traveled extensively and was beset in his last
years by scandals and financial problems.   Some critics dismiss
his writings as only popular literature as they are so readable.

Others accused him of being a "fiction factory" churning out novels wholesale with the help of collaborators under his name.

Gorman, Herbert Sherman. **The Incredible Marquis: Alexandre Dumas.** New York: Farrar & Rinehart, 1929. 466 p.
PQ2230.G6

Colorful Dumas was the subject of many second-rate biographies. Dumas is well served by Herbert Gorman's fascinating portrait of this great French romantic.

Maurois, André. **The Titans, a Three-Generation Biography of the Dumas.** Translated by Gerard Hopkins. New York: Harper, 1957. 508 p.
PQ2230.M3313

Dumas comes alive in this book as does his son of the same name. It is the father who is the real "titan" but Maurois also emphasizes the contributions of the son whom he feels he has been slighted in French literature. This is vintage Maurois, a well known biographer and especially successful with one of his own countrymen.

ELGAR, Edward (1857-1934), English composer

Edward Elgar is generally considered England's greatest native-born composer since Henry Purcell of the seventeenth century. His studies as a performer were mostly with his father, whom he succeeded as a church organist. As a composer he was self-taught. His marriage to a student transformed his creative life. During the three decades of his marriage he composed his greatest choral and orchestral music. His most popular pieces are his five "Pomp and Circumstance Marches." His output also included concertos, chamber music, piano music and some church music. He was the first major composer to systematically record his own music for the phonograph. After his wife died his later years were unproductive.

Kennedy, Michael. **Portrait of Elgar.** New York: Oxford University Press, 1968. 324 p.
ML410.E41.K5

Michael Kennedy writes well of a neurotic eccentric in this brilliant biography of a man at home in both salon music and musically deeper expressions. It is a very readable character study of the highlights and dark sides of Edward Elgar.

Moore, Jerrold Northrop. **Edward Elgar: A Creative Life.** New York: Oxford University Press, 1984. 841 p.
ML410.E41.M65 1984

This compendium of the life of Elgar details relentlessly the chronology of its subject. It is helpful in his pursuit of presenting Elgar always as man and artist to those who are most interested in this level of detail.

ELIOT, George (1819-80), English novelist

George Eliot, the pseudonym of Mary Ann Evans, wrote what is considered the most impressive Victorian novel, **Middlemarch,** in 1871-1872. The themes of her fiction concerned the moral choices people must make and the responsibility they have for their own lives. Other well-known titles include **Adam Bede** (1859), **Silas Marner** and the semi-autobiographical **The Mill on the Floss.**

Haight, Gordon Sherman. **George Eliot; a Biography.** New York: Oxford University Press, 1968. 616 p.
PR4681.H27

This is considered the definitive biography of George Eliot based on her personal papers and those of friends. Haight's focus is on what he considers to be her dominant personality trait, the need to be loved.

ELIOT, T.S. (Thomas Sterns) (1888-1965), English poet

"The Waste Land" of 1922 is his masterpiece. With this he ushered in the era known as literary modernism that displaced the less rational, more subjective romanticism. He was born in the United States but was studying in England when the First World War broke out and decided to stay there. He married a woman who was confined to mental institutions for the last fifteen years of their marriage, which caused him great anguish but during which time he produced some of his most profound poetry. He was a very well educated man who used this broad background in his very original approach to poetry. After his conversion to Anglo-Catholicism he wrote in a more religious vein and another of his masterpieces, **Four Quartets,** explores this area in a very personal manner. His drama, based on the murder of Thomas Becket, **Murder in the Cathedral** is still performed. Some feel he was as great a critic as a poet.

Ackroyd. Peter. **T.S. Eliot: A Life.** New York: Simon & Schuster, 1984. 400 p.
PS3509.L43.Z574 1984

Eliot was a profound man whose rather austere approach to life makes him difficult to reach. Added to this is the fact that the executors of the Eliot estate would not allow Ackroyd to

quote from his poetry, which illuminates the whole of the man.
It is a good biography of a man, who despite his poetic genius,
wrote comparatively little.

ERNST, Max (1891-1976), German painter

Max Ernst was a pivotal figure in the transition to
surrealism from dadaism. He was a self-taught artist and was
friends of well known French artists of the time with whom he
exhibited after moving to Paris in 1922. His particular
contribution to art was his collage. Two important collage books
are **The Woman with 100 Heads** of 1929 and **A Week of Goodness** in
1933. He spent the World War II years in the United States and
returned to Paris in 1949.

Russell, John. **Max Ernst: Life and Work.** New York: H.N.
Abrams, 1967. 359 p.
N6888.E7.R83 1967b

John Russell does an exceptional piece of work in this
biography, distinguishing the unique style of Ernst from that of
his contemporaries of the same school of artistic philosophy. It
is, as is usual with visual artists' biographies, well
illustrated.

ESENIN, Sergei Aleksandrovich (1895-1925), Russian poet

Esenin, also spelled Yesenin, was a tragic figure. He was
not an important poet, yet he spent so much of himself for his
poetry that he depleted his integrity, drank heavily and took his
own life. His poetry was of the peasant life and had a musical
lyricism. However, he might be better known in the West as being
briefly married to the famed dancer, Isadora Duncan.

McVay, Gordon. **Esenin: A Life.** Ann Arbor, Mich.: Ardis,
1976. 352 p.
PG3476.E8.Z774

More than ten years of research went into this tragic life.
The book overturns previous legends of Esenin as the saintly
peasant poet.

FAULKNER, William (1897-1962), American novelist

William Faulkner is considered among the great American
writers of the twentieth century. He won the Nobel Prize for
Literature in 1949 and two Pulitzer Prizes: one in 1954 for **A
Fable** and in 1962 for **The Reivers.** He used an imaginary county
called Yoknapatawpha as a microcosm of the loss of traditional

values and the anguish of post-Civil War Southern life. Faulkner began to write in his early teens. He was a voracious reader and well traveled. Among novels studied in American literature courses are his earlier and some feel his best: **The Sound and the Fury** (1929) demonstrated a variety of styles; **As I Lay Dying,** written the next year, is a masterpiece of the stream of consciousness technique and **Absalom, Absalom!** (1936) exhibits his ability with complex narrative.

Blotner, Joseph Leo. **Faulkner: A Biography.** New York: Random House, 1984. 778 p.
PS3511.A86.Z63 1984

This is a revised, condensed version of Blotner's 1974 two-volume work. It is a tighter, less sentimental look at Faulkner which incorporates new material and corrects and fills in the gaps of his older work, presenting a sharper profile.

Minter, David L. **William Faulkner, His Life and Work.** Baltimore, Md.: Johns Hopkins University Press, 1980. 325 p.
PS3511.A86.Z913

Minter looks more at the creative process of Faulkner and notes the role of his life in the composition of and content of his works.

Oates, Stephen B. **William Faulkner, The Man and the Artist: A Biography.** New York: Harper & Row, 1987. 363 p.
PS3511.A86.Z928 1987

Oates looks at the effect of Faulkner's writing upon Faulkner's life. The author puts forth an understanding of Faulkner in a truly literary biography.

Karl, Frederick R. **William Faulkner: American Writer, a Biography.** New York: Weidenfeld & Nicolson, 1989. 1,131 p.
PS3511.A86.Z8588 1989

Frederick Karl presents a portrait of a man who was torn between the love of the past in the South and the need for moving forward. He was a hard drinker to cover up his more sensitive approach to life and mask his real person to create the solitude he needed to write. Needless to say, 1,131 pages is a monumental work depicting a towering figure in American letters.

FEININGER, Lyonel (1871-1956), American painter

Feininger, an American cubist painter, spent most of his life in Europe. He is considered one of the most lyrical interpreters of that movement. He taught at the famed Bauhaus

interpreters of that movement. He taught at the famed Bauhaus from 1919 until 1933 when it was forced to close by the Nazis. His unique interpretation of cubism is more translucent as is seen in a series in the church in Gelmeroda. His later works using Manhattan as subject incorporate this approach.

Hess, Hans. **Lyonel Feininger**. New York: Abrams, 1961. 354 p.
ND237.F33.H43

This book, like most biographies of visual artists, contains less narrative on the life of the painter and more pages devoted to the catalog of his works and related documentary information. However, the life is enthusiatically written.

FIELDING, Henry (1707-54), English novelist; playwright

This eighteenth century English novelist was largely responsible for the emergence of the novel as a literary art form. His first writing attempts were in the form of satirical drama concerning the corruption in the politics at the time. These caused the drawing up of the Licensing Act of 1737, which effectively ended his career in that genre. He began writing novels and political pamphlets and essays. Out of this period came **Joseph Andrew** (1742), a comic prose, and his most famous **Tom Jones** (1749), an account of the coming of age of a young hero. He died, supposedly, from his strenuous duties as a principal magistrate in London.

Cross, Wilbur Lucius. **The History of Henry Fielding**. 3 vols. New Haven: Yale University Press, 1918.
PR3456.C8

This most thorough of works on the life and writings of Henry Fielding has been supplemented but not surpassed. When it came out to mixed reviews in 1919, the chief criticism was that Fielding comes across in what he did rather than what he was. Others felt that this was among the monuments of biography.

Rogers, Pat. **Henry Fielding, a Biography**. New York: Scribner, 1979. 237 p.
PR3456.R6

This is a very readable account of the man and varied career. Recent scholarship sheds new light and makes him more credible to contemporary readers. It is copiously illustrated.

Dudden, F. Homes. **Henry Fielding, His Life, Works, and Times**. 2 vols. Oxford: Clarendon Press, 1952.
PR3456.D8

This two-volume biography is more in the vein of Cross. Dudden did not take advantage of the research done since the publication of the Cross biography but does add Fielding's religious views.

FISHER, Dorothy Canfield (1879-1958), American novelist

Dorothy Canfield Fisher's works comprise eleven novels and more than one hundred short stories that reflect traditional American values. Her works are seldom noted now in surveys of American literature.

Washington, Ida H. **Dorothy Canfield Fisher: A Biography.** Shelburne, Vt.: New England Press, 1982. 258 p. PS3511.I7416.Z87 1982

Ida Washington has written a respectable biography of Dorothy Canfield Fisher despite her lack of prominence on the American literary scene. Fisher was a product of her social milieu which the biographer details for us.

FITZGERALD, Francis Scott Key (1896-1940), American novelist; short story writer

Fitzgerald was a chronicler of the period between the two world wars. Although he did not finish his studies there, Princeton influenced his writings. His life with his wife, Zelda, is portrayed in his work. Their disorderly existence increasingly damaged Fitzgerald. His best known work is **The Great Gatsby** of 1925 with its exploration of the conflict between materialism and idealism. His life with Zelda was a legend of its own. She, tragically, was hospitalized off and on for schizophrenia. During this time Fitzgerald's **Tender is the Night** was written in 1934 under very difficult circumstances.

Bruccoli, Matthew Joseph. **Some Sort of Epic Grandeur: The Life of F. Scott Fitzgerald.** New York: Harcourt Brace Jovanovich, 1981. 624 p. PS3511.I9.Z566

This book does much to correct the errors of previous biographers but at the same time develops a mythology of its own. This is the most thoroughly researched of the biographies so far.

Donaldson, Scott. **Fool for Love: F. Scott Fitzgerald.** New York: Congdon & Weed, 1983. 262 p. PS3511.I9.Z59 1983

This life, coming only two years after the Bruccoli book, offers little new information but a freshness of interpretation of what is already known of this unstable literary artist. Donaldson analyzes his works to get a fuller understanding of Fitzgerald's use of his fiction as autobiography.

Le Vot, André. **F. Scott Fitzgerald: A Biography.** Translated by William Byron. Garden City, N. Y.: Doubleday, 1983. 393 p.
PS3511.I9.Z68213 1983

Le Vot's unique contribution to the Fitzgerald canon is his look at the influence of French background upon the writings of Fitzgerald.

FLAUBERT, Gustave (1821-80), French novelist

Flaubert was the artist of the novel. He was a master stylist whose small output can be characterized as "poetic prose." His best known work is **Madame Bovary** (1857). The scandalous plot gave Flaubert notoriety that catapulted the book into an immediate success. He was an epileptic, unsuccessful in his family's eyes. His doctor father gave him an allowance which allowed him to pursue a writing career. He took years to write and rewrite his novels searching for "le mot juste." Among his other works was a masterpiece, **The Temptation of St. Anthony,** which took more than thirty years to complete in 1874. He also wrote several shorter pieces of fiction.

Lottman, Herbert. **Flaubert.** Boston: Little, Brown, 1989. 396 p.
PQ2247.L68 1989

Herbert Lottman gives us a chronicle of the writer whose dedication to his art is described as religious, spending up to eighteen hours a day working in a remote part of France. He uses Flaubert's own words and the words of his family and friends to describe Flaubert's chosen existence.

Bart, Benjamin F. **Flaubert.** Syracuse, N.Y.: Syracuse University Press, 1967. 791 p.
PQ2247.B3

More than twenty years of research went into this biography. Despite the scholarly approach it is a readable work.

Starkie, Enid. **Flaubert: The Making of the Master.** New York: Atheneum, 1967. (Sequel: **Flaubert: The Master.**) 403 p.
PQ2247.S77 1967b

Starkie, Enid. **Flaubert: The Master, a Critical and Biographical Study (1865–1880).** New York: Atheneum, 1971. 390 p. PQ2247.S78 1971b

These two volumes are an enthusiastic look at Flaubert, the man. The second examines Flaubert, the now famous novelist, and is considered to be the better of the two volumes. Despite its erudition it is written in straightforward, clear prose.

Sartre, Jean–Paul. **The Family Idiot: Gustave Flaubert, 1821–1857.** Translated by Carol Cosman. Chicago: University of Chicago Press, 1981, c1987. (1st of 5 vols. to be translated.) PQ2247.S313

This massive work is clearly worthy of its size. However, some reviewers feel that these volumes were not a biography of Flaubert but a philosophical problem to be analyzed, perpetuating Sartre's theory about Flaubert. Critics agree Carol Cosman did an exceptional job in translating all the nuances of Jean-Paul Sartre, a great writer in his own right.

Nadeau, Maurice. **The Greatness of Flaubert.** Translated by Barbara Bray. New York: Library Press, 1972. 307 p. PQ2247.N313

Nadeau was the editor of the eighteen volumes of the complete works of Flaubert. Despite his obvious interest in Flaubert he does not unduly praise him but gives us a life written with dispassion.

FORSTER, E.M. (Edward Morgan) (1879–1970), English novelist

Forster was educated at Cambridge and was an important member of the Bloomsbury Group. Among his better known works are **A Room With a View** (1908) and his most enduring novel **A Passage to India.** His novels contain his humanitarian concerns and characters and ideas overshadow plot.

Furbank, Philip Nicholas. **E.M. Forster: A Life.** 2 vols. New York: Oxford University Press, 1979, c1978. PR6011.O58.Z655 1979

Furbank knew Forster and his circle. His biography is written in elegant prose, not unlike that of his subject.

FRANCE, Anatole (1844–1924), French novelist

Anatole France was considered in his day to be a prominent French man of letters. He was elected to the French Academy in

1896 and won the Nobel Prize in 1921. His early fiction displayed both irony and charm as in **The Crime of Sylvestre Bonnard** (1881) and **At the Sign of the Reine Pédauque** (1893). His later writings were more political in nature.

Tylden-Wright. David. **Anatole France.** New York: Walker, 1967. 344 p.
PQ2254.Z5.T9 1967b

This important and impartial biography shows Anatole France as both a literary and political figure. He displayed more loyalty to his friends than his family. His fame made him autocratic and bitter, yet Paris reminded him of beauty and literature.

FRANCK, César (1822-90), Belgian-French composer

Belgian-born Franck settled permanently in Paris, where his organ improvisations drew many devotees. Many of his musical compositions, despite their distinctive style, were neglected for years. His "Three Chorales," written in his last year, are considered among the most important compositions for organ to come out of the nineteenth century. He is also known for his "Violin Sonata in A," dating from 1886, and "Symphonic Variations" (1885). He was a kind, gentle soul, revered by his pupils.

Indy, Vincent d'. **César Franck.** Translated by Rosa Newmarch. New York: Lane, 1909. 286 p.
ML410.F82.I63

The author of this biography was a pupil of Franck. At the time of its publication it was considered to be the writings of a disciple and has the flavor and style of the period of time. Unique and worthwhile for these reasons.

FREEMAN, Mary Eleanor Wilkins (1852-1930), American fiction writer

Mary Freeman was a minor figure in American literature, best known for her short stories. In **A Humble Romance and Other Stories** (1887) and **A New England Nun and Other Stories** (1891) she paints a grimly realistic and ironic portrait of rural New England.

Foster, Edward. **Mary E. Wilkins Freeman.** New York: Hendricks House, 1956. 220p.
PS1713.F6

Edward Foster writes a sympathetic life based on interviews of Mary Freeman's friends and relatives and her correspondence. He gives meticulous attention to her background, which formed the backdrop of her short stories.

FRENCH, Daniel Chester (1850-1931), American sculptor

Daniel French became famous in his early twenties with the 1873-75 bronze sculpture, "The Minute Man," in Concord, Massachusetts. America's unsurpassed sculptor of public monuments, he was an artist who went from triumph to triumph and lived an upright and happy life. His classic gigantic seated "Abraham Lincoln" in the Lincoln Memorial took eleven years to execute, 1911-22.

Cresson, Margaret French. **Journey into Fame; the Life of Daniel Chester French.** Cambridge: Harvard University Press, 1947. 316 p.
NB237.F7.C7

Margaret Cresson writes an unpretentious, pleasant account of the modest Yankee Puritan, her father. It is a bright, charmingly readable account of an artist whose place in American sculpture she did not fully realize.

FROST, Robert (1874-1963), American poet

Robert Frost is quintessentially American. He won the Pulitzer Prize four times. His poems, although regional in flavor, were universal in theme. He was a pioneer of unique interplay of rhythm, meter, everyday language, the experimental and the traditional. His early life in Massachusetts produced little poetry as he also taught and operated a dairy farm for ten years. He went to England for three years in 1912 to get his literary career established. He returned to live in New Hampshire, where he continued to write to wide acclaim and did some lecturing. **North of Boston,** published in 1914, contains some of his most powerful works. Among his most frequently studied poems is "Stopping by Woods on a Snowy Evening." The poem "The Road Not Taken" is in a philosophical mode.

Thompson, Lawrence. **Robert Frost:** 3 vols. New York: Holt, 1966-1976.
PS3511.R94.Z953

This three-volume set is by the poet's official biographer, who knew Frost as a college student. It is exhaustive in documentation. His dissection of Frost's public life was met with a storm of disagreement. Thompson presents a demythologized

Frost showing his darker side and harshness within his family circle. Unfortunately, the second volume is not widely available.

Pritchard, William H. **Frost: A Literary Life Reconsidered.** New York: Oxford University Press, 1985, c1984. 286 p. PS3511.R94.Z89 1984

Pritchard aims to revise the persona set forth in the Thompson biography. He exhibits a greater understanding of his poetry and the integration of his life and art. It may be necessary to read the Thompson book in order to understand what Pritchard was revising.

GAINSBOROUGH, Thomas (1727-88), English painter

Gainsborough was greatly influenced by Van Dyck in his portrait paintings, which were distinguished by their elegance. His favorite subject was the landscape and he produced some of the first landscape paintings in England. However, it was his portraitures upon which his fame was established. His most celebrated work is "The Blue Boy" (1770). In 1774 he became one of the founding members of the Royal Academy of Arts in London.

Woodall, Mary. **Thomas Gainsborough, His Life and Work.** British Painters Series. New York: Chanticleer Press, 1949. 128 p. NK497.G2.W6 1949

This is a brief, scholarly biography of Gainsborough, showing how he was influenced economically to paint portraits rather than, as he would have chosen, landscapes.

GARCIA LORCA, Federico (1898-1936), Spanish poet; playwright

Garcia Lorca is considered twentieth century Spain's most illustrious poet and playwright despite his brief life, ending during the Spanish Civil War. His prosperous family gave him exceptional educational opportunities and occasions to meet major avant-garde persons. He was the center of a group of poets known as the Generation of 1927, celebrating the three hundredth anniversary of the death of a Spanish Baroque poet. His most famous poem, "Gypsy Ballads" (1928), helped make him famous throughout the Spanish-speaking world. After a brief stay in New York, he returned to write plays, among them **The House of Bernarda Alba** in 1936. His works probe Spanish society and the treatment of women and social groups within Spain. His fame also rests on his tragic death by a firing squad, a martyr of the

Republican cause. His works are universal in theme and are noted for their mastery of language.

Gibson, Ian. **Pain Singing Behind a Smile: A Life of Frederico Garcia Lorca.** New York: Pantheon Books, 1989. 551 p.
PQ6613.A763.Z647713 1989

Nearly twenty years of research is incorporated into this biography of Garcia Lorca. Gibson had access to materials not available to earlier biographers. Ian Gibson is the authority on Garcia Lorca, and this volume is a condensation of a two-volume biography published in Spain in 1985 and 1987.

GASKELL, Elizabeth Gleghorn (1810-65), English novelist

This Victorian novelist was moved by the lives of the laborers in Manchester where she lived with her minister-husband. Dickens praised her work and asked her to contribute to one of the periodicals he edited. She was the author of a sensitive biography of her friend Charlotte Brontë in 1857.

Hopkins, Annette Brown. **Elizabeth Gaskell, Her Life and Work.** London: J. Lehmann, 1952. 383 p.
PR4711.H6

This still is considered the definitive biography of Gaskell. Annette Hopkins had access to her private papers. The quality of this biography is credited for a renewed interest in its subject's works.

GAUGUIN, Paul (1848-1903), French painter; woodcut artist

Gauguin's four years of his childhood in Peru had a great influence upon his later artistic career. He was at first an "amateur" painter with a full-time job as a stockbroker, supporting his wife and children. An encounter with Camille Pissarro, which improved his technique, and a period of unemployment moved him to become an artist, abandoning his wife and children in Denmark, where he had been unsuccessful. He was at first allied with the impressionists but then moved to the synthetist theory using flat planes and unnatural coloring as in "The Yellow Christ." He moved to Tahiti where he did his best works, depicting the beauty of the native peoples. He was poor and desperate at the end of his life.

Andersen, Wayne V. **Gauguin's Paradise Lost.** New York: Viking Press, 1971. 371 p.
ND553.G27.A74 1971

This is not strictly a biography but rather a fusion of the works and life of Gauguin.

GERSHWIN, George (1898-1937), American composer

George Gershwin began his career as a musician at the age of fifteen as a "song-plugger" in New York's Tin Pan Alley. He wrote many popular songs with his brother, Ira. His significant contribution was an American opera **Porgy and Bess** in 1935. His "Rhapsody in Blue", a piano concerto, and **An American in Paris** established his reputation as an American classical composer, mixing the indigenous jazz with folk music.

Ewen, David. **George Gershwin, His Journey to Greatness.** Englewood Cliffs, N.J.: Prentice-Hall, 1970. 354 p. ML410.G288.E87 1970

This is an important biography by one of America's most prolific writers in music. David Ewen did considerable research and had the cooperation of Ira in compiling this book, which traces his development as a composer.

Jablonski, Edward. **Gershwin.** New York: Doubleday, 1987. 436 p. ML410.G288.J29 1987

This biography is considered as close to definitive as possible. As did Ewen, Edward Jablonski had the cooperation of Ira Gershwin.

GIACOMETTI, Alberto (1901-66), Swiss sculptor; painter

The unusual proportions and monumental scale mark the very unique style of Giacometti. He was the son of a painter and at an early age was exposed to an extensive variety of art. He, at first, incorporated the cubist style, then he turned to bronze figuration with surfaces that appear eroded. Among the examples of his elongated figures is his "Man Walking II" of 1960.

Lord, James. **Giacometti, a Biography.** New York: Farrar, Straus, Giroux, 1985. 575 p. NB553.G4.L67 1985

This biography came out to mixed reviews. It is an introspective study of the sculptor. However it is also filled with more gossip than one might feel to be worthy of an otherwise real contribution to an understanding of Giacometti.

GIDE, André (1869-1951), French novelist

Gide's influence to French literature was more as a theorist than a practioner. However, his contributions to the French fiction are fairly significant, the most important being his only novel, **The Counterfeiters** of 1925, which encompasses his view of life and art.

O'Brien, Justin. **Portrait of André Gide, a Critical Biography.** New York: McGraw-Hill, 1953. 390 p.
PQ2613.I2.Z6568

This is a far-reaching analysis of Gide, the man. He is observed and assessed by the portraits of heroes he created, which show his intellectual development.

Painter, George Duncan. **André Gide; a Critical Biography.** New York: Atheneum, 1968. 147 p.
PQ2613.I2.Z657 1968b

Painter looks closely at the life of Gide as Gide claims he experienced it and finds a legitimacy for his life as a work of art.

Delay, Jean. **The Youth of André Gide.** Abridged and translated by June Guicharnaud. Chicago: University of Chicago Press, 1963. 498 p.
PQ2613.I2.Z6183

Jean Delay is a psychiatrist and this is a penetrating psychological study of Gide's youth. Delay was also a friend of his in his last years.

Fowlie, Wallace. **André Gide: His Life and Art.** New York: Macmillan, 1965. 217 p.
PQ2613.I2.Z6275

This is primarily an introduction to Gide, written in a readable style.

GILBERT, W.S. (William Schwenck) (1836-1911), English playwright; poet

It is difficult to think of Gilbert without Sullivan. Their operettas were exceptionally successful, noted for their wit and tuneful music. William Gilbert's unique contribution was the underlining satire and wit of the operettas. Among the best known are **The Mikado** (1885) and earlier ones, **H. M. S. Pinafore** (1878) and the next year, **The Pirates of Penzance.** Despite the harmony in their productions their relationship was not always harmonious.

Dark, Sidney and Rowland Grey. **W.S. Gilbert, His Life and Letters**. New York: George H. Doran, 1923. 269 p.
PR4714.D3

This is the first true biography of Gilbert. It meets a definition of modern scholarship and the authors avoided being caught up in the overenthusiasm of his public reception.

Pearson, Hesketh. **Gilbert, His Life and Strife**. New York: Harper, 1957. 276 p.
PR4714.P4 1957a

This is considered the biography that most fully uses the private papers of Gilbert. Gilbert was a temperamental person who wanted to be taken as a serious dramatist and was not.

GIRAUDOUX, Jean (1882-1944), French playwright; novelist

In his youth Giraudoux traveled extensively. He wrote five novels and some short stories, but his international fame rests upon his dramatic works, some fifteen plays. He used mythology, fantasy, political and psychological themes with a rich style, to voice his concern about the lack of morality in human nature. Among his best known works are **Tiger at the Gates** (1935), **Electra** (1937) and the popular **The Madwoman of Chaillot** (1945).

Inskip, Donald Percival. **Jean Giraudoux, The Making of a Dramatist**. New York: Oxford University Press, 1958. 194 p.
PQ2613.I74.Z65

This book is not a biography in the strict sense of the word but traces the development of Giraudoux as a dramatist. This is the first book in English which gives some background on the man whose reputation as a playwright preceded him.

GLASGOW, Ellen Anderson Gholson (1873-1945), American novelist

There has been a resurgence of interest in Ellen Glasgow recently thanks to the feminist movement. She won the Pulitzer Prize in 1942 for **In This Our Life**. Her theme is the reshaping of the South after the Civil War. **Barren Ground,** considered her best novel, depicts the emotional and economic drain on a young woman working a failing farm. She struggled with deafness all of her life.

Godbold, E. Stanly. **Ellen Glasgow and the Woman Within.**
Baton Rouge: Louisiana State University Press, 1972. 322 p.
PS3513.L34.Z665

Godbold looks at Ellen Glasgow against the backdrop of
Southern literary history. Her inhibitions and her literary
opinions are both scrutinized in this authoritative, well written
narrative. Godbold has been criticized for reading too much
autobiography into her novels.

GOETHE, Johann Wolfgang von (1749-1832), German poet; playwright;
novelist

Goethe is considered to be one of the great geniuses of all
time, not only as a literary artist and a major influence on
romanticism but as a creative thinker. He wrote exceptionally
lyrical poetry and his novels had a far-reaching influence. His
dramatic poem, **Faust,** the writing of which spanned his years from
1808 through 1832 and synthesized philosophy and art, continues
to challenge readers today.
Goethe was educated by his father until he began at the
university in Leipzig. He started writing during that time and
practiced law for four years with his father after his studies,
then he was a legal council for ten years in the court of Karl
Augustus of Saxe-Weimar. After a trip to Italy in 1788 he
returned to Germany, recognizing that he must pursue his artistic
calling. The height of his career and in German letters was his
collaboration with Friedrich Schiller from 1794 until 1805. He
continued his creative output until into his seventies. His
contribution to the sciences was his concept of morphology, now
fundamental to the theory of evolution.
Numerous works of his were exceptional contributions to
literature. Besides **Faust,** a dramatic poem, there was **The
Apprenticeship of Wilhelm Meister** of 1796, a prototype of the
German novel.
Goethe was a celebrity in his own time. He left a large
output of very literate autobiographical materials which spurred
many biographies. Listed below are those considered to
measure up to the standards of scholarly, literary biographies.
However, some older biographies have their place in the corpus of
Goethe.

Grimm, Hermann Friedrich. **The Life and Times of Goethe.**
Translated by Sarah Holland Adams. Boston: Little, Brown, 1880.
559 p.
PT2051.G73

The significance of this biography is that it opened up a
whole area of the literary research of Goethe.

Bielschowsky, Albert. **The Life of Goethe.** Translated by William A. Cooper. 3 vols. New York: Putnam, 1905-1908.
PT2051.B55

This is one of the most enduring of the Goethe biographies that were coming out very frequently at the end of the nineteenth and the beginning of the twentieth century.

Robertson, John George. **The Life and Work of Goethe, 1749-1832.** New York: E.P. Dutton, 1932. 350 p.
PT2049.R6 1932a

This remains a fairly substantial contribution and readable by today's standards.

Ludwig, Emil. **Goethe: The History of a Man.** Translated by Ethel Colburn Mayne. New York: Blue Ribbon Books, 1928. 647 p.
PT2051.L82 1928b

This was the most popularly written work with a bit of the sensational added.

Lewes, George Henry. **The Life and Works of Goethe.** 2 vols. London: D. Nutt, 1855; rpt. **The Life of Goethe.** New York: F. Ungar, 1965.
PT2049.L4 1965

This is considered to be one of the best biographies of any man in any language. It is well researched and eloquently written. However, Lewes' literary judgments are no longer valid and his neglect of the aged Goethe is unfortunate with the considerable research taking place concerning creativity into old age.

Friedenthal, Richard. **Goethe, His Life and Times.** Cleveland: World Pub., 1965, c1963. 561 p.
PT2051.F713 1965

For many critics, this continues to be the best modern biography of Goethe. Friedenthal probes in a lively, readable style all the social, political, scientific and cultural influences experienced by Goethe.

Fairley, Barker. **A Study of Goethe.** Oxford: Clarendon Press, 1947. 280 p.
PT2049.F33

This is an examination of the development of the inner life of Goethe. This compact biographical study is particularly useful as an introduction to Goethe's works.

GOGH, Vincent van (1853-90), Dutch painter

Vincent van Gogh is a major artist of the nineteenth century and is the best known of the postimpressionists. Today his works are bringing exhorbitant prices at auction houses. His sunflower series of 1888 is among the best known works by any painter. His style is so distinctive that it is easily recognizable. In his first period, the Dutch period, the paintings were more somber-toned. He moved to Paris and, influenced by Pissarro and other major artists of the time, lightened his pallette. At Arles where he spent more than two years in frenzied activity, ending his life in suicide, he painted his most famous canvases, despite his being confined intermittently to hospitals because of bouts of insanity. His early life gave little indication of what he would so-called "do with his life." He worked in some odd jobs and did some theology and was a lay missionary briefly before recognizing his true call. In this short career he did more than seven hundred paintings and over fifteen hundred drawings.

Hammacher, Abraham Marie and Renilde Hammacher. **Van Gogh, a Documentary Biography.** New York: Macmillan, 1982. 240 p. ND653.G7.H255 1982

Despite the importance of this artist, there is no really good biography that brings this man alive. This is the best attempt insofar as it is biography and not primarily a study of the man through his works. The Hammachers' work is scholarly, giving us the artistic and intellectual milieu in which van Gogh worked. However, there is no interpretation nor synthesizing of their research to portray the person. His letters, which they quote, are available in other sources.

GOGOL, Nikolai Vasilevich (1809-52), Russian fiction writer

A most original writer of the early nineteenth century whose literary style took a very different turn from his fellow countryman, Pushkin. His themes and style influenced the absurdist movement. He published a poem to disastrous reviews, then took up acting, worked in government while studying painting. His next literary attempt was much more successful in which he incorporated the folklore of his native Ukraine. His themes took a much more complex style incorporating his religious views and despair over human weakness. This dark vision, lightened by a comical view of the world, brought forth two of his masterpieces, a drama, **Inspector General** of 1836 and his novel **Dead Souls,** with its morbid plot. He worked on a second part to **Dead Souls** but destroyed it in a fit of despair toward the end of his life.

Magarshack, David. **Gogol, a Life.** New York: Grove Press, 1957. 329 p.
PG3335.M25 1957a

Needless to say the tortured life of Gogol inspired much biographical outpouring. Most of it does not have the detached, detailed approach that Magarshack brings to his subject.

GOLDSMITH, Oliver (1728-74), Anglo-Irish novelist; playwright

Goldsmith's well known contribution to the English novel was his only work in that genre, **The Vicar of Wakefield.** This 1766 work is a mixture of satire and the melodrama and sentimentality he criticized in contemporary drama. His greatest poem, "The Deserted Village," written in 1770, laments the loss of the simplicity of rural life by large landowners.

Wardle, Ralph Martin. **Oliver Goldsmith.** Lawrence: University of Kansas Press, 1957. 330 p.
PR3493.W3

Wardle looks at previous biographical attempts of Oliver Goldsmith and evaluates them, noting their deficiencies. He had access to manuscripts and personal papers not available to these previous biographers. This is considered the first biography of Goldsmith to use modern research methods in its production and conclusions.

GORKY, Maksim (1868-1936), Russian novelist; short story writer; playwright

Gorky's life reads like a Dickens novel. He was on his own at a very young age. Maksim Gorky is a pseudonym, "Gorky" means bitter in Russian. His writings would contain the themes of his life, a passionate humanitarianism and the need to subordinate his characters to ideology. His first and greatest play, written in 1902, was **The Lower Depths.** The 1905 Revolution forced him into exile and he wrote **Mother** in 1906, a revolutionary novel. He was involved with the politics of the day at the expense of his writing. However, his masterpiece, **The Life of Klim Samghin** (1927-36), a four-part novel, which was in process the last ten years of his life, more firmly established him as the father of Soviet literature.

Levin, Dan. **Stormy Petrel; the Life and Work of Maxim Gorky.** New York: Appleton-Century, 1965. 332 p.
PG3465.L38

This full-length biography also gives critical reviews of his works. Levin looks at the political orientation of Gorky, which has come under criticism, stating that Gorky was unaware of the reality of the brutality of Stalin.

Troyat, Henri. **Gorky.** Translated by Lowell Bair. New York: Crown Publishers, 1989. 216 p.
PG3465.T7613 1989

Henri Troyat is a biographer of literary masters. He examines his brutal childhood as well as his later political activities and how these influenced his literary output. This is a thoroughly readable biography which portrays Gorky honestly.

GRAHAM, Martha (1894-   ), American choreographer

A living legend in her own time who was still working in the field of dance in her nineties is Martha Graham. She was the creator of modern dance, and her choreography incorporates a new vocabulary of movement. She started with the Denishawn School. After eleven years she opened up her own studio and discarded the more romantic interpretation in favor of the angular, more abstract. "Appalachian Spring" in 1944, based on Aaron Copland's music of the same name is a world-renowned classic. She also explored mythology in "Cave of the Heart" in 1946 and "Errand into the Maze" the following year. Due to her preservationist attitude about her dancing role, her company nearly went into collapse. However, into the 1980's she was still choreographing.

Stodelle, Ernestine. **Deep Song: The Dance Story of Martha Graham.** New York: Schirmer Books, 1984. 329 p.
GV1785.G7.S86 1984

This is a definitive biography of Martha Graham, dancer and choreographer. Ms. Stodelle goes into great detail about her life as well as her art. The photographs add drama to this personal narrative.

GRAVES, Robert (1895-1985), English poet

Robert Graves was one of the many artists shattered by the trauma of World War I. He was seriously wounded in France. He spent his convalescence expressing his feelings about the war in poetry. He took a degree at Oxford and spent his life as a teacher, creative writer and literary critic. His best known novels were **I, Claudius** and **Claudius the God,** written in 1934. He published more than fifteen volumes of poetry, but **Collected Poems, 1959** represented what he wished to preserve. He may best be known to college students as the author of **Greek Myths** (1955), containing translations and commentary. He spent most of his life on the island of Majorca.

Seymour-Smith, Martin. **Robert Graves, His Life and Work.**
London: Hutchinson, 1982. 607 p.
PR6013.R35.Z783 1982

This biography came out to very mixed reviews. The author is a poet and was a friend of Graves. Seymour-Smith's opinions are quite authoritative in his interpretation of the life of Robert Graves. Robert Graves' life is a most interesting combination of highs and lows, and this Seymour-Smith seems to render but without the probing that could have taken place.

Graves, Richard Perceval. **Robert Graves, the Assault Heroic, 1895-1926.** New York: Viking, 1987, c1986. 387 p.
PR6013.R35.Z717 1987

This is a book by the poet's nephew. What holds one's interest is the engrossing life of Robert Graves who seems to survive the, at times, excessive minutiae.

GRAY, Thomas (1716-71), English poet

Intensity, lyricism and wit characterize the poetry of Thomas Gray, a retiring history professor at Cambridge. His 1751 short poem "Elegy Written in a Country Churchyard" is one of the most celebrated poems in the English language by a person who did not consider himself a poet by vocation but saw poetry as something to be pursued in his "spare time." So little did he perceive himself as a poet that he refused the title of poet laureate.

Ketton-Cremer, Robert Wyndham. **Thomas Gray; a Biography.**
Cambridge: Cambridge University Press, 1955. 310 p.
PR3503.K4 1955

This biography is based on the charming letters and other personal papers of Gray. It looks at his creative life, his relationships, his secluded life and the problems he had with handling his jeering undergraduates.

GRECO (1541?-1614), Greek-Spanish painter

El Greco is considered the most outstanding painter of the sixteenth century Spanish school. He went to Italy to study art. He moved on to Toledo and took on an important series of commissioned religious paintings such as "The Disrobing of Christ" (1577-79). He moved from a more realistic painting style to his distinctive elongated figures such as in "The Agony in the Garden" (1597-1603). His paintings also exhibited such an intensity and mystical quality that his style was not easily transmitted. A renewed interest in his art came about at the end of the nineteenth century.

Vallentin, Antonina. **El Greco**. Translated by Andrew Révai and Robin Chancellor. Garden City, N. Y.: Doubleday, 1955, c1954. 316 p.
ND813.T4.V355 1955

There is not a great deal of scholarly documentation according to the norms of modern research. Antonina Vallentin brings everything she can to this worthwhile book.

GREENAWAY, Kate (1846-1901), English illustrator

Kate Greenaway holds a special place in art as one of the most influential and still popular illustrators of children's books. Her finely detailed, delicately colored illustrations are in books still in print. Her **Mother Goose or The Old Nursery Rhymes** of 1881 probably has few rivals.

Engen, Rodney K. **Kate Greenaway, a Biography**. New York: Schocken Books, 1981. 240 p.
ND1942.G8.E54

Unfortunately this book is marred by the poorly reproduced illustrations by Greenaway. The author is an authority on Victorian illustrators and is able to portray the struggling Kate Greenaway who suffered greatly during a relationship with John Ruskin, the English author and art critic, and whose illustrations for children's books belie the rather sterile emotional existence she led.

GREENE, Graham (1904-   ), English novelist

Graham Greene is one of this century's most widely read English novelists. He writes not only serious novels, reflecting his moral concerns but is also noted for his spy stories and comedies. His style is highly visual and distinctive. His conversion to Catholicism resulted in his two best novels, **The Heart of the Matter** (1948) and **The End of the Affair** (1951). He wrote short stories and several screenplays.

Sherry, Norman. **The Life of Graham Greene**. vol. 1- New York: Viking, 1989-
PR6013.R44.Z845 1989

In this first of a two-volume work, Norman Sherry traces the first thirty-five years of Graham Greene. Sherry literally went to the places where Greene lived at various times in order to get a real feel for his subject. This is a very worthwhile in-depth look at an adventurous life.

GRIFFES, Charles Tomlinson (1884-1920), American composer

Griffes studied piano and composition in Germany but was also influenced by French and Russian music as well as that of the Orient. He returned home to spend his working days teaching music at a private school. His best-known piano work is the familiar "White Peacock" from "Four Roman Sketches" of 1915-16. He also wrote orchestral, chamber and vocal music.

Maisel, Edward. **Charles T. Griffes, the Life of an American Composer**. rev. ed. New York: Knopf, 1984. 399 p. ML410.G9134.M2 1984

This is an exceptionally well written biography by an American musicologist which gives us a vivid picture of this impressionist composer.

H.D. (Hilda Doolittle) (1886-1961), American poet

H.D. was a poet of the imagism school and was influenced by Ezra Pound, to whom she was briefly engaged. She moved to England and married the poet-novelist Richard Aldington. Her imagist style moved toward the more classical, using the Greek myths and exploring archetypes.

Guest, Barbara. **Herself Defined: The Poet H.D. and Her World**. Garden City, N. Y.: Doubleday, 1984. 360 p. PS3507.O726.Z68 1984

This is not the most well written of biographies but it is the best of those about H.D., whose life is quite fascinating. It is the authorized biography and is based on personal recollections and private letters of H.D.'s contemporaries and her personal papers. It is a book full of famous names and unconventional relationships.

HANDEL, George Friederich (1685-1759), English composer

Handel was one of the greatest composers of the Baroque era. He was born in Germany and worked as a musician and composed there but moved to England where he lived most of his adult life. He was influenced by his stay in Italy and composed some Italian operas but his fame rests on his English oratorios, especially the universally known "Messiah" of 1741. His other important contribution is in the area of the concerto.

Hogwood, Christopher. **Handel**. New York: Thames & Hudson, 1985, c1984. 312 p.
ML410.H13.H57 1985

This recent biography is by a noted English musician, who has written a scholarly work using all available documents and modern research methods. Hogwood is excellent in integrating the artist with his career. It is addressed to the serious layman and can be used as a reference book.

Deutsch, Otto. **Handel, a Documentary Biography**. New York: W.W. Norton, 1955. 942 p.
ML410.H13.D47 1955a

This, too, is a scholarly biography but more readable. It contains much material for further study of the man and his music.

Lang, Paul Henry. **George Frideric Handel**. New York: W.W. Norton, 1966. 731 p.
ML410.H13.L16

Handel inspires a serious approach and this is seen in this critical biography which also contains some interpretation of his music by the musicologist Paul Henry Lang. Like the other two books mentioned above the myths and distortions about Handel are stripped away with the more modern approach to research.

HARDY, Thomas (1840-1928), English novelist; poet

Thomas Hardy is a major English novelist who bridged the gap between the nineteenth and twentieth centuries. He introduced into Victorian literature the concept of fatalism, the human limitation of adapting to a changing environment. His major contributions to literature are three of his novels, **The Return of the Native** (1878), **Tess of the D'Urbervilles** (1891) and **Jude the Obscure** (1895). He was influenced by the Latin classics, the Bible and architecture. Most importantly, philosophically, was Darwin's **Origin of Species** (1859). The outrage against his treatment of sexuality in **Jude the Obscure** (1895) and **Tess of the D'Urbervilles** caused him to return to poetry, which has been considered to be more significant than his fiction. However, the response to his novels has overshadowed his poetry.

Millgate, Michael. **Thomas Hardy, a Biography.** New York: Random House, 1982. 637 p.
PR4753.M54 1982

This is a superb biography by the editor of the letters of Thomas Hardy. He probes the character of Hardy and how it influenced his writings as well as how he was influenced by the public and critics on the future course of his choice of genres. There is also criticism of Hardy's works, but the main thrust of the book is his life.

HARRIS, Joel Chandler (1848-1908), American fiction writer

Joel Chandler Harris is among America's finest humorists and local color writers. His Uncle Remus, a former slave, relates stories about authentic life of Southern blacks drawing upon folklore, dialect and humor.

Cousins, Paul M. **Joel Chandler Harris; a Biography.** Southern Literary Studies. Baton Rouge: Louisiana State University Press, 1968. 237 p.
PS1813.C6

Paul Cousins' scholarly biography was researched and written over a forty-year period. He interviewed contemporaries of Joel Chandler Harris and then put the book away to look at it again forty years later using the intervening scholarship and a different perspective.

HARTE, Bret (1836-1902), American short story writer; poet

Bret Harte was a writer of the American West. He is best known for his short story "The Outcasts of Poker Flat," written in 1870. He was not as successful as a writer for the **Atlantic Monthly,** and financial and personal problems made him decide to leave his family and live in Europe in order to concentrate on Western fiction. He died in London.

O'Connor, Richard. **Bret Harte; a Biography.** Boston: Little, Brown, 1966. 331 p.
PS1833.O3

This offers nothing new about Bret Harte but puts his story in a wonderfully descriptive narrative and clearly delineates the periods of Harte's life.

Stewart, George Rippey. **Bret Harte, Argonaut and Exile;**
Being an Account of the Life of the Celebrated American Humorist.
Boston: Houghton Mifflin, 1931. 384 p.
PS1833.S7

This is still considered the definitive biography of Bret
Harte. It is a rich presentation of Harte's character and
personality in a readable form.

HAWTHORNE, Nathaniel (1804-64), American fiction writer

Hawthorne is best known for his 1850 novel, **The Scarlet**
Letter, in which he applied a judgment in artistic terms to
Puritanism. He felt that most American literature of the day was
based on British models so he sought to create an authentic
national idiom. To support himself he had to work outside the
field of literature. After a second stint outside his field he
had his most productive period from 1849-1852, during which time
he wrote **The House of the Seven Gables. The Marble Faun** (1860)
was written after a European stay. He lived briefly at the
utopian Brook Farm and in Concord during the period of Ralph
Waldo Emerson and Henry David Thoreau.

Stewart, Randall. **Nathaniel Hawthorne, a Biography.** New
Haven: Yale University Press, 1948. 279 p.
PS1881.S67

Although using other sources, this biography is primarily a
reworking of the notebooks of Hawthorne's wife. It is thoroughly
researched but does not truly get to the depths of Hawthorne to
present a live portrait.

Turner, Arlin. **Nathaniel Hawthorne, a Biography.** New York:
Oxford University Press, 1980. 457 p.
PS1881.T79

Arlin Turner had been a Hawthorne scholar for thirty years
before writing this full-length life. This is a most readable
biography.

HAYDN, Joseph (1732-1809), Austrian composer

Franz Joseph Haydn, as he is more commonly known, was one of
the masters of the classical period. When he was nearly thirty
he entered the service of the Princes Esterházy, who were to be
his patrons for the rest of his life. During this time this
prolific composer wrote most of his 107 symphonies, many of his
eighty-three string quartets and most of his twenty-five operas.
His works of the "Sturm and Drang" period (storm and stress) from
1768-1774 are particularly significant in their inventiveness.

He was a friend of Wolfgang Amadeus Mozart and a teacher of Ludwig van Beethoven. Among his choral works the most famous is "The Creation" of 1798. The finest of his symphonic works were composed during a sojourn to England in the early 1790's.

Landon, H.C. Robbins. **Haydn, a Documentary Study.** New York: Rizzoli, 1981. 224 p.
ML410.H4.L257

This is an illustrated biography of Haydn which portrays Haydn as a composer in clear, vivid prose. This book is the result of the ongoing research of H.C. Robbins Landon on the life and music of Haydn.

Geiringer, Karl. **Haydn: A Creative Life in Music.** 3rd ed. Berkeley: University of California Press, 1982. 403 p.
ML410.H4.G4 1982

This third edition of a biography, written in collaboration with Irene Geiringer, continues to be a significant source on the life of Haydn.

HEBBEL, Friedrich (1813-63), German playwright

This German dramatist was also a poet and a short story writer. His dramas, particularly his trilogy **Die Nibelungen** (1862), are considered his greatest works. He influenced the works of Henrik Ibsen, August Strindberg and George Bernard Shaw in his themes of the struggle between the new and the old order and the psychological refinement of his characterization.

Purdie, Edna. **Friedrich Hebbel: A Study of His Life and Work.** London: Oxford University Press, 1932. 276 p.
PT2296.P8

Much of the best biographical material often remains in the original language of the creative artist. This scholarly work, the most penetrating study of Hebbel in English, provides good biographical insights and interpretations of his art.

HEINE, Heinrich (1797-1856), German poet

Heinrich Heine belongs among the greats of German literature. Numerous famous composers set his poems to music. Despite his German roots his enthusiasm for the July Revolution in France moved him to make Paris his home from 1831 until his death. His greatest poetry was written during the last eight years of his life as he lay paralyzed from syphilis.

Butler, E.M. (Eliza Marian). **Heinrich Heine, a Biography.**
London: Hogarth Press, 1956. 291 p.
PT2328.B8

This is a sympathetic, objective portrayal, concentrating on
the personality and life of Heine. Heine may demand a more
psychoanalytically oriented approach as he was a man of many
contradictions but this is, nevertheless, a competent biography.

Kossoff, Philip. **Valiant Heart: A Biography of Heinrich
Heine.** New York: Cornwall Books, 1983. 217 p.
PT2328.K58 1983

This vivid biographical work of one of the greatest literary
personalities in German literature shows the man as he was with
all the rough edges, questionable motivations and behavior.

HELLMAN, Lillian (1906-1984), American playwright

Lillian Hellman was one of the foremost women dramatists of
the first half of the twentieth century. Her first play **The
Children's Hour** achieved instant fame. Her success continued
with the **The Little Foxes** (1939). These and other plays dealt
with social issues, and some were made into films.

Rollyson, Carl E. **Lillian Hellman: Her Legend and Her
Legacy.** New York: St. Martin's Press, 1988. 613 p.
PS3515.E343.Z87 1988

This book borders on the "celebrity" biography. However, it
is serious in its appraisal of Lillian Hellman's view of herself
as seen in her life and memoirs. It may have more details than
are necessary to bring her to life, but it is a contribution to
the understanding of a significant playwright.

HEMINGWAY, Ernest (1889-1961), American novelist; short story writer

Hemingway was one of the great American writers of the
twentieth century. With the publication of his novel, **The Sun
Also Rises** (1926), he became a voice for the "lost generation,"
the American expatriates in Paris. His direct, terse style set
forth plots featuring courageous people. His life had a
celebratory character with much traveling, four marriages, poor
health, and suicide. Among his other well known novels are **A
Farewell to Arms** (1929) and **For Whom the Bell Tolls** (1940). He
settled in Cuba where he wrote the short novel **The Old Man and
the Sea,** which won a Pulitzer Prize.

Baker, Carlos. **Ernest Hemingway; a Life Story.** New York: Scribner, 1969. 697 p.
PS3515.E37.Z575 1969

This remains the most authoritative biography, written with the assistance of his widow, Mary, with access to unpublished manuscripts and letters.

Brian, Denis. **The True Gen: An Intimate Portrait of Ernest Hemingway by Those Who Knew Him.** New York: Grove Press, 1988. 356 p.
PS3515.E37.Z58264 1988

This is another important biography based upon interviews with relatives and close friends. Brian tries to separate the man from the myth, the myth that plays a large part in the Hemingway saga.

HENRY, O. (1862-1910), American short story writer

O. Henry, a pseudonym, is the name that the Library of Congress now uses for William Sidney Porter. He began his writing career after serving a prison term for embezzling. In 1902 he settled in New York and continued to write the short stories which became known for their unexpected conclusions. His more than three hundred stories were published in several volumes.

Langford, Gerald. **Alias O. Henry; a Biography of William Sidney Porter.** New York: Macmillan, 1957. 294 p.
PS2649.P5.Z7126

Langford gives us a fine piece of work in intertwining the life and work of O. Henry.

Long, E. Hudson. **O. Henry, the Man and His Work.** Philadelphia: University of Pennsylvania Press, 1949. 158 p.
PS2649.P5.Z714

This is another look at O. Henry, less detailed than the Langford work but nevertheless of a scholarly quality.

Smith, C. Alphonso. **O. Henry Biography.** Garden City, N.Y.: Doubleday, Page, 1916. 258 p.
PS2649.P5.Z8

This remains, despite its age, the most authoritative biography of O. Henry. Not only was it well researched, but it is an excellent example of a truly literary biography.

HESSE, Hermann (1877-1962), German novelist

Hermann Hesse was at his height of popularity during the 1950's especially with the younger generation, with his emphasis on the spiritual in man and a criticism of middle-class values. His best known novels are **Siddhartha** (1922), **Steppenwolf** (1927), and **Magister Ludi,** which won him the Nobel Prize in 1946.

Freedman, Ralph. **Hermann Hesse, Pilgrim of Crisis: A Biography.** New York: Pantheon Books, 1978. 432 p. PT2617.E85.Z6955

This account is the most authoritative to date in English of the life of Hermann Hesse. It may not be the liveliest of biographies but then neither was Hesse the liveliest of men. The complex workings of the author's mind and how that translated into his art are seen in this sensitive portrayal.

HICKS, Edward (1780-1849), American painter

Edward Hicks is known primarily as the painter of more than forty versions of "The Peaceable Kingdom." He was also a well known Quaker preacher.

Ford, Alice. **Edward Hicks, His Life and Art.** New York: Abbeville Press, 1985. 276 p. ND237.H58.F6 1985

This biography of Hicks is well illustrated. Alice Ford probes the social and philosophical background of the artist-preacher.

HINDEMITH, Paul (1895-1963), German composer

Paul Hindemith is considered one of the most important and prolific composers of the twentieth century and a dominant theoretical force in music. He was a professor of composition in Berlin when the Nazis banned his music. At the invitation of the Turkish government he went to that country to help reorganize the study of music there. He then came to the United States, where he was a professor at Yale University but spent his last years in Switzerland. His music is known for its linear, contrapuntal style in the contemporary idiom. His best known work is his opera, **Mathis der Maler.** He also wrote chamber music, operas and sonatas and the song cycle, "The Life of Mary."

Skelton, Geoffrey. **Paul Hindemith: The Man behind the Music: A Biography.** New York: Crescendo, 1975. 319 p. ML410.H685.S6 1975b

Geoffrey Skelton gives us a fine portrayal of Hindemith's personality and adventurous life, using letters and reminiscences, which captured his wry humor as well as his recalcitrant character.

HOGARTH, William (1697-1764), English engraver

One of the greatest artists of the eighteenth century, Hogarth was known primarily as a satirical engraver and to a lesser extent as a painter. He was apprenticed to an engraver and gained distinction in 1731 with several versions of the "Beggar's Opera." His "A Harlot's Progress" of 1732 marked his interest in morality as a subject. He was also an art theorist.

Paulson, Ronald. **Hogarth: His Life, Art, and Times.** 2 vols. Studies in British Art. New Haven: Published for the Paul Mellon Centre for Studies in British Art (London) by the Yale University Press, 1971.
ND497.H7.P38

This is a very erudite biography, not always easy reading. Paulson not only portrays the artist but writes of English intellectual life and art of Hogarth's time. A biography written for the scholar.

HOUSMAN, A.E. (Alfred Edward) (1859-1936), English poet

A.E. Housman failed his examinations at Oxford but continued to study the classics while employed as a clerk in London. Despite his lack of success at Oxford his scholarly publications won him a Latin professorship at University College in London and then at Trinity, Cambridge. He is chiefly remembered as a poet of three brief volumes, **A Shropshire Lad** (1896), **Last Poems** (1922) and the posthumously published **More Poems** (1936). His style and themes were narrow, yet he was able to communicate the universal.

Graves, Richard Perceval. **A.E. Housman: The Scholar-Poet.** London: Routledge & Kegan Paul, 1979. 304 p.
PR4809.H15

Graves explores the dual role of Housman as professor and poet, drawing upon correspondence and other personal papers. The aim of Graves' book is to encourage the reading of Housman's poetry.

Page, Norman. **A.E. Housman, a Critical Biography.** New York: Schocken Books, 1983. 236 p.
PR4809.H15.P33 1983

Norman Page evaluates earlier biographies of Housman, criticizes Graves as being overspeculative and then proceeds to do what he criticized Graves for doing—speculating. It is a good work and as authoritative as can be expected, given the enigmatic character of Housman and his complex intellectual and personal life.

HOWELLS, William Dean (1837-1920), American novelist

William Dean Howells was considered one of the greatest American novelists in his time. He was a prolific writer who influenced the development of realism in American Literature. His best known novels are A Modern Instance (1882) and The Rise of Silas Lapham (1885). As an editor of the Atlantic Monthly he was instrumental in encouraging such writers as Mark Twain and Henry James. His writings came to be considered too decorous despite the universal themes he explored.

Cady, Edwin H. The Road to Realism; the Early Years, 1837-1885, of William Dean Howells. Syracuse: Syracuse University Press, 1956. 283 p.
PS2033.C25

Cady, Edwin H. The Realist at War; the Mature Years, 1885-1920, of William Dean Howells. Syracuse: Syracuse University Press, 1958. 299 p.
PS2033.C23

These two volumes give the most complete picture of any of the biographies written. Cady emphasizes the family influence and sees his career as divided into three parts. He explores the reasons for the decline of popularity of Howells.

HUGHES, Langston (1902-67), African-American poet

Langston Hughes realistically portrayed the lives of African- Americans in his poetry. He was a prominent member of the Harlem Renaissance movement. His genius was in his ability to merge the comic with the pathetic and in his belief in the commonality of all cultures. Among his best known poems are "The Weary Blues" (1926) and "Fine Clothes to the Jew" (1927). He also wrote some fiction.

Rampersad, Arnold. The Life of Langston Hughes. 2 vols. New York: Oxford University Press, 1986-1988.
PS3515.U274.Z698 1986

Hughes presents a challenge to a biographer in that he was a very private figure behind his public image. The author looks at a radical life that left behind Columbia University for a boat to Africa, a poet more esteemed outside America than in it. Arnold Rampersad writes a thorough biography that is essential reading.

HUGO, Victor Marie (1802-85), French poet; novelist; playwright

Victor Hugo is best known to the English-speaking world as the author of the novels, **The Hunchback of Notre Dame** (1831) and **Les Misérables.** He was to the French the outstanding lyric poet of the nineteenth century. His most intense period of creativity followed his successful collection of poems **Odes and Ballads** (1826). This seventeen-year period of creativity ended upon the failure of a verse drama followed by the death of his daughter. He accepted a post in the government but after Napoleon's seizure of power he went into exile. He wrote his most mature poetry during this time, among them **Contemplations,** considered his finest. He returned to Paris, to politics and continued his poetry. His funeral was a state occasion. His works have been plagued with controversy and critical indifference.

Josephson, Matthew. **Victor Hugo, a Realistic Biography of a Great Romantic.** Garden City, N. Y.: Doubleday, Doran, 1942. 514 p.
PQ2293.J6

This is a very readable, popular biography with a focus on the public life of Hugo both as a writer and political figure. It is intended for the general reader.

Grant, Elliott Mansfield. **The Career of Victor Hugo.** Harvard Studies in Romance Languages..., vol. 21. Cambridge: Harvard University Press, 1945. 365 p.
PQ2293.G7

The emphasis of the Grant biography is on the literary career of Hugo, and it notes facts on his family life only as it impacted on his writings. The style and organization are clear.

Maurois, André. **Olympio; the Life of Victor Hugo.** New York: Harper, 1956. 498 p.
PQ2293.M353 1956a

This massively researched work by a French literary figure in his own right is the most complete biography of Hugo and one of Maurois' best analyses of a creative artist. The style is intense but not complex and would interest the scholar as well as the serious general reader.

HURSTON, Zora Neale (1901-60), African-American writer

Zora Hurston, a student of anthropology and folklore, wrote the African-American folktales, **Mules and Men** (1935) and **Tell My Horse** four years later. Her novels were unique but realistic celebrations of African-American life, employing humor. **Jonah's Gourd Vine** (1934) and **Their Eyes Were Watching God** (1937) are two novels of note.

Hemenway, Robert E. **Zora Neale Hurston: A Literary Biography.** Urbana: University of Illinois Press, 1977. 371 p. PS3515.U789.Z7

This readable work is a fine piece of biography which interweaves the life and art of Zora Hurston. It looks at her actual ambivalence as an African-American despite her ability to grasp this reality artistically.

IBSEN, Henrik (1828-1906), Norwegian playwright; poet

Henrik Ibsen is considered to be one of the most influential modern playwrights. His early plays were met with hostility in Norway, so he went to Italy and then to Germany where he wrote the realistic plays for which he is best known, **Peer Gynt** (1867), **A Doll's House** (1879), **Ghosts** (1881) and **Hedda Gabler** (1890). The drama of his late period was more introspective and less popular, although powerful. His masterpiece from this period is considered to be **The Wild Duck**, a play of complex relationships. He also wrote poetry of consistently high quality.

Meyer, Michael Leverson. **Ibsen, a Biography.** Garden City, N.Y.: Doubleday, 1971. 865 p. PT8890.M47

This is a massive work. It not only looks thoroughly at Ibsen's life but also at his intellectual exploration of the unconscious. Ibsen was not without his faults but Meyer emphasizes his exceptional contribution to the theater and his single minded triumph over many internal and external obstacles. A thorough consideration of his plays along with commentaries of major literary figures on Ibsen is included.

IRVING, Washington (1783-1859), American fiction writer

Washington Irving was a writer of many talents. Under the pseudonym of Diedrich Knickerbocker he wrote the great book of comic literature **A History of New York** (1809). He is best known to students of American literature, even young students, as the author of two tales, "Rip Van Winkle" and "The Legend of Sleepy

Hollow." His biography of George Washington, written during the years 1855-59, runs to five volumes. His essays have a gentle satirical quality.

Williams, Stanley Thomas. **The Life of Washington Irving.** 2 vols. New York: Oxford University Press, 1935. PS2081.W45

This 1935 biography is still considered to contain the most complete picture of the multi-talented Irving. This two-volume set is based on extensive research into his personal papers and has some criticism of his works.

ISHERWOOD, Christopher (1904-86), English novelist

Isherwood's novels are largely autobiographical. He spent some time in Germany with his lifelong friend W.H. Auden. What critics consider to be his best novel, **Down There on a Visit** (1962), centers on his visits to that country.

Finney, Brian. **Christopher Isherwood: A Critical Biography.** New York: Oxford University Press, 1979. 336 p. PR6017.S5.Z65

Finney has written an excellent biography, thoroughly researched, based on personal papers and interviews of Isherwood's friends. The prose is clear and vivid.

IVES, Charles (1874-1954), American composer

Charles Ives was an insurance man who composed nights and weekends. Despite this dual life he is considered a most prolific and original American composer. His more than 350 finished pieces include long, complex works incorporating folk idioms with polytonality and polyrhythms. Ives composed for a variety of instrumental combinations as well for voice. Of particular note is his "Second Piano Sonata: Concord, Mass., 1840-60" which was in process from 1909 until 1915. A brief, unique orchestral piece, "The Unanswered Question," was written in 1908.

Cowell, Henry and Sidney Cowell. **Charles Ives and His Music.** New York: Oxford University Press, 1955. 245 p. ML410.I94.C6

This is not a definitive work but an exploratory look at the life and work of Charles Ives, written before his death and based on interviews of Ives and friends. It explores his dual role as composer and very successful businessman and the frustrations of a creative artist earning a living in an unrelated field.

Rossiter, Frank R. **Charles Ives and His America.** New York: Liveright, 1975. 420 p.
ML410.I94.R68

This book is broader in concept than his life. It looks at his milieu and mind set, the conflicting forces and psychic demons, which seem to reside with great frequency within the creative artist and how these seemed to interact in his life establishing his choices and priorities. His inability to accept the importance of his life as a composer led him to live a life of self-imposed isolation.

JAMES, Henry (1843-1916), American novelist

Henry James was from an exceptionally cultured and talented family. He was born in New York City but traveled in Europe extensively. His early novels compared his perceptions of the naiveté of Americans to the sophistication of the Europeans. **Portrait of a Lady** (1881) is an example of this view. His masterpieces were written toward the end of his life, **The Ambassadors** (1903) and **The Golden Bowl** (1904). James, one of the great masters of the novel, is noted for his subtle characterizations and complex style. He also wrote other creative fiction and was a noted critic.

Edel, Leon. **Henry James.** 5 vols. Philadelphia: Lippincott, 1953-1972.
PS2123.E33

Leon Edel is a master biographer. He spent nineteen years on this work. For this exceptional literary effort Edel was awarded the Pulitzer Prize and, for volumes two and three, the National Book Award for Nonfiction. The documentation available on Henry James is staggering. There are 15,000 extant letters of James as well as family papers, part of Houghton Library at Harvard University. Despite his scholarly efforts, Edel has been criticized for being too enamored of his subject and too Freudian in interpreting both James and his characters as they relate to James' life. Still, few biographies match the quality of this one.

Edel, Leon. **Henry James, a Life.** New York: Harper & Row, 1985. 740 p.
PS2123.E353 1985

This is a shortened edition of the five-volume biography. Despite the considerable condensation, it still has the impact of the larger work. The core of the original remains.

JANACEK, Leos (1854-1928), Czech composer

Janácek is considered the greatest Czech composer since Antonin Dvorak. He composed many works before he won recognition at the time of the successful production of his opera **Jenufa,** thirteen years after it was written. His reputation, particularly for his most original vocal works, continues to grow.

Vogel, Jaroslav. **Leos Janácek: A Biography.** Revised and edited by Karel Janovickby. New York: W.W. Norton, 1981. 439 p.
ML410.J18.V712 1981

This is a revision of a 1963 biography. Jaroslav Vogel was a conductor of Janácek's works and has written an exemplary work. It is not the most clear prose but is worth the effort to read because of the quality and organization of the research.

JEFFERS, Robinson (1887-1962), American poet

Jeffers was a controversial poet. He had a master's degree in literature and studied medicine for three years. He combined his knowledge of the classics, the Bible and his meditative experience of nature in his art.

Bennett, Melba Berry. **The Stone Mason of Tor House; the Life and Work of Robinson Jeffers.** Los Angeles: W. Ritchie Press, 1966. 264 p.
PS3519.E27.Z572

This is not the definitive biography of Jeffers but is a fine introduction to his personality. Melba Bennett spent a number of months at Tor House while Jeffers and his wife were still alive. Jeffers' wife began the research for a biography of her husband but died before she could write it. Bennett incorporated her research in his book.

JOHNSON, Samuel (1709-84), English man of letters

Samuel Johnson was not primarily a creative writer. His
poetry takes a back seat to his work as a lexicographer, essayist
and critic. However so exceptional is James Boswell's **Life of
Johnson** that Johnson must be included in any study of biography.
And so great was his influence upon the English language and
literature that the period of time in which he lived is called
the Age of Johnson.

Boswell, James. **Life of Johnson**. 4 vols. Edited by George
Birbeck Hill. Oxford: Clarendon Press, 1887.
PR3533.B6 1887

There are several editions of the **Life of Johnson**. This
one, edited by George Birbeck Hill, is considered the best.

Boswell was a friend of Johnson's and was so enthralled by
him as a person that he kept a running chronology of his life
from the time he met him. Despite the length of this work, it
primarily concerns Johnson's life after Boswell met him with
little mention of his early life and family.

Bate, Walter Jackson. **Samuel Johnson**. New York: Harcourt
Brace Jovanovich, 1977. 646 p.
PR3533.B334

Samuel Johnson was fortunate to have another exceptional
biography written of him. This much more recent work is more
balanced in its coverage of the whole of Johnson's life.

Wain, John. **Samuel Johnson**. London: Macmillan, 1974. 388 p.
PR3533.W33 1974

This biography is based on Boswell's and is written by a
poet-novelist. It is geared toward the general reader.

JONSON, Ben (1573?-1637), English playwright; poet

Ben Jonson is considered one of the greatest comic
dramatists of all times as well as one of the great poets of the
seventeenth century. He tried acting but was unsuccessful at
that but his career as a dramatist was meteoric. He wrote a
number of plays with a variety of themes and styles but his
best known are his "comedy of humors" among them **Volpone** (1606)
and **The Alchemist** (1610). He then moved into the art form of
court masques in which he worked brilliantly. Jonson continued
to write poetry. So great was his influence that a group of
young admirers called the "Sons of Ben" continued after his
death. In his day he was as famous as Shakespeare.

Riggs, David. **Ben Jonson: A Life.** Cambridge, Mass.: Harvard University Press, 1989. 399 p.
PR2631.R54 1989

David Riggs sees Jonson as a man of paradoxes: a womanizer with a criminal record but a great model of classical austerity as a writer and in his writings. Using the rather speculative psychoanalytical approach, Riggs sees his drives being channeled

into his art. Despite the opportunity for a biographical exposé Riggs handles his personal excesses with tact.

Chute, Marchette Gaylord. **Ben Jonson of Westminster.** New York: Dutton, 1953. 380 p.
PR2631.C53

This biography is written for the general reader and serves more as an introduction to the life and times of Jonson. It is nevertheless reliable and balanced and sets Jonson's plays in their context.

JOYCE, James (1882-1941), Irish novelist; poet

One of the great innovators of twentieth century fiction, James Joyce's best known works, **Ulysses** (1922), and **Finnegans Wake,** written two years before his death, continue to be sources of seemingly inexhaustible literary challenges. **Ulysses** is in the "stream of consciousness" vein, and the technique of **Finnegans Wake** overshadows the plot to the puzzlement of many readers. He was born in Dublin but lived most of his life on the continent, the post-World War I years in Paris. Yet it is his birthplace and early life that he incorporates into his fiction. He also wrote poetry at different times off and on and a play, **Exiles,** in 1918. Joyce had many operations on his eyes and died following surgery in Zurich.

Ellmann, Richard. **James Joyce.** rev. ed. New York: Oxford University Press, 1982. 887 p.
PR6019.O9.Z5332 1982

Richard Ellmann is a major biographer and in Joyce he finds a pre-eminent subject. This is the revised edition of the 1959 work that won the National Book Award when it first appeared. Critics felt this edition was not sufficiently updated to merit being called "revised." However, there is some new material and many more illustrations.

Gorman, Herbert Sherman. **James Joyce.** New York: Farrar & Rinehart, 1939. 358 p.
PR6019.O9.Z547

This biography, which does not begin to compare with Ellmann's, is, nevertheless, worthwhile. It was written in such close collaboration with its subject that it could be called autobiographical.

KAFKA, Franz (1883-1924), Czech novelist; short story writer

One of the major twentieth century literary figures, Kafka is noted for his lucid, precise prose full of angst, emotional oppression and labyrinthine complexity. He was virtually unknown during his lifetime because he did not have much of his work published. Some of his short fiction, such as "The Metamorphosis," was published before his death. All his novels, among them the masterpieces, **The Trial** and **The Castle**, were published posthumously by his friend, Max Brod. Many of his works were not translated into English until years after their publication. He was an important asset to an insurance firm, where he worked until his health forced him to retire. He seemed unable to break the emotional ties with his parents and never married Felice, to whom he proposed more than once.

Hayman, Ronald. **Kafka: A Biography** (Previously published as **K, a Biography of Kafka**). New York: Oxford University Press, 1982. 349 p.
PT2621.A26.Z74622 1982

This is the first of three biographies of Kafka published in the 1980's. Hayman writes with sensitivity but is exhaustive in detailing the life of Kafka. It is a full-length portrait of Kafka but some reviewers at the time of its publication felt that he does not come alive.

Pawel, Ernst. **The Nightmare of Reason: A Life of Franz Kafka**. New York: Farrar, Straus, Giroux, 1984. 466 p.
PT2621.A26.Z8155 1984

Pawel had access to more sources than Max Brod did in writing his biography even though Brod was Kafka's friend. With this background Pawel disputes some of the insights offered by Max Brod. It is brilliantly written but at times a bit too strident in tone.

Mailloux, Peter Alden. **A Hesitation before Birth: The Life of Franz Kafka**. Newark: University of Delaware Press, 1989. 622 p.
PT2621.A26.Z7696 1989

This is a fascinating in-depth exploration of the tormented life of Kafka. The title of the book is exceptionally appropriate. One has a real feel for Kafka as a person and the inner conflict that he experienced in his interpersonal relations, his need for the more unstructured existence than working in an office would allow and his compulsive pursuit of the woman he would never marry.

KAHLO, Frida (1907-1954), Mexican painter

Frida Kahlo may be better known as the wife of Diego Rivera, the Mexican painter. She was, however, an artist in her own right who, as a result of a serious accident, used art as therapy. She became an art teacher, and her work has been exhibited not only in her native country but also in the United States and France. Besides the physical sufferings she endured throughout her life as a result of the accident, she experienced great emotional turmoil as the wife, ex-wife, and then wife again of Diego Rivera.

Herrera, Hayden. **Frida, a Biography of Frida Kahlo.** New York: Harper & Row, 1983. 507 p.
ND259.K33.H47 1983

Hayden Herrera has access to the primary sources of Kahlo's life as well as extensive interviews with Kahlo's circle. At times it may seem to be that Herrera makes her subject a celebrity. In reality Kahlo was a courageous artist who lived a painful life.

KEATS, John (1795-1821), English poet

During John Keats' short life he wrote some of the greatest poems in English literature. He was of the second generation of British romantic poets. Orphaned at an early age, apprenticed to a surgeon at the age of sixteen, he abandoned medicine for poetry two years later and at the young age of eighteen began a six-year writing career that produced some of the most powerful lyric poetry in English. Among his best known poems is the long allegory "Endymion" (1818). After he had contracted tuberculosis and as a result of his poor health could not marry the woman he loved, he wrote his six great odes among which are the well-known "Ode on a Grecian Urn" and "Ode to a Nightingale."

Bate, Walter Jackson. **John Keats.** Cambridge: Belknap Press of Harvard University Press, 1963. 732 p.
PR4836.B3

This work is a Pulitzer Prize winner. It most skillfully interweaves the life of Keats with his works. Bate's criticism of his poetry is insightful.

Gittings, Robert. **John Keats.** Boston: Little, Brown, 1968.
469 p.
PR4836.G49 1968

This is the British complement to Bate's biography. It
is a readable work that sheds light on the life and poetry of
Keats.

Ward, Aileen. **John Keats; the Making of a Poet.** New York:
Viking Press, 1963. 450 p.
PR4836.W3

This book is addressed to the general reader and is written
in an accessible style.

KIPLING, Rudyard (1865-1936), English poet; fiction writer

India-born Rudyard Kipling was a literary giant in his
time. He is best known now for his children's **Jungle Books.** His
most characteristic medium was the short story. He went back and
forth between India and England during his lifetime.

Carrington, Charles Edmund. **The Life of Rudyard Kipling.**
Garden City, N. Y.: Doubleday, 1955. 433 p.
PR4856.C35

This definitive biography by Carrington is based on private
papers and interviews with Kipling's contemporaries. It is
readable and generally objective. Some critics feel Carrington
lacks a sound literary perspective.

KLEE, Paul (1879-1940), Swiss painter; graphic artist

Klee is as elusive to write about as his art is to
interpret. He was a sophisticated art theoretician whose works
exhibit a kind of innocence and whimsy which appears at variance
to his intellectual probings. He studied the violin but chose to
follow a career in art, a difficult decision. His work is
influenced by his study of various periods of art from early
Byzantine to Francisco de Goya and James Ensor. His early works
were mostly etchings with such descriptive titles as "Virgin in a
Tree" (1913) and "Two Men Meet, Each Believing the Other to be of
Higher Rank". He settled in Germany with his wife and taught at
the Bauhaus. He returned to Switzerland when the Nazis
considered his work to be "degenerate." This move changed the
lightheartedness of his work to somberness.

Haftmann, Werner. **The Mind and Work of Paul Klee.** New York: Praeger, 1954. 213 p.
ND588.K5.H314 1954a

Klee has many facets to his art and life that more than challenge the biographer. Hartmann has produced a fine work that explores the many talents and moods of Klee.

KLEIST, Heinrich von (1777-1811), German poet; playwright

Kleist is considered one of the greatest poets in German literature. During his lifetime he did not achieve the fame he desired and resorted to suicide. He was not unnoticed during his career, but his work was ahead of its time. He was also a playwright whose masterpiece is considered to be **The Prince of Homburg** (1810). The meaning of his works continued to be debated by both existentialists and Marxists.

Maass, Joachim. **Kleist: A Biography.** Translated by Ralph Manheim. New York: Farrar, Straus, & Giroux, 1983. 313 p.
PT2379.M1513 1983

This is a detailed but readable biography of a complex literary artist. Its significant feature is the excellent portrayal of Kleist and his circle by an established novelist.

KLEMPERER, Otto (1885-1973), German musician

One of the twentieth century's outstanding conductors of major orchestras in Europe and the United States, Klemperer was considered to be a most influential musician and significant interpreter of the orchestral repertoire. He also composed symphonies, string quartets and a mass.

Heyworth, Peter. **Otto Klemperer, His Life and Times; v 1, 1885-1933.** New York: Cambridge University Press, 1983. 492 p.
ML422.K67.H53 1983

This is an exceptional biography of an interpreter of music. This first volume details his years in Germany. Heyworth explores his supposed manic-depressive personality and the legend that has surrounded his magnetism as a symphony conductor.

KODALY, Zoltán (1882-1967), Hungarian composer

Kodály is the foremost Hungarian composer of the twentieth century after Béla Bartók. He, like Bartók, explored the folk idiom of his country and based much of his music on this research. His approach was more conservative than Bartók's. Among his most popular works is the 1926 "Háry János," a comic opera. He wrote both instrumental and vocal music.

Young, Percy. M. **Zoltán Kodály, a Hungarian Musician.** London: E. Benn, 1964. 231 p. ML410.K732.Y7

This is a well-crafted biography of a musician, thoroughly researched and a pleasure to read. All aspects of Kodály's life as a person and artist are thoroughly examined as well as his place in the broader musical scene in his own country and in Western music.

KOKOSCHKA, Oskar (1886-1980), Austrian painter; author

Oskar Kokoschka was a visual artist who expressed himself in various media and locales. He was an expressionist but his highly personal style within this school is characterized by a psychological tension reflecting prewar Vienna. He moved to Berlin but returned to be in the Austrian army in World War I, during which he was wounded. After his painful convalescence he traveled through Europe, North Africa and the Near East where the subjects of his paintings were spatially distorted urban scenes. He moved to London, became a British citizen but settled in Switzerland the last twenty years of his life.

Whitford, Frank. **Oskar Kokoschka, a Life.** New York: Atheneum, 1986. 221 p. ND511.5.K6.W48 1986

Whitford concludes from the documents on Kokoschka's life that he saw himself as a victim of criticism and had to move on to preserve his artistic integrity.

KOLLWITZ, Käthe (1867-1945), German graphic artist; sculptor

Käthe Kollwitz was a graphic artist whose realistic portrayals of poverty and oppression strongly captured her political and social statements. Among these is "Blue Shawl" (1903). Her woodcuts, such as "Death" (1934-35), have an expressionistic style. Käthe Kollwitz was also the sculptor of a significant war monument, unveiled in 1933 in a Belgian cemetery.

Klein, Mina C. and H. Arthur Klein. **Käthe Kollwitz; Life in Art.** New York: Holt, Rinehart & Winston, 1972. 183 p. NC251.K6.K55

This book looks at her painful life and how she expressed what she felt and saw in powerful artistic statements.

LAWRENCE, D.H. (David Herbert) (1885-1930), English novelist

D.H. Lawrence wrote in other genres, including poetry, but it is in the novel that he achieved his greatest impact upon literature. His reputation began notoriously. His **The Rainbow** (1915) and **Lady Chatterley's Lover** were banned. Lawrence claimed union with nature and sexual fulfillment to be the antidotes to dehumanizing industrialization. Despite his influence upon the novel some critics preferred his short stories as they were less polemic in tone. His was a kind of vagabond life. Leaving England in 1919 he returned only for brief visits. He traveled through Europe and lived in Australia and New Mexico, experiences which produced some fine travel writing. During his lifetime he was considered a literary pornographer, and his works did not receive much sympathetic criticism until more than twenty years after his death. The early **Sons and Lovers** (1913) is considered by some to be his finest novel.

Nehls, Edward (ed.). **D.H. Lawrence: A Composite Biography.** 3 vols. Madison: University of Wisconsin, 1957-59. PR6023.A93.Z73

This biographical study has a rather unique approach. Nehls uses autobiography, biography and Lawrence's writings to portray Lawrence's life without editorial comment. It is the most complete biography of Lawrence to date.

LEWIS, Sinclair (1885-1951), American novelist

In 1930 Sinclair Lewis became the first American to win the Nobel Prize for Literature. Among his most significant novels are **Main Street** (1920), **Babbitt** (1922) and **Arrowsmith** (1925). His theme was a satire on midwestern middle-class urban life. His later novels did not achieve the success of those of the 1920's. He spent his last two years in Rome.

Schorer, Mark. **Sinclair Lewis, An American Life.** New York: McGraw-Hill, 1961. 867 p. PS3523.E94.Z78

Mark Schorer has been a major critic of Sinclair Lewis and therefore eminently qualified to write his biography. This very readable account of the life and work of Lewis is based not only on primary documents but also on interviews with hundreds of Lewis' contemporaries.

LEWIS, Wyndham (1886-1957), English painter; novelist

Despite Lewis' large body of work as a visual artist and
numerous creative writings, the man and his work are not well
known. It is the whole corpus that must be looked at in regard to
its controversial, iconoclastic aspect. He founded the vorticism
movement, which aimed at developing a machine-age aesthetic
during its brief (1913-19) existence. His novels **Tarr** (1918) and
The Revenge for Love (1937) are strong social commentaries which
also delve into the life of an artist.

Meyers, Jeffrey. **The Enemy: A Biography of Wyndham Lewis.**
London: Routledge & Kegan Paul, 1980. 391 p.
PR6023.E97.Z75

This is a most interesting, well-written biography of a man
whom the author felt was, despite his genius, unfocused in his
pursuit of the arts and in his need to make political and social
statements. His was an improbable career with self-destructive
tendencies.

LISZT, Franz (1811-86), Hungarian composer

Considered the greatest pianist in his time and one of the
greatest of all times, Liszt was one of the major composers of
the romantic period, especially for the piano. After
concertizing for a number of years he settled in Weimar to devote
himself to composing. Among his best known works are two piano
concertos, "Totendanz" for piano and orchestra and the monumental
"Faust Symphony," which dates from 1854-1857. He lived with a
countess and then later with a princess. After separation from
the latter, he turned to writing religious music, received minor
orders and was made an abbé by Pope Pius IX. His later music,
misunderstood at the time, anticipated that of the twentieth
century. He performed the large, difficult works of Chopin and
Schumann when they were no longer able to do so and assisted
other composers in having their music performed. He was also a
most distinguished piano teacher.

Walker, Alan. **Franz Liszt.** vol. 1- New York: Knopf, 1983-
ML410.L7.W27 1983

Alan Walker is enamored of his subject in this projected
three-volume biography. However, the publication will probably
be considered the definitive biography of Liszt and despite its
scholarly detail, readable. An incredible achievement.

Taylor, Ronald. **Franz Liszt, the Man and the Musician.** New
York: Universe Books, 1986. 285 p.
ML410.L7.T35 1986

This is also a serious, well-researched biography which portrays movingly the person and art of Franz Liszt. Taylor works through the legends and opens to the reader a man, who at the end of his life, despite his successful musical career, found his existence meaningless.

LONGFELLOW, Henry Wadsworth (1807-82), American poet

Who has not read "Evangline" or "The Song of Hiawatha"? These poems and many others made Longfellow the most popular American poet of the nineteenth century and the poet who made Europe take note of American literature. He was well educated and was a professor at Harvard from 1835 until 1854. Several years later he received honorary degrees from Oxford and Cambridge and two years after his death became the first American to be honored in the Poets' Corner of Westminster Abbey, London. He was widowed twice. His second wife and mother of their six children died tragically. His reputation has declined during the twentieth century, but he remains popular although he is no longer considered a major poet.

Wagenknecht, Edward. **Longfellow: A Full-Length Portrait.** New York: Longmans, Green, 1955. 370 p.
PS2281.W17

This is a revisionist study of Longfellow, a rethinking and more thorough reading of the primary documentation of the life and work of Longfellow. At times too detailed, it nevertheless portrays a lively account of Longfellow, especially during his very happy second marriage.

LOWELL, Amy (1874-1925), American poet

Amy Lowell was from a distinguished New England family. It was not until 1913 that she went to England and found her distinctive style as a leader of the imagists. Among her most significant contributions are **Sword Blades and Poppy Seeds** (1914) and the poem for which she won a Pulitzer, "What's O'Clock" (1925).

Damon, S. Foster. **Amy Lowell, a Chronicle, with Extracts from her Correspondence.** Boston: Houghton Mifflin, 1935. 773 p.
PS3523.088.Z64

This remains the definitive biography by a friend of Lowell's. Despite the proximity, Damon writes dispassionately both of the poet and her works. It contains much material from her letters and is so organized as to allow Lowell to speak for herself.

LUNT, Alfred (1892-1977), American actor
(LUNT) FONTANNE, Lynne (1887-1983), American actress

During their forty-year career they were considered the best
acting couple on the American stage in such plays as those by
George Bernard Shaw, William Shakespeare and Noel Coward.

Brown, Jared. **The Fabulous Lunts; a Biography of Alfred Lunt
and Lynne Fontanne.** New York: Atheneum Pubs., 1986. 523 p.
PN2287.L8.B76 1986

This is one of the rare biographies of substance on
interpreters of the arts. Brown, a theater historian, has
written an impressive work that details their wonderful artistry
together.

McCULLERS, Carson (1917-67), American novelist; short story
writer

Carson McCullers used her small town, southern origins as the
basis of her novels. Her best known novel is her first, **The
Heart Is a Lonely Hunter**, which is a psychological study of the
isolation of a deaf-mute. Her other works are noted for her
sensitive portrayals of the characters.

Carr, Virginia Spencer. **The Lonely Hunter: A Biography of
Carson McCullers.** Garden City, N. Y.: Doubleday, 1975. 600 p.
PS3525.A1772.Z58

This is a serious biography that nevertheless appeals to the
general reader. Carson McCullers emerges as a warm, alive
individual, a very complex personality involved in the lives of
many people. The author interviewed more than five hundred
people in the seven years of research for this biography.

MAHLER, Gustave (1860-1911), Austrian composer; conductor

Mahler set conducting standards that have become legendary.
So rigorous were his musical demands that he constantly moved
from opera house to opera house. He was a noteworthy composer
especially of his song cycles, "Songs of a Wayfarer" (1883-85),
"Kindertotenlieder" (1901-04) and "Das Lied von der Erde" (1911).
He spent the years 1907-10 in New York before returning to
Vienna, where he died from overwork.

Blaukopf, Kurt. **Gustave Mahler.** Translated by Inge Goodwin.
New York: Praeger, 1973. 297 p.
ML410.M23.B63

This well-translated book contains important insights into the life of this musician, as well as the times during which he lived.

MALRAUX, André (1901-76), French novelist; writer

Better known for his social and philosophical writings, André Malraux incorporated his views into his fiction. In 1933 he won the prestigious Goncourt Prize for **Man's Fate**. Two of his previous novels incorporated his philosophical bent with political events. His more specific philosophy of art was in his final novel **The Walnut Trees of Altenburg** (1948). He then went on to write a series of critical works based on the theme of art. His **Anti-Memoirs** of 1967 is an exceptional autobiography.

Payne, Robert. **A Portrait of André Malraux**. Englewood Cliffs, N. J.: Prentice-Hall, 1970. 481 p.
PQ2625.A716.Z79

This book is based on Malraux's autobiography. Payne takes his rather fragmented musings and reorganizes them into an engrossing portrait, primarily of Malraux's public life. This is a good introduction to a fascinating man who lived a rich life.

Lacouture, Jean. **André Malraux**. Translated by Alan Sheridan. New York: Pantheon Books, 1975. 510 p.
PQ2625.A716.Z686813 1975

Lacouture does an exceptional piece of work in this very thorough biography of a twentieth century Renaissance man. He shows how Malraux evolved intellectually. He discreetly touches upon his tormented personal life. The flaw of the work is, unfortunately, the rather poor translation. Despite this it is an important biography.

MANN, Heinrich (1871-1950), German novelist

Heinrich Mann was the author of several novels of social criticism such as **Professor Unrat** (1905), translated as **The Blue Angel** in 1932. His finest work of fiction is considered to be **The Patrioteer** (1921). He was in the shadows of his more illustrious brother, Thomas.

MANN, Thomas (1875-1955), German novelist

Thomas Mann is one of the outstanding figures in German literature in the twentieth century. His fame was established by his very first novel at the age of twenty-six, **Buddenbrooks**

(1901). The theme of **Death in Venice** (1912) is creativity and neurosis as it is for his major novel **The Magic Mountain** twelve years later.

Hamilton, Nigel. **The Brothers Mann: The Lives of Heinrich and Thomas Mann, 1871-1950 and 1875-1955.** New Haven: Yale University Press, 1979, c1978. 422 p.
PT2625.A43.Z647 1979

It seemed that the lives of these two literary brothers were so intertwined that to study one is to study both. With this thesis in mind, Hamilton has given us this joint biography in clear, readable prose.

MANSFIELD, Katherine (1888-1923), English short story writer

This New Zealand-born author, influenced by Chekhov, was a master of the short story. She moved to London at an earlier age to establish herself as a writer after considering a career in music. Her first collection of short stories was written after convalescing in Bavaria, **In a German Pension** (1911). **Bliss and Other Stories** established her reputation in 1920. After her marriage to John Middleton Murry in 1918 she became a member of a literary circle which included Virginia Woolf and D. H. Lawrence.

Alpers, Antony. **The Life of Katherine Mansfield.** New York: Viking Press, 1980. 466 p.
PR9639.3.M258.Z58

Antony Alpers wrote an earlier biography of Katherine Mansfield in 1954. This is not a revision of it but a new life based on a wealth of new material. He develops her life as a woman whose artistic maturing is cut short by her death at thirty-four. It makes for a moving story of a complex life.

Tomalin, Claire. **Katherine Mansfield: A Secret Life.** New York: Knopf, 1988, c1987. 292 p.
PR9639.3.M258.Z89 1988

Less detailed than Alpers' life, Tomalin's work has its own merits. It is a study of the artist as a woman. It is insightful and readable.

MARQUAND, John P. (John Phillips) (1893-1960), American novelist

Marquand started out as a successful writer of slick adventure fiction. He then turned to his more noteworthy theme of the upper-class elite of Boston. **The Late George Apley**

(1937), his first novel with this theme, won him a Pulitzer
Prize.

Bell, Millicent. **Marquand: An American Life.** Boston: Little,
Brown, 1979. 537 p.
PS3525.A6695.Z57

Millicent Bell has written a scholarly yet sympathetic
portrayal of Marquand. She had full access to his personal
papers and files of his publisher. She penetrates his life and
mind in a graceful style.

Birmingham, Stephen. **The Late John Marquand; a Biography.**
Philadelphia: Lippincott, 1972. 322 p.
PS3525.A6695.Z59

This reads like one of John Marquand's novels as is hinted
by the "late" in the title. Birmingham explores his early life
and notes the relationship between it and his later unsuccessful
family life.

MATISSE, Henri (1869-1954), French painter; sculptor

Matisse, along with Picasso, is considered among the most
important artists of the twentieth century. Matisse belonged to
the schools of impressionism, postimpressionism and fauvism. His
last years saw him making brilliant paper cut-outs, some feel his
best and most original works, and decorating a French chapel with
joyful themes. He began working as a law clerk until he took art
lessons. Masterpieces from his early works are "Woman with a
Hat: Madame Matisse" (1905) and "The Dance" (1910). Influenced
by cubism he became more sober with "The Piano Lesson" (1917).
He also worked in the so-called decorative arts bringing his
mastery to design.

Barr, Alfred Hamilton. **Matisse, His Art and His Public.** New
York: Museum of Modern Art, 1951. 591 p.
ND553.M37.B34

This is a monumental work, considered by some book reviewers
to be one of the finest monographs written during the lifetime of
an artist. As with all visual artists there are many pages of
plates. The book does contain biographical material, possibly
not of the scope and organization that one would find with a
literary artist.

Schneider, Pierre. **Matisse.** Translated by Michael Taylor and
Bridget Strevens Romer. New York: Rizzoli, 1984. 752 p.
N6853.M33.S3513 1984

Again more of a study of the artist, copiously illustrated, than a birth-to-death biography, this book is nevertheless most insightful into Matisse and in a way mirrors the excesses of its subject.

MAUGHAM, William Somerset (1874-1965), English novelist; playwright; short story writer

One of a number of artists who trained in medicine and then turned to writing, Maugham is among the most popular English writers of the twentieth century. Among his plays are the classic drawing-room comedies, **Our Betters** (1915), **The Circle** (1921) and **The Constant Wife** (1927). His best-known novel, **Of Human Bondage** (1915), mirrors his own unhappy youth. Most of his short stories were set in the Far East. He also wrote critical essays.

Morgan, Ted. **Somerset Maugham.** London: J. Cape, 1980. 711 p.
PR6025.A86.Z5568

Ted Morgan's life leaves out little as he has access to many primary documents. He is sympathetic toward his subject, yet objective.

MAUPASSANT, Guy de (1850-93), French fiction writer; playwright

Guy de Maupassant is one of the great masters of the short story whose works translate gracefully into English. He had an unhappy childhood, served in the Franco-Prussian War and then went to Paris to study law. His mentor was Gustave Flaubert, who also introduced him to Emile Zola and Henry James. He wrote over 300 short stories among them the collections **La Maison Tellier** in 1881, **Mademoiselle Fifi**, the following year and **Miss Harriet** in 1884. His six novels are lesser known. A man of sexual excess, he died of syphilis in an insane asylum.

Steegmuller, Francis. **Maupassant, a Lion in the Path.** New York: Random House, 1949. 430 p.
PQ2353.S8

This is also a study of the writer as well as a biography. Included are four short stories that had not been translated into English. Despite the painstaking scholarship, the book is as readable as one of Maupassant's more morbid short stories.

MELVILLE, Herman (1819-91), American novelist

Melville's name is nearly synonymous with his novel, one of the greatest ever written, **Moby-Dick**. This 1851 work is based on his experiences as a whaler in the South Seas. Besides the whaling theme, it is steeped in symbolism. Despite its later distinction, it was poorly received during his lifetime. He had to support himself as a customs inspector and was in poor health. His fame came posthumously, nearly thirty years after he died in poverty and obscurity.

Howard, Leon. **Herman Melville, a Biography**. Berkeley: University of California Press, 1951. 354 p.
PS2386.H6

This is the most authoritative of the biographies of Melville. Despite its rather stilted prose, it presents a credible account of Melville's life, putting into focus the life events that lead to the creation of Melville's writings.

MENDELSSOHN-BARTHOLDY, Felix (1809-47), German composer

This German romantic composer of oratorios, piano and orchestral music was a child prodigy who wrote twelve symphonies for string orchestra and a major work, the Overture to **Midsummer Night's Dream** by the age of seventeen. He maintained a classical form imbued with expressive lyricism. He organized the Leipzig Conservatory in 1842-43, a world renowned center of music education, and at the same time concertized as a pianist and conductor especially in England. Of his symphonies, the most popular are the "Scottish," composed during the years of 1830 through 1842, "Italian" (1833), and "Reformation" (1830-32). His violin concerto (1844) is one of the most well known for that instrument.

Blunt, Wilfrid. **On Wings of Song; a Biography of Felix Mendelssohn**. New York: Scribner, 1974. 288 p.
ML410.M5.B62

This is a very readable, charming biography. It may border on the anti-intellectual as hinted by its title, but nevertheless, it is a good introduction to the milieu which brought forth one of the nineteenth century musical geniuses.

MEREDITH, George (1828-1909), English novelist; poet

Although not a household name as are his compatriots, George Eliot, Charles Dickens, and Alfred Lord Tennyson, George Meredith is one of the major Victorian writers. He started his

worklife apprenticed to a lawyer but turned to journalism,
contributing poetry and essays to periodicals. Meredith
considered his finest work to be **Beauchamp's Career** (1875), which
concerns the life of an idealistic but radical politician.
Other critics feel **The Egoist** (1879) to be his masterpiece. His
greatest poems are found in **Poems and Lyrics of the Joy of Earth**,
written in 1883. His genius in this genre is his metaphor,
lyricism and meter.

Stevenson, Lionel. **The Ordeal of George Meredith, a
Biography.** New York: Scribner, 1953. 368 p.
PR5013.S7

There may never be a definitive biography of Meredith, a man
who lived an intensely intellectual existence, not easily
penetrated or chronicled. Nevertheless this biography is
illuminating and written with clarity, thanks to meticulous
scholarship.

MILLAY, Edna St. Vincent (1892-1950), American poet

As well known for her bohemian lifestyle as for her poetry,
Edna St. Vincent Millay won a Pulitzer for the poem "The Harp
Weaver" in 1924. Her poetry is intensely lyrical. Her life in
Greenwich Village became increasingly more politically involved.
Cynicism is seen in her poetry beginning with the World War II
years.

Gould, Jean. **The Poet and Her Book; a Biography of Edna St.
Vincent Millay.** New York: Dodd, Mead, 1969. 308 p.
PS3525.I495.Z64

Millay was the subject of numerous anecdotal biographies
that emphasized her bohemian existence. Jean Gould writes a more
balanced account of her life and creativity. It is considered to
be the major work on her life and has many interesting
photographs.

MILTON, John (1608-74), English poet

John Milton is considered to be one of the greatest literary
figures in Western literature. His epic poem, "Paradise Lost,"
first published in 1667 and then revised in 1674, was written
with the help of secretaries, as he had at this point lost his
sight. "Paradise Lost" continues to be thoroughly studied and is
compared with the great epics of Homer and Dante. A companion
poem, "Paradise Regained," was written during the revision of
"Paradise Lost" as was "Samson Agonistes." He also wrote
important religious and political tracts. The latter caused

great controversy, and he was jailed for his beliefs concerning the restoration of the monarchy. His last years were spent in the company of his family and friends who read to him and with whom he enjoyed his other great love, music.

Wilson, A.N. **The Life of John Milton.** New York: Oxford University Press, 1983. 278 p.
PR3581.W47 1983

A.N. Wilson, a prize—winning novelist, writes a fine biography of a difficult subject. His handling of Milton's sensitive family life is well done, and his insights into the creativity of the poet are refreshing. The political career of Milton is less well served.

Masson, David. **The Life of John Milton: Narrated in connexion with the Political, Ecclesiastical, and Literary History of His Time.** 7 vols. New York: Peter Smith, 1877–1896.
PR3581.M3

This may be the longest biography of a creative artist. Needless to say, it is comprehensive and rich in the social and cultural milieu of his times.

Parker, William Riley. **Milton: A Biography.** 2 vols. Oxford: Clarendon Press, 1970.
PR3581.P27

This is considered the definitive biography of Milton despite the great length of the Masson one. The first volume is the biographical section; the second provides the documentation.

MODIGLIANI, Amedeo (1884-1920), Italian painter; sculptor

Amedeo Modigliani settled in Paris in 1906. He was particularly influenced by Cézanne and Brancusi with their deliberate distortions. Despite his fame today he was hardly acknowledged during his brief lifetime and died racked by drug addiction and poverty. Among his best known paintings is "The Jewess" (1908) and among his sculptures, "Head" (1912) and "Caryatid" (1914). He returned to painting at the end of his life and did his best work as seen in "Nude" (1917).

Sichel, Pierre. **Modigliani; a Biography of Amedeo Modigliani.** New York: Dutton, 1967. 597 p.
ND623.M67.S5

This well researched biography avoids dwelling upon the excessive bohemianism that made Modigliani a legend in his time. However, the personalities and haunts of his brief life are recorded to bring out a complete portrait of the life of the painter and sculptor.

MOLIERE, Jean Baptiste Poquelin (1622-73), French playwright

This seventeenth century French dramatist was the author of a number of French comedies which are still very popular today. He began his career as an actor, then founded a company which was to be the forerunner of the famous Comédie Française. His plays are noted for their excessive caricatures. Among these famous satires are **Tartuffe** (1664) and **The Misanthrope** (1666). One of his farces is **The Doctor in Spite of Himself** (1666).

Palmer, John L. **Molière.** New York: Brewer and Warren, 1930. 494 p.
PQ1852.P3

This is a straightforward presentation of the life and times of Molière. John Palmer paints a thorough and objective portrait.

MORRIS, William (1834-96), English poet; artist

William Morris was both a visual and literary artist. He had a very full career and quite a dramatic personal life, providing much fodder for biographical musings. He was a founder and leading exponent of the late nineteenth-century Arts and Crafts Movement. His most important venture was the Kelmscott Press, which printed exquisitely illustrated books. Although no one work of art stands out in Morris' career, the cumulative effect of all that he contributed both theoretically and practically to the visual arts is significant. For his poetry, popular in its time, little enthusiasm remains.

Mackail, J.W. **The Life of William Morris.** 2 vols. New York: Longmans, Green, 1899.
PR5083.M25

Mackail's book remains the classic biography of Morris despite more recent works. Mackail had the advantage of being both a personal friend of Morris and an eloquent writer.

Henderson, Philip. **William Morris: His Life, Work, and Friends.** New York: McGraw-Hill, 1967. 388 p.
PR5038.H4 1967b

This book draws upon primary documents not available to Mackail. It delves more into Morris' rather troubled personal life and political views, which Mackail touched only in passing.

MOZART, Wolfgang Amadeus (1756-91), Austrian composer

Mozart is considered to be the greatest musical genius to have ever lived. At the age of five he was already composing minuets. His first works, four sonatas for clavier with violin accompaniment, were published when he was eight, his first symphony at nine. At his death at thirty-five he had composed 626 works, including piano pieces, piano concertos, symphonies and operas such as the The Marriage of Figaro (1786), Don Giovanni (1787) and The Magic Flute. He fell from fame despite his exceptional output during his last years and died of kidney failure while composing a requiem. His music lives no less so now than when it was composed. Because his life was his music, most books about Mozart are studies of his work.

Hildesheimer, Wolfgang. Mozart. Translated by Marion Faber. New York: Farrar, Straus, Giroux, 1982. 408 p. ML410.M9.H433 1982

This thought-provoking book, based upon the letters of Mozart, is the closest to a definition of a biography. It presents an intriguing evaluation of Mozart, tearing down the many facades of this popular composer's life.

NORRIS, Frank (1870-1902), American novelist

Frank Norris's novels were statements of his social beliefs. In The Octopus (1901) he attacked the railroad industry and did the same to the wheat industry with The Pit two years later.

Walker, Franklin. Frank Norris, a Biography. Garden City, N.Y.: Doubleday, Doran & Co., 1932. 317 p. PS2473.W3

This straightforward volume, despite being nearly sixty years old, is still considered the standard Norris biography. It contains a wealth of material, showing exceptional research and careful writing.

O'CASEY, Sean (1884-1964), Irish playwright

Sean O'Casey grew up in the slums of Dublin. He was largely self-taught. After some time in an activist role before the Easter Rebellion of 1916 he withdrew to devote himself to his writing. His early plays, depicting the grim life of Irish slums, may be considered his greatest — The Shadow of the Gunman (1923), Juno and the Paycock (1924) and the play that caused a riot in the Abbey Theatre, The Plough and the Stars (1926). After his break with Ireland, largely because of the reaction to the latter play, he moved to England where he continued as a successful dramatist, in his later years writing in a comic vein.

O'Connor, Garry. **Sean O'Casey: A Life.** New York: Atheneum, 1988. 448 p.
PR6029.C33.Z7823 1988

Garry O'Connor disputes O'Casey's claim to his impoverished upbringing. He also sets straight a number of other details that the cantankerous O'Casey in his six-volume autobiography distorts to his own advantage. He is less kind about the quality of his dramatic writing than others have been. A very interesting life written quite unsympathetically at times.

O'CONNOR, Frank (1903-66), Irish short-story writer

He fought in the Irish Civil War and was a director of the Abbey Theatre during the 1930's. His major contribution to Irish literature are his short stories, penetrating but tender portrayals of Irish life.

Matthews, James H. **Voices: A Life of Frank O'Connor.** New York: Atheneum, 1983. 450 p.
PR6029.D58.Z76 1983

With a style bordering on the brilliant, Matthews writes a model biography using currently accepted research in presenting a vivid portrait of a minor Irish writer.

ODETS, Clifford (1906-63), American playwright

Clifford Odets was primarily a dramatist of social protest. His first produced play was a success and his next two even more so. **Awake and Sing!** (1935) is an optimistic play and his most popular is **Golden Boy** (1937). His work influenced Tennessee Williams and Arthur Miller.

Brenman-Gibson, Margaret. **Clifford Odets, American Playwright: The Years from 1906 to 1940.** New York: Atheneum, 1981. 748 p.
PS3529.D46.Z58 1981

This first volume covers the most dynamic years of Odets artistic development. Brenman-Gibson, a psychoanalyst turned biographer, uses her background to probe the mind of her close friend.

O'HARA, John (1905-70), American novelist; short story writer

John O'Hara was a popular author whose acerbically penetrating view of American life produced such novels as **Appointment in Samarra** (1934) and **A Rage to Live** (1949). Many critics, however, regard his short stories as his finest writings.

Bruccoli, Matthew Joseph. **The O'Hara Concern: A Biography of John O'Hara.** New York: Random House, 1975. 417 p. PS3529.H29.Z59

This critical biography looks at the life and art of John O'Hara as well as his stature in American literature. Bruccoli feels that O'Hara was underestimated in more academic circles. This distinguished work is well researched and well written with the aid of O'Hara's widow.

O'KEEFFE, Georgia (1887-1986), American painter

Georgia O'Keeffe ranks among the foremost modernist painters. Although her subjects were from nature, she developed a unique abstract style. Especially well-known are her series of large flowers and the "Pelvis Series" of 1943, animal bones set against an abstract background. The noted photographer, Alfred Stieglitz, nourished her career and later became her husband.

Lisle, Laurie. **Portrait of an Artist: A Biography of Georgia O'Keeffe.** Albuquerque: University of New Mexico, 1986. 408 p. ND237.O5.L57 1986

This biography is strongest on the early years of Georgia O'Keeffe's life. Laurie Lisle shows how O'Keeffe, although helped by Stieglitz in launching her career, had to find her own way artistically.

OLIPHANT, Margaret (1828-97), English fiction writer

Margaret Oliphant was a minor writer with a major output. She was a contributor, as a literary critic, to the periodical **Blackwood's** for forty-six years. Her biographies and literary histories are noteworthy, but her reputation as a writer rests with her many novels of Scottish life and especially **The Rector and the Doctor's Family,** a chronicle of life in an English province.

Williams, Merryn. **Margaret Oliphant: A Critical Biography.** New York: St. Martin's Press, 1986. 217 p. PR5114.W5 1986

Williams draws a compelling portrait of Margaret Oliphant as
the most prolific Victorian writer, a serious career woman. The
literary assessments unfortunately take up more room in the book
than one would like.

O'NEILL, Eugene Gladstone (1888-1953), American playwright

O'Neill is generally acclaimed as the foremost American
playwright. His numerous plays continue to be performed. Among
his most noteworthy are his first Pulitzer winner **Beyond the
Horizon** (1920) and another of his early period, **Desire Under the
Elms** (1924). **The Iceman Cometh** (1946) is considered his finest.
He won another Pulitzer Prize, posthumously in 1956, for **Long
Day's Journey into Night**, his autobiographical masterpiece, left
in manuscript form at his death. His life was filled with family
difficulties and poor health, which are reflected in his powerful
dramas.

Alexander, Doris. **The Tempering of Eugene O'Neill**. New York:
Harcourt, Brace & World, 1962. 300 p.
PS3529.N5.Z556

This well-researched biography covers the first thirty-two
years of O'Neill's life and is exceptionally fine in this period,
portraying the playwright's father, an important figure in
O'Neill's life. Alexander looks at the intellectual development
of the artist and his evolution as well as the people and events
that shaped his early career.

Gelb, Arthur, and Barbara Gelb. **O'Neill**. New York: Harper,
1962. 970 p.
PS3529.N5.Z653

This is a very significant contribution to the study of the
life and works of O'Neill. More than four hundred people were
interviewed for this book, and the authors had the cooperation of
the three wives of O'Neill as well as access to his papers at
Yale.

Schaeffer, Louis. **O'Neill, Son and Playwright**. Boston:
Little, Brown, 1968. 543 p.
PS3529.N5.Z797

Schaeffer, Louis. **O'Neill, Son and Artist**. Boston: Little,
Brown, 1973. 750 p.
PS3529.N5.Z797

These two volumes are considered to be the definitive
biography of O'Neill. Schaeffer used many of the primary
documents available to previous biographers but corrected earlier

errors and emphasized the unhealthy relationship O'Neill had with his parents who are the key to understanding O'Neill and his plays.

ORPEN, William, Sir (1878-1931), English painter

William Orpen was an Edwardian portrait painter. A minor figure in the Irish renaissance, Orpen is noted for his great technical virtuosity and historical interest. His best known work is "Homage to Manet" (1909).

Arnold, Bruce. **Orpen, Mirror to an Age.** London: J. Cape, 1981. 448 p.
ND497.O8.A76

Bruce Arnold has written a major biography of Orpen that is sumptuously illustrated. This underrated painter is the fortunate subject of this beautifully written, historically fascinating book, which surely will re-establish his artistic contribution to early twentieth century England.

ORWELL, George (1903-50), English fiction writer

George Orwell, the pen name of Eric Arthur Blair, was born in India, educated in England, served in the Indian Civil Service in Burma and spent some time in Spain. His literary essays have been considered to be on a par with the greatest written in English. However, he is best known for his two novels, **Animal Farm** (1946) about the failure of communism and the prophetic **Nineteen Eighty-Four** (1949). These two works brought him his first fame and almost his only source of income as a writer.

Crick, Bernard. **George Orwell, a Life.** Boston: Little, Brown, 1980. 473 p.
PR6029.R8.Z627 1980

George Orwell is well served in this thoroughly researched biography by Crick. One is left with a clear portrait of a man who genuinely tried to live by and communicate the principles that guided his life.

Stansky, Peter, and William Abrahams. **The Unknown Orwell.** New York: Knopf, 1972. 316 p.
PR6029.R8.Z79

Stansky, Peter, and William Abrahams. **Orwell, the Transformation.** New York: Knopf, 1980, c1979. 302 p.
PR6029.R8.Z78980

These two volumes chronicle the life of Orwell. The first spans his life through the publication of his memoirs after serving in Burma. The second continues the development of his unique identity—his need to have a pseudonym as well as insights into the rest of his life and writings.

OWEN, Wilfred (1893-1918), English poet

Wilfred Owen is one of the "war poets," English poets killed in World War I who wrote in the trenches of their experiences. Most of his writing, though, took place in 1917 while he was recovering from wounds. His poems are remarkable in their use of rhythm and sound patterns.

Stallworthy, Jon. **Wilfred Owen**. London: Oxford University Press, 1974. 333 p.
PR6029.W4.Z855

This is considered the standard biography of Owen. Despite his brief and rather limited existence, he was a great letter writer and from these letters and interviews of his relatives and acquaintances, Stallworthy, a poet and former soldier, has brought together enough material to enrich both the scholar and general reader.

Hibbard, Dominic. **Owen the Poet**. Athens: University of Ohio Press, 1986. 244 p.
PR6029.W4.Z66 1986

This biography covers some of the material that Stallworthy did but puts greater emphasis on his early life and intellectual influences.

PASTERNAK, Boris Leonidovich (1890-1960), Russian poet; novelist

Pasternak became a universal symbol of artistic integrity. Born into a cultured family, with subsequent formal study in music and philosophy, Pasternak gave his poetry a unique lyricism and an intellectual passion. **Over the Barriers** (1916) and **My Sister, Life** established his poetic reputation. The repressive atmosphere of the 1930's and 40's turned his literary energies to translating Shakespeare and other major Western poets. His masterpiece, the novel **Doctor Zhivago,** was finished in 1955. It had to be published out of the country. For this epic work of twentieth-century Russia, he won the Nobel Prize but was unable to accept it and spent his last days in his home outside Moscow.

Mallac, Guy de. Boris Pasternak, His Life and Art. Norman: University of Oklahoma Press, 1981. 449 p.
PG3476.P27.Z736

This is a thoroughly researched life of Pasternak, possibly the best available in any language. Pasternak, his life, his intellect and the milieu in which he lived and worked are difficult to capture. The book is most absorbing in its coverage of the time following the Nobel Prize. The last part of the book contains literary analysis and is less satisfactory.

Hingley, Ronald. Pasternak: A Biography. New York: Knopf, 1983. 303 p.
PG3476.P27.Z687 1983

This biography complements the Mallac one: its interpretation of this great writer is quite different. It is more anecdotal and less adulatory in its approach. It lacks the detail of the Mallac book.

PAVLOVA, Anna (1881-1931), Russian dancer

Pavlova is synonymous with ballet. Despite her sickly childhood and the poverty of her family, she was determined to be a dancer. Could she have been anything else? It was through her exceptional genius as an interpreter of the dance and her willingness to travel extensively to promote the art that she has earned the reputation of being, possibly, the most highly acclaimed ballerina of the twentieth century.

Money, Keith. Anna Pavlova, Her Life and Art. New York: Knopf, 1982. 425 p.
GV1785.P3.M66 1982

Well-researched biographies of interpreters of the arts are few and far between. Keith Money spent six years compiling this scholarly biography, written in a poetic prose befitting its subject. Despite the thoroughness of the approach, Pavlova remains an enigma.

PERROT, Jules (1810-92), French choreographer

Jules Perrot was one of the most prolific choreographers of the French romantic ballet. He began as a dancer with the Paris Opéra and after being dismissed from the company because of the jealousy of his partner, he began to choreograph. He did "Ondine" in 1843 in London and "Pas de Quatre" in 1845. He went on to the Imperial Theater in St. Petersburg (now Leningrad) as a dancer and choreographer for eleven years.

Guest, Ivor Forbes. **Jules Perrot: Master of the Romantic Ballet**. New York: Dance Horizons, 1984. 383 p.
GV1785.P417.G84 1984

Ivor Guest, a ballet scholar, has written an animated book on the life and times of Jules Perrot. This richly illustrated book is enhanced by photographs and memorabilia of his work in the dance.

PICASSO, Pablo (1881-1973), Spanish sculptor; painter; graphic artist

Picasso is considered one of the foremost figures in twentieth century art; but some feel he was also an egotistical celebrity. He began his art studies in Barcelona but moved on to Paris as a leader in the School of Paris. He was prolific, creative and was a major influence in the direction of modern art with his cubism and abstraction. To his "blue period" belongs "The Old Guitarist" (1903). In 1907 he painted his most significant work in the development of cubism "Les Demoiselles d'Avignon." His next landmark work was "Guernica," incorporating the themes of war and opposition to fascism. He worked until his death at the age of ninety-one, his later years devoted to other media and lighter subjects. His personal life was as controversial and colorful as his art.

Penrose, Roland. **Picasso: His Life and Work**. 3rd ed. Berkeley: University of California Press, 1981. 517 p.
ND553.P5.P42 1981

This biography appeals to both the popular taste and the student. This book seems to be the best in terms of scholarship. The minutiae of his life at times may put some readers off, but the cumulative effect of this approach intensifies the uniqueness of Picasso.

PLATH, Sylvia (1932-63), American poet

Sylvia Plath became one of the most celebrated poets of her generation after the posthumous publication of **Ariel** two years after her suicide. Her introspective poetry came from the extremes of emotion that she experienced. Her marriage is said both to have nurtured and destroyed her creativity. And the creative force in her life may have been the destruction of her life. There is so much conjecture about such a promising woman who took her own life at a young age.

Butscher, Edward. **Sylvia Plath, Method and Madness**. New York: Seabury Press, 1976. 388 p.
PS3566.L27.Z59

There are psychoanalytical overtones in this sympathetic but detailed account of the life of Plath.

Stevenson, Anne. **Bitter Fame: A Life of Sylvia Plath.** Boston: Houghton Mifflin, 1989. 413 p.
PS3566.L27.Z9134

This biography paints the dark side of Plath. It explores her family, her marriage and first attempt at suicide as well as how this all influenced her poetry and other creative writing. Again, because of her age at her death there is much posthumous psychoanalysis.

POE, Edgar Allan (1809-49), American short story writer

Poe is considered the father of the modern detective story as seen in "The Murders in the Rue Morgue" (1841). He was also an editor, a witty critic and his poetry is noted for its musicality and imagery such as in "The Bells." Above all he is known as one of the most brilliant and original writers of short stories such as "The Mask of the Red Death" and "The Fall of the House of Usher." He was orphaned at an early age and put in the care of foster parents who were most concerned about a good education for him. However, his stints at the new University of Virginia and West Point were short-lived. His literary executor defamed his personal life and he was falsely accused of being an alcoholic and lazy. His literary reputation was better established during his lifetime in France than in his own country.

Symons, Julian. **The Tell-Tale Heart: The Life and Works of Edgar Allan Poe.** New York: Harper and Row, 1978. 259 p.
PS2631.S95

This thorough biographical study of Poe probes the false accusations of his literary executor. Symons writes a straightforward life of this wonderfully complex and creative writer.

POLLOCK, Jackson (1912-56), American painter

Controversy over Jackson Pollock's "drip" technique and the psychoanalytical interpretations of the artist still rage more than thirty years after his death. His violent art, such as his 1947 "Full Fathom Five," used the technique of hurling paint onto a canvas on the floor. He was a central figure in the abstract expressionist movement, forcing new definitions of art and its techniques.

Solomon, Deborah. **Jackson Pollock: A Biography.** New York:
Simon & Schuster, 1987. 287 p.
ND237.P37.S65 1987

This is a balanced view of the painter which covers new
material about the evolution of Pollock's technique and the
influences upon him. It is an objective biography with an
emphasis on his wife, whose artistic career flowered after his
death.

Landau, Ellen G. **Jackson Pollock.** New York: Harry N. Abrams,
1989. 283 p.
ND237.P73.L36 1989

This book comes out about the same time as another by Steven
Naifeh and Gregory White Smith. This latter book, which is not
included here, has had great notoriety, overshadowing this more
modest and intelligent biography. Landau approaches Pollock like
the academic art historian she is, although his works literally
invite psychoanalysis.

POPE, Alexander (1688-1744), English poet

Alexander Pope is considered to be the greatest of all
English verse satirists. Despite his limited formal education he
was a prodigy, writing his first poem at the age of twelve. His
physical disabilities limited his activities, so, as an
adolescent, he read great literature. His first period of
writing consisted of classically based poems of which his 1714
"Rape of the Lock" is an exceptional example. He translated
Homer and wrote a great deal of literary criticism in a satirical
vein.

Quennell, Peter. **Alexander Pope; the Education of Genius,
1688-1728.** New York: Stein & Day, 1968. 278 p.
PR3633.Q4

Some artists' careers are so exceptional that it is
necessary to limit the scope of a biography. The title of
this book speaks of such a necessity. Quennell's book is steeped
in knowledge of the times of Pope. This balanced approach to the
artist and his problematic life is written in a clear prose.

Sherburn, George Wiley. **The Early Career of Alexander Pope.**
Oxford: Clarendon Press, 1934. 326 p.
PR3633.S45

Again another book looking only at the early career of Pope.
Unfortunately the sequel was never published. Volume I is

considered to be the most complete and authoritative analysis of that period.

Mack, Maynard. **Alexander Pope: A Life.** New York: W.W. Norton in association with Yale University Press, 1986. 975 p. PR3633.M27 1986

The emphasis in this book is on the later years of Alexander Pope, taking over where the Sherburn book left off. It looks at the two sides of the Pope persona: the desire to withdraw into the countryside and his active commitment to the political issues of the time.

PORTER, Katherine Anne (1890-1980), American short story writer; novelist

Katherine Porter's best-seller, **Ship of Fools,** may have been her most popular work, but her best work is in short story. The **Collected Short Stories of Katherine Anne Porter** won a Pulitzer Prize for fiction in 1966.

Givner, Joan. **Katherine Anne Porter: A Life.** New York: Simon & Schuster, 1982. 572 p. PS3531.O752.Z64 1982

This is the only complete biography of Katherine Porter to date. It was commissioned by the author and explodes Porter's myth of herself. Givner attempts to look at her creative works in relation to her life. The essence of Katherine Anne Porter is lost in the minutiae.

POTTER, Beatrix (1866-1943), English children's author

Beatrix Potter is known for her delicately illustrated books about animals that have been favorites of children since their first publication. **The Tale of Peter Rabbit** (1901) is not only still read but her artwork from this book continues to be put on souvenirs. Her very restrictive life with her parents and her small animals was psychologically very unfulfilling but literarily and artistically successful. She married when she was nearly fifty and wrote little of consequence after that.

Lane, Margaret. **The Tale of Beatrix Potter: A Biography.** rev. ed. New York: F. Warne, 1978. 173 p. PR6031.O72.Z6 1968

This tiny book reminds one of the subject's books. Margaret Lane, who has written another book called **The Magic Years of Beatrix Potter**, draws a full portrait of the woman in her wealthy but closed-in existence in which she wrote successfully as opposed to her happily married period which seemed not to help her creatively.

Taylor, Judy. **Beatrix Potter: Artist, Storyteller and Countrywoman.** New York: Viking Penguin, 1986. 224 p.
PR6031.O72.Z85 1986

Judy Taylor has written a biography of Beatrix Potter that, despite the amount of primary research, might also appeal to high school students. Again the emphasis is on the contrast of her response to her change in lifestyles from that of a very dutiful ageless daughter to an astute businesswoman and wife in middle age.

POUND, Ezra (1885-1972), American poet

Ezra Pound was one of the most influential and controversial figures in twentieth century poetry; both as a poet and theorist. For his political broadcasting in Italy, he was confined to a mental institution in the United States, being pronounced unfit to stand for trial in this country. He returned to Italy but ceased to write and seldom even spoke. He influenced and assisted many literary figures during his life. His major poems are "Homage to Sextus Propertius" (1918) and **Cantos**, which were written from the period 1925 until 1960.

Carpenter, Humphrey. **A Serious Character: The Life of Ezra Pound.** Boston: Houghton Mifflin, 1988. 1005 p.
PS3531.O82.Z5526 1988

In this massive biography Humphrey Carpenter sifts through the details of Pound's life, leaving most of them in. He has a fresh approach to the impact on his career and life. In this work Pound is given the space to play out his complex existence.

PROKOFIEV, Sergey (1891-1953), Russian composer

Prokofiev's music continues to be analyzed and played to large audiences. His first attempts at composing came at age five. He entered the St. Petersburg Conservatory at thirteen, studying with major musical figures. His style departs from the romantic through its emotional restraint and rhythmic momentum. Although his later compositions were more accessible, he maintained a basic neoclassical style throughout his productive life. Among his best known works are the "Classical Symphony" (1916-17), the opera **The Love for Three Oranges** (1921) and an equally interesting, rather humorous concept of "Lieutenant Kije"

of 1934. His last years were lived under the unhappy shadow of
the restrictive atmosphere of Stalin.

Robinson, Harlow Loomis. **Sergei Prokefiev: a Biography.** New
York: Viking, 1987. 573 p.
ML410.P865.R55 1987

This very readable book draws from previously untranslated
Russian primary sources. Robinson writes a fast-paced book about
a man who traveled a great deal as a pianist and conductor and
composed some of the most well known twentieth century music.

PROUST, Marcel (1871-1922), French novelist

Marcel Proust is essentially a single-work author, despite
his other published writings. So much of himself went into the
seven-volume novel, **Remembrance of Things Past,** written from the
years 1913 until his death. It is said he wrote himself to death
with this work, part of which was still in manuscript form at his
death and not completed for publication until 1927. He was a
frail but brilliant child whose devotion to his mother was so
excessive that after her death he withdrew into a cork-lined
room, there to ponder and write his masterpiece and other works.

Painter, George Duncan. **Proust.** 2 vols. Boston: Little,
Brown, 1959-1965.
PQ2631.R63.Z7896

Needless to say the eccentric Proust lived a biographer's
delight of a life. His whole life was lived to produce
Remembrance of Things Past. The attachment to his mother, his
life following her death make for wonderful probings. George
Painter gives us the minutiae as did Proust. Painter writes an
absorbing account of this French author.

PUSHKIN, Aleksandr Sergeevich (1799-1837), Russian poet; prose writer

It has been said that all of Russian literature has been
influenced by Pushkin, who died in a duel over his wife's
reputation. He has been the subject of many novelistic,
speculative biographies. He was of an impoverished but cultured
aristocratic family who valued education. He had an active
social life, yet he was able to ponder the deeper realities of
existence through his writings. Today his writings may be better
known to non-Russians as operas, **Eugene Onegin** from the 1823
through 1831 years, his light verse fairy tale, **Ruslan and
Ludmila** (1820) and his major drama **Boris Godunov** (1831). His
later years were devoted to prose such as his popular novel, **The
Captain's Daughter** (1834).

Simmons, Ernest Joseph. **Pushkin.** Cambridge: Harvard University Press, 1937. 485 p.
PG3350.S52 1937

In this highly readable biography Simmons studies the man, his art and his milieu. It is thoroughly researched and, despite more recent biographies, continues to be the most authentic.

RANSOM, John Crowe (1888–1974), American poet

John Crowe Ransom may be better known as the founder and editor for twenty-one years of the **Kenyon Review,** an influential literary periodical. As a poet, however, his writing is noted for its elegant but impersonal style. His **Selected Poems** of 1963 won the National Book Award for Poetry the next year.

Young, Thomas Daniel. **Gentleman in a Dustcoat: A Biography of John Crowe Ransom.** Southern Literary Studies. Baton Rouge: Louisiana State University Press, 1976. 528 p.
PS3535.A635.Z9185

This is a fine biography of John Crowe Ransom who lived a long and interesting life. Thomas Daniel Young based this book on his personal knowledge of Ransom, which resulted in an exhaustive but sympathetic account.

RAVEL, Maurice (1875–1937), French composer

Maurice Ravel, along with Claude Debussy, is considered among the two most influential French composers of the early twentieth century. His original, fluid but demanding music has a very distinctive style. After a stint in World War I he lived a rather isolated life in the French countryside where he composed full-time and collected mechanical toys. His genius was recognized in his lifetime and he toured England and the United States.

Stuckenschmidt, Hans Heinz. **Maurice Ravel; Variations on His Life and Work.** Translated by Samuel R. Rosenbaum. Philadelphia: Chilton Book Co., 1968. 271 p.
ML410.R23.S753

This continues to be considered the best biography of Ravel in English. It is a well written, thoughtful approach to a very creative composer. Stuckenschmidt explores the Basque heritage of his mother and the Swiss heritage of his father to explain the uniqueness in Ravel's style. Letters of Ravel are quoted, giving the book a real feel for the person and music of the man. There is some analysis of his works.

RAY, Man (1890-1976), American painter; photographer

Man Ray was a unique artist involved in both the
surrealist and dada movements and celebrated for his paintings,
photographs and films. He was a significant contributor to the
advancement of photography as an art form. Criticism of
photography had been concerning its excessive realism; Ray moved
it into the realm of the abstract. He was a portrait
photographer in Paris. In 1922 he published **Delicious Fields,** an
album of abstract photographs, employing his rayographic
technique, which did not require the use of the camera.

Baldwin, Neil. **Man Ray, American Artist.** New York: C.N.
Potter, 1988. 449 p.
N6537.R3.B3 1988

Neil Baldwin wrestles with the enigma of Man Ray and does
not quite capture him. Despite his bizarre, attention-grabbing
art, Ray was a private person. Baldwin also does not
satisfactorily explore Ray's artistic expression with respect to
his background and influences of Paris as one of the many
expatriates after World War I.

REMBRANDT HARMENSZOON van RIJN (1606-69), Dutch painter

One of the greatest painters in any age in any country was
Rembrandt. His portraits are without equal; his use of light,
breathtakingly beautiful. His output was prodigious; over six
hundred paintings, three hundred etchings and two thousand
drawings. After a period of time in a studio in Amsterdam,
Rembrandt returned to his native Leiden where he taught and did
portrait painting. He did nearly one hundred self-portraits
which show his evolution as a painter. His wife's position
afforded him wealth and access to society for his greater
development. The year his wife died he painted "The Night
Watch" (1642). Her death left him without his beloved partner
and his former social position. Despite this he continued to
paint masterpieces, such as "Aristotle Contemplating the Bust of
Homer" (1653) and "The Polish Rider." He was less fashionable as
an artist toward the end of his life but continued to receive
commissions until his death.

Mee, Charles. **Rembrandt's Portrait: A Biography.** New York:
Simon & Schuster, 1988. 336 p.
ND653.R4.M356 1988

This biography of Rembrandt, which also discusses some of
his works, supersedes earlier ones. Mee makes use of the most
recent studies on Rembrandt in this well-balanced work.

REYNOLDS, Joshua, Sir (1723-92), English painter

Joshua Reynolds, considered one of the greatest English painters, was besieged by commissions to paint portraits—he did nearly two thousand of the most notable figures of the time. He also did much to raise the status of the artist in England during the eighteenth century. He is known for the Grand Style in his later works. Of significance is "Samuel Johnson" (1772) and the finely done "Nelly O'Brien" (1762-63). His "Self-Portrait" in the Grand Style in 1780 is an homage to past artists such as Rembrandt and Michelangelo.

Hilles, Frederick Whiley. **The Literary Career of Sir Joshua Reynolds.** New York: The Macmillan Co., 1936. 318 p. ND497.R4.H5

This biography is a unique undertaking. Despite his enormous all-absorbing, painterly talent, Reynolds also wanted to be a great writer. This book looks at the conflict he experienced in this dilemma, an artist involved in more than one art.

RICHARDSON, Ralph, Sir (1902-83), English actor

Ralph Richardson went to an art school before he decided on an acting career. His most memorable performances were in 1944 as Peer Gynt in the play of the same name and as Falstaff in **Henry IV.** He was also known for his exquisite cameo roles. He played on Broadway and in film.

O'Connor, Garry. **Ralph Richardson: An Actor's Life.** New York: Atheneum, 1982. 260 p. PN2598.R46.O26 1982

This is a model biography based on contemporary research methods of an interpreter of the arts. O'Connor gives us fine insights into the process of acting. A charming portrait comes through in this, at times, riveting biography.

RICHARDSON, Samuel (1689-1761), English novelist

Samuel Richardson is considered to be the first major English novelist. His portrayal of his characters is of an emotionally complex nature. The format he used was epistolary and among his best known works are **Pamela** (1740), **Clarissa** (1747-48), considered the greatest fictional work of the eighteenth century, and his final work **The History of Sir Charles Grandison** (1753-54). His portrayal of women is especially sympathetic. He worked as a printer until he was fifty and had a passion for letter-writing.

Eaves, T.C. Duncan, and Ben D. Kimpel. **Samuel Richardson: A Biography.** Oxford: Clarendon Press, 1971. 728 p.
PR3666.E2

Eaves and Kimpel have written a biography that does an exceptional job of looking at the background, profession, personal life and the literary art of Richardson. This portrait of Richardson is based on his and others' writings.

RILKE, Rainer Maria (1875-1926), German poet

Rainer Maria Rilke is considered the most influential poet of modern Germany. His poems are characterized by lyrical beauty and a combination of sublime tragedy and mystical vision. From his early period his best known work is **Book of Hours** (1905). His **Duino Elegies** (1911-12) contain his mystical and tragic feelings. His posthumously published **Late Poems** are among his major achievements. He was married briefly but felt that neither his wife nor he was called to marriage so they separated to devote themselves to art, and their child was raised by her maternal grandparents.

Hendry, J.F. **The Sacred Threshold: A Life of Rainer Maria Rilke.** Manchester: Carcanet New Press, 1983. 184 p.
PT2635.I65.Z74215 1983

This book has been characterized as primarily an introduction to Rilke and his work. Hendry, who is also a poet, is able to convey the importance to Rilke of the inseparability of life and art.

Leppmann, Wolfgang. **Rilke: A Life.** Translated in collaboration with the author by Russell M. Stockman. New York: Fromm International Pub. Corp., 1984. 421 p.
PT2635.I65.Z782313 1984

This has been considered the standard biography of Rilke. It is faulted for being too detailed, but it is an exceptional portrait of the poet, who was always renewing his approach to life and writing.

RIMBAUD, Arthur (1854-91), French poet

Arthur Rimbaud was a child prodigy. His significant contribution to poetry ended at the age of nineteen after the breaking up of his homosexual relationship with Paul Verlaine.

He was one of the creators of free verse and used a great deal of visualization in his poems, which were precursors of the surrealist movement. He prematurely stopped writing and became a trader and gunrunner in Africa.

Petitfils, Pierre. **Rimbaud**. Translated by Alan Sheridan. Charlottesville: University Press of Virginia, 1987. 388 p. PQ2387.R5.Z754513 1987

Petitfils is a Rimbaud scholar who has unearthed and pondered over Rimbaud and his work for more than forty years. He analyzes his years of being a poet, his ability to change the direction of French poetry with his small body of work, and how he abandoned it all despite his precocious talent.

RODIN, Auguste (1840-1917), French sculptor

Auguste Rodin was a prolific sculptor who employed many people to assist in his undertakings. So realistic were his human forms that he was accused of casting his works from living people. He received a commission from the French government for the "Gates of Hell," a set of sculptures he worked on in his studio all of his life. He never finished the whole work but completed one hundred eighty-six parts of it some of which are works in their own right such as "Adam and Eve" (1881) and the world-renowned "The Thinker" (1879-1900). He also sculpted more intimate works such as "The Kiss" (1886) as well as many portraits of the most important personalities of his time. Although not a participant, World War I brought hard times to him, and his physical and mental health rapidly deteriorated.

Grunfield, Frederic V. **Rodin: A Biography**. New York: Holt, 1987. 738 p.
NB553.R7.G78 1987

This is a good biography of Rodin, written for the general reader. Unfortunately Grunfield gives equal time to trivia as well as to more important aspects of the man as artist.

ROSSETTI, Christina Georgina (1830-94), English poet

Christina Rossetti wrote childhood verses which were printed on a family press. Her best work is in **Goblin Market and Other Poems** (1862), which is described as melancholic, fantastic and lyrical. She was of a highly cultured family background and was the sister of Dante Gabriel Rossetti, a pre-Raphaelite painter-poet. Christina was a deeply religious person who lived a reclusive life.

Battiscombe, Georgina. **Christina Rossetti, a Divided Life.**
New York: Holt, Rinehart & Winston, 1981. 233 p.
PR5238.B32 1981

This beautifully written book is based on primary
documentation of her life and not on a reading of her poetry,
which was the basis of earlier biographies. Battiscombe is still
unable to say anything new about Christina.

ROSSINI, Gioacchino (1792-1868), Italian composer

Rossini is best known as a composer of operas. His comic
masterpiece is **The Barber of Seville** (1816). His thirty-ninth
and last opera was **William Tell**, composed thirty-nine years
before he died. He continued to compose, but on a much smaller
scale, piano pieces and songs. During this time he wrote two
significant religious works, "Stabat Mater" (1842) and "Short
Solemn Mass" (1864). He lived in Paris, then Italy, then Paris
again, where he died at the age of seventy-six.

Weinstock, Herbert. **Rossini, a Biography.** New York: A.A.
Knopf, 1968. 560 p.
ML410.R8.W35

This biography contains nearly two hundred pages of
documentation. However, the narrative is a fascinating study of
the life of Rossini, incorporating the composer's humor.

RUBENS, Peter Paul, Sir (1577-1640), Flemish painter

Rubens is considered one of the foremost painters in Western
art. His output was enormous, more than two thousand paintings.
He had a large workshop in which he employed numerous associates
but his genius originated all the paintings. The associates only
worked on his ideas. He was in the diplomatic corps and in his
travels had the opportunity to paint numerous members of the
nobility. His themes are both religious and a "joie de vivre."
Of his religious paintings, "Raising of the Cross" and "Descent
from the Cross," 1610 and 1611, respectively, are among his best
known. His more secular themes can be seen in his joyful "The
Judgement of Paris" and "Three Graces," painted near the end of
his life. His work is influenced by the Italian Renaissance and
the lusty colorfulness of the Flemish school.

White, Christopher. **Peter Paul Rubens: Man and Artist.** New
Haven: Yale University Press, 1987. 310 p.
ND673.R9.W48 1987

Christopher White is a contemporary leading scholar in the
field of Flemish painting. The mostly colored plates are a feast
for the eyes. The book is most informative on the life of Rubens
as artist and his significant diplomatic and peacemaking
contributions.

SACKVILLE-WEST, V. (Victoria) (1892-1962), English novelist; poet

Victoria Sackville-West was a prize-winning poet and member
of the famed Bloomsbury Group. She wrote under the name "Vita."
It is her novels, though, that are the more enduring. Among her
best are **The Edwardians** (1930) and **All Passion Spent**, written the
following year. She was also a biographer.

Glendinning, Victoria. **Vita: The Life of V. Sackville-West.**
New York: Knopf, 1983. 436 p.
PR6037.A35.Z68 1983

"Vita" was known as an arrogant, self-centered woman.
Glendinning is a sympathetic biographer who is realistic in her
approach to the flaws of character in her subject. Her attempt
at this biography has mixed results, but it is as good a portrait
as possible, absorbing in places, a kind of an adventure story
"Vita" might like to have written of herself.

SAINT-EXUPERY, Antoine de (1900-44), French prose writer

Saint-Exupéry is best known for his well-loved children's
story **The Little Prince,** which is based on his aviation
experiences. He also wrote some autobiographical novels of his
flying experiences. He vanished on a reconnaissance flight
between Corsica and the Alps.

Cate, Curtis. **Antoine de Saint-Exupéry.** New York: Putnam,
1970. 608 p.
TL540.S18.C37

"Saint-Ex" was a very colorful personality who was hard to
contain in a book. The book came out to mixed reviews. What
emerges is a nearly definitive biography of an adventuresome,
appealing but, at times, very mercurial personality.

SAINT GAUDENS, Augustus (1848-1907), American sculptor

Saint Gaudens is best known as a sculptor of public portrait
monuments. He began his career as a cameo cutter, which
supported his formal studies in America. He then traveled to
France and Italy for further studies. His first triumph is in

Madison Square Park, "Admiral David Farragut" (1878-81). His "Abraham Lincoln" in Chicago's Lincoln Park is exceptionally expressive of that president.

Wilkinson, Burke. **Uncommon Clay: The Life and Works of Augustus Saint Gaudens.** San Diego: Harcourt Brace Jovanovich, 1985. 428 p.
NB237.S2.W55 1985

This book is for the general reader. It is a very readable account of the artist and his art. This well-researched work is a lively portrayal of America's most outstanding public sculptor.

SAND, George (1804-76), French novelist

George Sand was a most unconventional but prolific writer of nineteenth century France. Her masculine attire and name, a pseudonym for Aurore Dudevant, did not shroud her exploration of the full gamut of the feminine in her fiction and non-fictional writings. She had to support herself and her two children with her literary endeavors after the breakup of her marriage to Baron Dudevant. Of her many novels, **Indiana** (1832) and **Lélia**, a year later, are her best known. She may be better remembered for having the composer Frédéric Chopin as a lover as well as the artist Jules Sandeau. Despite her other writings, her letters and journals in **My Life** are considered to be her finest writings (1854-55). Needless to say all of this lends itself to not just a few biographies.

Seyd, Felizia. **Romantic Rebel; the Life and Times of George Sand.** New York: Viking Press, 1940. 286 p.
PQ2412.S47

When this book came out in 1940 reviewers called it fascinating and said that it presented a fine literary and cultural backdrop for the life of George Sand, a period of time not unlike the Paris of one hundred years later. It is comprehensive and straightforward and not without wit.

Maurois, André. **Lélia, the Life of George Sand.** Translated by Gerard Hopkins. New York: Harper, 1953. 482 p.
PQ2412.M313 1953a

The title of this book refers to one of George Sand's more explicit novels. Maurois is considered to be a writer of the "biographie romancée." It is a well researched tome with an interesting sifting of the facts to bring about a unique portrait of George Sand.

Cate, Curtis. **George Sand: A Biography.** Boston: Houghton Mifflin, 1975. 812 p.
PQ2413.C3

This most recent of the three biographies captures the spirit of George Sand, audacious with a conservative strain. It is the most comprehensive to date, but George Sand was even a fuller personality than is seen here, and she may never be captured no matter how probing the approach.

SANDBURG, Carl (1878-1967), American poet

Carl Sandburg did write an historical novel and a popular biography of Abraham Lincoln, for which he received a Pulitzer for the last four of the six volumes. However, he is best known as a Pulitzer Prize-winning poet who incorporated, to the shock of poetry readers, street language and an irregular verse, drawing upon his varied interests and concerns on the American social scene. All of his poetry has been anthologized.

Callahan, North. **Carl Sandburg, Lincoln of our Literature: A Biography.** New York: New York University Press, 1970. 253 p.
PS3537.A618.Z538

Carl Sandburg's work and life are the subject of many studies. This book comes closest to a full-length biography. It was written with the help of Sandberg and is sympathetic toward him.

SARGENT, John Singer (1856-1925), American painter

Although considered an American painter, John Singer Sargent was born in Florence, Italy. He studied there as well as in Paris. He came to the United States at the age of twenty but returned to Europe after one of his paintings caused a scandal. He did return again to America in his thirties when he was at the height of his fame, continuing his portraiture, landscapes and watercolors. He is best known for his portraits of well-known social personalities, whom he painted with uncommon technique in a most complimentary way.

Olson, Stanley. **John Singer Sargent, His Portrait.** New York: Macmillan, 1986. 309 p.
ND237.S3.O4 1986b

This exceptionally well-researched biography is primarily aimed at the scholar. The reproductions are poor and the reader may wish to consult other studies of the artist and his works. Despite its scholarship it is gossipy and humorous. It also contains interesting information about his circle of friends and acquaintances.

SATIE, Erik (1866-1925), French composer

Erik Satie was a member of the famous "les six" group of composers in France. His musical style stood out from this group in its abstraction and harmonic innovations, anticipating the neoclassicism of Stravinsky. He was influenced by, and he influenced, Claude Debussy. Satie worked as a café pianist and lived in abject poverty. The titles of his short piano pieces exhibit a unique witticism as did his use of unconventional "instruments." Considered his most outstanding work is "Socrates" written in 1918.

Harding, James. **Erik Satie.** New York: Praeger, 1975. 269 p.
ML410.S196.H3 1975

Erik Satie was a most interesting character. His approach to composing and his musical insights were unique. James Harding's prose is smooth and a real French flavor pervades the book.

SAYERS, Dorothy L. (Dorothy Leigh) (1893-1957), English story writer

Dorothy Sayers was one of the first woman graduates of Oxford University. She was a classical scholar and a significant translator of Dante, but we all know her as the author of the detective novels featuring Lord Peter Wimsey. Dorothy Sayers developed her plots and characters uncommonly well. Among her best books are **The Nine Tailors** (1934) and a year earlier, **Murder Must Advertise.**

Brabazon, James. **Dorothy L. Sayers: A Biography.** New York: Scribner, 1981. 308 p.
PR6037.A95.Z62

Dorothy Sayers requested that no biographies be written of her until fifty years after her death. James Brabazon was able to get the cooperation of her son in putting this work together, and it is as definitive a biography as possible considering that much material is yet to be released for research.

SCHOENBERG, Arnold (1874-1951), Austrian composer

Arnold Schoenberg is one of the universally accepted great innovators of twentieth century music. He developed the twelve-tone system, also called serial music. He began to study the violin at the age of nine, the same year he started composing. His first notable work and one which possibly remains most popular is "Verlärte Nacht" or "Transfigured Night," composed in 1899. In 1921 he began to compose in the twelve-tone system and continued in that mode for the rest of his life. He taught at the Prussian Academy of the Arts in Berlin, a most prestigious post but was dismissed because he was Jewish. He immigrated to the United States,where he became a citizen in 1941 and taught in California. He continued to compose, producing a piano concerto in 1942 but died before finishing his opera **Moses and Aron** started in 1932, considered to be his legacy to the opera world.

Stuckenschmidt, Hans Heinz. **Schoenberg: His Life, World, and Work.** Translated by Humphrey Searle. New York: Schirmer, 1978, c1977. 581 p.
ML410.S283.S93 1978

Although this touches upon the style of musical composition of Schoenberg it is primarily biographical and was commissioned for the centenary of the birth of the composer. It is very detailed and came out to mixed reviews. Nevertheless, it is the book to read to get a complete picture of the personal life of one of the greatest twentieth century composers.

SCHUBERT, Franz (1797-1828), German composer

Schubert was a very prolific composer who lived a full life in thirty-one years. He was the proponent of romanticism and was outstanding as a composer of the song; his "Die Winterreise" (1827) is considered among the most important song cycles in vocal literature, employing the piano as an equal instrument in these compositions. He also wrote symphonies and some of the most lyrical piano solo works, such as the "The Wanderer Fantasy" (1822) and the "Impromptus" five years later. His chamber music is among the most romantic written, especially as heard in his "Octet" for strings in 1828 and the great String Quintet in C Major of the same year. He did not teach nor is he considered a major influence to succeeding generations of composers, but his music lives in the repertoire of contemporary interpreters.

Brown, Maurice John Edwin. **Schubert, a Critical Biography.** New York: St. Martin's Press, 1958. 414 p.
ML410.S3.B7

No real definitive biography seems to exist, at least in English. This is a chronology of the composer's life and music. It is authoritative and brings together a kind of portrait of the composer.

Marek, George Richard. **Schubert.** New York: Viking, 1985.
254 p.
ML410.S3.M18 1985

This is a highly readable documentary of the life of
Schubert, who will continue to elude a biographer. It is shy on
discussion of his music, but because of his short life and
prolific output one cannot ignore Schubert, the musician.

SCHUMANN, Robert (1810-56), German composer

Robert Schumann was a leader of the German romantic music
tradition. The first part of his composing life was taken up
with piano works, among his most brilliant, "Carnaval" and
"Fantasiestücke," composed before the age of thirty. He then
concentrated on orchestral music and songs, in the latter using
the piano as an equal. His orchestral work, "Rhenish Symphony"
(1850), contained such emotional intensity that musicologists
look upon it as a precursor of his own eventual breakdown. He
married a well-known pianist, Clara Wieck, with whom he had eight
children. Despite family responsibilities he moved frequently,
displaying an unstable temperament which ultimately caused him to
spend his last two years in a mental institution. He composed
for nearly every musical form. Much that he wrote remains in the
repertoire of contemporary musicians.

Taylor, Ronald. **Robert Schumann, His Life and Work.** New
York: Universe Books, 1982. 354 p.
ML410.S4.T2 1982

This biography is addressed to the general reader. Taylor
explores the writings of Schumann and diffuses earlier myths but
reveals the pain of his life.

SCHWARTZ, Delmore (1913-66), American poet

Delmore Schwartz has been characterized as an intellectual
poet. He taught on the university level. His themes of
alienation and his near obsession with the past suffuse his
poetry, highlighted by his allusive language. His best poems are
in the 1960 Bollinger Prize winner **Summer Knowledge: New and
Selected Poems 1938-58.**

Atlas, James. **Delmore Schwartz: The Life of an American
Poet.** New York: Farrar, Straus & Giroux, 1977. 417 p.
PS3537.C79.Z56

James Atlas finds in the emotional disarray of Schwartz a talent burned out. His auspicious beginnings deteriorated into chaos at the end of his life.

SCOTT, Walter, Sir (1771-1832), Scottish novelist; poet

Walter Scott realized unprecedented prominence as an historical novelist and narrative poet. Among his most noteworthy novels and still read today are **Ivanhoe** (1820) and his first, **Waverly**, published anonymously in 1814. However, he began his working life with his father, a lawyer, rising to a significant legal appointment. Among his most popular poems is "Lady of the Lake" written in 1810. He was involved in publishing ventures that were faltering financially. His efforts to stave off this failure caused him to write incessantly to earn the necessary funds. Such overwork caused the decline in his health that led to his death. He married at the age of twenty-six and had four children.

Lockhart, J. G. **Memoirs of the Life of Sir Walter Scott, Bart.** 2 vols. Philadelphia: Carey, Lea, & Blanchard, 1837. PR5332.L6 1837

This edition is abridged from seven volumes. It is considered, like James Boswell's **Life of Samuel Johnson,** to be one of the best literary biographies of all time. Modern scholarship, however, has since disproved some of the more "creative" elements in this work.

Johnson, Edgar. **Sir Walter Scott; the Great Unknown.** 2 vols. New York: Macmillan, 1970. PR5332.J6

Edgar Johnson's biography is considered the "other" biography of Sir Walter Scott. It has the advantage of additional primary materials.

Buchan, John. **Sir Walter Scott.** New York: Coward-McCann, 1932. 384 p. PR5332.B83 1932a

This is the most accessible of the biographies, and as all good biographies of artists must do, makes the reader turn to his works.

Grierson, Herbert John Clifford. **Sir Walter Scott, Bart.** New York: Columbia University Press, 1938. 320 p. PR5332.G73

Another revisionist of the Lockhart work, Grierson brings an expertise backed by editing twelve volumes of his letters. He brings out the financial problems experienced by Sir Walter Scott as they so profoundly affected his creativity and life.

SHAW, George Bernard (1856-1950), Irish playwright

So pervasive has been Shaw's influence that there is an adjective to describe his ideas and approach—"Shavian." This long-lived playwright, who began his writing career as a novelist, went on to be a music critic for some London newspapers, then a drama critic for the **Saturday Review of Literature**, etc. He revolutionized the Victorian stage with, among others, the "unpleasant" play **Mrs. Warren's Profession**, a jibe at attitudes toward prostitution, written in 1893. His best plays were written in the early 1900's, **Man and Superman** (1905) and **Major Barbara** of the same year. **Pygmalion** (1913) is considered his most enduring. Of his later plays, **Saint Joan** (1923) is his best known. He was a Renaissance man in the breadth of his knowledge and his views of the world and his intellectual life moved through several philosophical trends.

Holroyd, Michael. **Bernard Shaw: Volume I 1856-1898: The Search for Love**. New York: Random House, 1988. 486 p. PR5366.H56 1988

Holroyd, Michael. **Bernard Shaw: Volume II 1898-1918: The Pursuit for Power**. New York: Random House, 1989. 421 p. PR5366.H56 1989

The third volume of this trilogy is in process as of this writing. The trustees of Shaw's estate have commissioned Michael Holroyd to write this biography. Holroyd is up to the task but his attempt is not without its critics.

Henderson, Archibald. **George Bernard Shaw: Man of the Century**. New York: Appleton-Century Crofts, 1956. 969 p. PR5366.H43

Henderson was the authorized biographer of Shaw until Holroyd. This is the third biography of Shaw written by Henderson, this time without the living Shaw supervising its content. It is considered invaluable as a source of the whole of his career and life.

SHELLEY, Mary Wollstonecraft (1797-1851), English novelist

Mary Wollstonecraft Shelley, the second wife of the poet Percy Shelley, wrote the chilling, ever-popular **Frankenstein**

(1818), a novel with a philosophical import dwarfed by its harrowing tale. Her husband and Lord Byron were also challenged to write similar stories but she alone persisted. After the death of her husband she edited his writings and her own.

Sunstein, Emily W. **Mary Shelley: Romance and Reality.** Boston: Little, Brown, 1989. 478 p.
PR5398.S86 1989

Emily Sunstein writes of the life of the woman, Mary Wollstonecraft Shelley, daughter of a significant philosopher, who ran off with Shelley while his wife was still living, who spoke five languages before she was twenty-five yet lived in the shadow of her husband, Percy Shelley. This is a seminal work of the life of a brilliant woman, the author of one of the world's masterpieces, **Frankenstein.**

SHELLEY, Percy Bysshe (1792-1822), English poet

Shelley was of the great English romantic tradition of Coleridge, Keats and Byron. Shortly after marrying Mary Wollstonecraft Godwin he settled in Italy, never to return to England. He drowned at the age of twenty-nine but not before going through three distinct periods in his literary career. His first period was devoted to pamphlets and poems with radical themes. His brilliant lyrical poetry shines through his second period culminating in **Prometheus Unbound** (1819), a four-act lyrical drama. His major achievements of his last period were "Adonais," a pastoral elegy of 1821 and the unfinished "The Triumph of Life."

Holmes, Richard. **Shelley: The Pursuit.** New York: E.P. Dutton, 1975, c1974. 829 p.
PR5431.H65 1975

This is a full-scale biography, bringing to life his personality and adding new insights to his existence. Holmes is a revisionist, but his own book is somewhat dated as well.

White, Newman Ivey. **Shelley.** 2 vols. New York: Alfred A. Knopf, 1940.
PR5431.W5

Although this is considered to be the standard biography of Shelley, Holmes' book complements it in bringing up to date some of the more recent research. As Holmes brings Shelley's personality to light, White gives us the facts and allows the reader to draw her or his own conclusions.

SITWELL, Edith, Dame (1887-1964), English poet

Edith Sitwell was one of three siblings of an aristocratic family who attained a kind of literary fame. She was the most established as a poet and biographer.

Glendinning, Victoria. **Edith Sitwell; a Unicorn among Lions.** New York: Knopf, 1981. 393 p.
PR6037.I8.Z59 1981

This biography, written by the author of other biographical studies, shows the complex, contradictory nature of her subject. Of importance in Edith Sitwell's life is the long, stormy relationship she had with Tchelitchev, a Russian artist to whom Glendinning brings a perceptive analysis.

SLOAN, John (1871-1951), American painter

Sloan began his career as a newspaper artist. In 1904, after the encouragement of Robert Henri with whom he studied, he moved to New York and used that city as the inspiration for the new social realism movement. He exhibited with the Ashcan School (1908) and in the famed 1913 Armory Show. He was also a popular teacher.

Brooks, Van Wyck. **John Sloan; a Painter's Life.** New York: Dutton, 1955. 246 p.
ND237.S57.B7

John Sloan is fortunate to have Van Wyck Brooks as the author of his biography. This historian-critic brings warmth and sensitivity to the life and times of John Sloan and to the critical years of the formation of the American art scene.

SMETANA, Bedrich (1824-84), Czech composer

Smetana is best known for his cycle of six symphonic poems "Má Vlast," translated as "My Country," composed during the years 1874-79. He was a precocious musician, performing in public and composing at the age of eight. His family moved a great deal and he drew his inspiration for his music from Bohemia, newly independent from Austria. He settled in Prague, studied composition and taught. Other significant works are the opera **The Bartered Bride** (1866), still in today's repertoire and the autobiographical chamber piece "From My Life" (1876). He suffered from increasing deafness and depression, dying in a mental institution.

Large, Brian. **Smetana**. New York: Praeger, 1970. 473 p.
ML410.S63.L4 1970b

This fresh approach to the life of Smetana is addressed both
to the specialist as well as the general reader. There is quite
a bit of emphasis on his music but enough of his life to address
the question of whether Smetana was the victim or architect of
his circumstances.

SOLZHENITSYN, Aleksandr Isaevich (1918-   ), Russian novelist

Although a writer of the nineteenth century tradition,
Solzhenitsyn is considered one of the foremost Russian
novelists of the twentieth century. He was sentenced to hard
labor for eight years for having written critical remarks about
Stalin in a letter to a friend. His first novel to be published
in the Soviet Union was **One Day in the Life of Ivan Denisovich**
(1962), which brought him first acclaim because of its subject
matter and then disfavor. He found it almost impossible to have
his works published in his own country. After more
confrontations concerning censorship and after winning the Nobel
Prize in 1970, he was forced to immigrate to the West, finally
settling in the United States. During that time he finished the
three-part **The Gulag Archipelago** (1973-78).

Scammell, Michael. **Solzhenitsyn: A Biography**. New York:
Norton, 1984. 1051 p.
PG3488.O4.Z873 1984

This massive biography grippingly details the life of its
subject. Michael Scammell has done an exceptional piece of
research in exposing Soviet misinformation about him.

STEIN, Gertrude (1874-1946), American fiction writer

Gertrude Stein was part of the group of expatriate artists
who settled in Paris. After studying for, but not finishing, a
medical degree at Johns Hopkins University, Gertrude Stein spent
four decades writing in her very unconventional style, living
with her lifelong companion, Alice B. Toklas, befriending other
artists and amassing an exceptional collection of modern art.
Getting her work published was somewhat difficult but her best-
selling **The Autobiography of Alice B. Toklas** put her in the
public eye. She tried to incorporate both art and music in theme
and style in her writing.

Mellow, James R. **Charmed Circles: Gertrude Stein and
Company**. New York: Praeger, 1974. 528 p.
PS3537.T323.Z72

149

Her interesting life has made her the subject of numerous, but not so well executed biographies. The emphasis of the Mellow work is on her as a writer and her impact upon the art world at that time. This is enjoyable prose.

STEINBECK, John (1902-68), American fiction writer

John Steinbeck's contribution to American letters won him the Nobel Prize in 1962. His life experiences among the migrant workers in California manifested themselves in his novels, often sympathetic to the alienated in society. Among his most outstanding works are **Of Mice and Men** (1937), concerning the lives of itinerant workers and the Pulitzer Prize-winning **The Grapes of Wrath,** (1939) not only an exceptionally well written novel but one in which the plight of the dispossessed farmer was brought to the fore. Of his later works, **East of Eden,** written in 1952 and made into a film three years later, is most significant. His subsequent novels were anticlimatic to this powerful, creative work using the Biblical story of Adam as a backdrop to the story of his mother's family.

Kiernan, Thomas. **The Intricate Music; a Biography of John Steinbeck.** Boston: Little, Brown, 1979. 331 p.
PS3537.T3234.Z716

This fine biography really comes to grips with the artistry of the novelist, his personality and the kind of a statement he wanted to make through his fiction. It is readable and popular, and Kiernan has been criticized by reviewers for his failure to recognize that not all of Steinbeck's work was of the same stature.

Benson, Jackson J. **The True Adventures of John Steinbeck, Writer: A Biography.** New York: Viking Press, 1984. 1116 p.
PS3537.T3234.Z616 1984

This book came out to mixed reviews; it was called everything from "definitive" to "simplistic." However, a genuine human being emerges from this huge biography, a man very grounded in his environment with a kind of missionary zeal to publish all he felt.

STEVENSON, Robert Louis (1850-94), Scottish novelist; poet

Robert Louis Stevenson's popularity rests on classics of juvenile literature, such as **Treasure Island,** written while looking for a congenial climate for his lifelong tubercular disease. **Dr. Jekyll and Mr. Hyde** (1886) is a frightening allegorical classic, and **Kidnapped** was written the same year.

Financially secure, he spent his last years in Samoa, where he died before completing what many critics feel was his finest prose, **Weir of Hermiston.**

Calder, Jenni. **Robert Louis Stevenson: A Life Study.** New York: Oxford University Press, 1980. 362 p.
PR5493.C25 1980

This is mainly a psychological study of Stevenson, his seeming preoccupation with his health, and his relationship with his wife, Fanny, as a husband who was a wanderer and an artist.

Furnas, J.C. (Joseph Chamberlain). **Voyage to Windward; the Life of Robert Louis Stevenson.** New York: Sloane, 1951. 566 p.
PR5493.F8

This is considered a standard and very readable biography of Stevenson. Furnas uses letters as the basis of his research. He probes the unevenness of Stevenson's writings.

Pope-Hennessy, James. **Robert Louis Stevenson.** New York: Simon & Schuster, 1975, c1974. 320 p.
PR5493.P6 1975

Pope-Hennessy emphasizes the milieu in which Stevenson worked. This biography is not without its biases but includes rich details not found in other works, especially concerning his travels and his relationship with his wife.

STRAUSS, Richard (1864-1949), German composer

Richard Strauss was a musical child prodigy, playing the piano by four, composing at six. He started out professionally as a conductor, which gave him the opportunity to introduce some of his own orchestral compositions. Of his tone poems during that time "Thus Spake Zarathustra" (1896) was the most significant. After 1900 he concentrated on operas, one of which brought fame to its librettist, Hugo von Hofmannsthal—**Der Rosenkavalier** (1911). During a period of financial struggle, his composing was less significant. Because his librettist for the opera **Die schweigsame Frau** (1935) was Jewish, this work was banned. His daughter-in-law and grandsons were also Jewish, which again caused him to be involved in political conflict. He went to England where he continued to compose.

Marek, George Richard. **Richard Strauss: The Life of a Non-Hero.** New York: Simon & Schuster, 1967. 350 p.
ML410.S93.M4

This is a commendable biography and very readable. Marek delves into the enigma of the creative block during the political oppression that Strauss endured because of his association with Jews as his librettist and his daughter-in-law's family. His major compositions are the subject of Marek's commentaries.

STRINDBERG, August (1849-1912), Swedish novelist; playwright; poet

Strindberg was an exceptionally complex man, complex enough to generate a nine-volume autobiography. He is listed as a literary artist and yet his paintings are coming to the auction block at high prices. His family life did not nourish a healthy personality, nor was the repressive Swedish Oscarian society a better milieu. Summers spent on an island off Stockholm brought forth a notable attempt at a play and the publication of a novel. He made enough money from these attempts so that he was able to use his writing as his sole financial support. His marital attempts were disasters which influenced the themes of some of his dramas, notably, **Miss Julie** (1888). He wandered all over Europe, dabbled in the occult and returned to die in Stockholm. His "inferno" years were marked by more than sixty plays as well as theoretical works, novels and nearly all other forms of literary expression. This period was prepared by voracious reading. His works sometimes span more than one literary genre and have been criticized as being of uneven quality. He was a forerunner of expressionism, surrealism and the psyche-probing play in the "Theater of the Absurd." Other significant works are **A Dream Play** (1902), and **The Ghost Sonata** (1907), to name two in his herculean output.

Lagercrantz, Olof Gustav Hugo. **August Strindberg.** Translated by Anselm Hollo. New York: Farrar, Straus, Giroux, 1984. 398 p.
PT9815.L313 1984

There is less emphasis in this book on Strindberg the dramatist than as a writer in other genres. It scrutinizes his forced creative leaps and private battles with living.

Meyer, Michael Leverson. **Strindberg.** New York: Random House, 1985. 651 p.
PT9815.M4 1985

Meyer looks at Strindberg, the dramatist. It is a shocking portrayal of Stindberg's aligning himself with iniquity to "conjure up" his writing.

STUART, Gilbert (1755-1828), American painter

One of the many portraits of George Washington painted by Gilbert Stuart is on the American one dollar bill. This portrait painter is considered among the greatest ever to work in America. During the American Revolution he studied in England, then debts drove him to Ireland. He returned to America to the acclaim of many famous people. He painted the first six presidents with a technique straightforward and natural in its execution.

Mount, Charles Merrill. **Gilbert Stuart, a Biography.** New York: W.W. Norton, 1964. 384 p.
ND237.S8.M65

Charles Mount is also a portrait painter and brings a unique sensitivity to Stuart. He corrects early inaccuracies about the man and adds new material from primary sources unavailable to earlier biographers and critics. He addresses the issues of patronage and commissioning as they affect the artist. Key paintings are analyzed thoughtfully.

SULLIVAN, Arthur (1842-1900), English composer

Arthur Sullivan is part of the Gilbert and Sullivan team, whose operettas with their satire, farcical plots and characters and singable music continue to delight the whole spectrum of music lovers. Among the delights are their **H. M. S. Pinafore** (1878), **Patience** (1881) and **The Mikado** (1885). Sullivan was knighted for his work and died trying to save a drowning woman.

Jacobs, Arthur. **Arthur Sullivan, a Victorian Musician.** New York: Oxford University Press, 1984. 470 p.
ML410.S95.J28 1984

This is a biography for the general reader, written in a lively style as well as meticulously researched. Sullivan emerges as a fine fellow, kind, courteous, a man on his own terms but not always the perfect partner.

SUTHERLAND, Graham Vivian (1903-80), English painter

Graham Sutherland was a well-known portrait painter whose modus vivendi did not always please his patrons nor the art world of the time. His early work is pastoral in form. The best known of his works is a portrait of Somerset Maugham done in 1949. His religious themes are most eloquently seen in the tapestry of Coventry Cathedral.

Berthoud, Roger. **Graham Sutherland: A Biography.** London: Faber & Faber, 1982. 328 p.
ND497.S95.B47 1982

This biography is like a Sutherland portrait, somewhat aloof, candid, carefully designed, official. It is well documented and organized, but real people do emerge.

SWIFT, Jonathan (1667-1745), Anglo-Irish satirist

Jonathan Swift may be the omnipotent satirist in English letters. His irony may be at its best or worst in suggesting that the poverty in Ireland might be erased by raising children as a cash crop in **A Modest Proposal** (1729). He is the author of **Gulliver's Travels,** a book for all ages — and lost on a child. **A Tale of a Tub** scorns religion and learning. As editor of the famous **Examiner** he was part of the political scene. A change in English government forced him to Ireland, where he lived out his life. Swift expressed his views in the third person, making it difficult to know just whose ideas are being expressed.

Ehrenpreis, Irvin. **Swift: The Man, His Works, and the Age.** 3 vols. Cambridge: Harvard University Press, 1962-1983.
PR3726.E37

Ehrenpreis took many years to write this enormous work, and his views of the man evolved over time, which makes it one of the great biographies of our times. Ehrenpreis tunes into Swift's mind and psyche so deeply as to produce a worthy literary feat.

SWINBURNE, Algernon Charles (1837-1909), English poet

Swinburne's father underwrote the beginning of his literary career after Swinburne left Oxford without a degree. He was involved in organizations of radical politics and religious skepticism. The first publisher of his **Poems and Ballads, First Series** written in 1866 withdrew them from sale after a controversy arose about their sometimes perverse content. His poetry is now looked upon as being a bit overdone but during its heyday he and his literary outpourings were a sensation. Some of his literary criticism is still relevant. His life lends itself to numerous biographical works.

Gosse, Edmund. **The Life of Algernon Charles Swinburne.** New York: Macmillan, 1917. 363 p.
PR5513.G6

This is considered the major biography despite its age. It is very accurate in its depiction of his inordinate creative energy. Gosse knew his subject and at times the book is overly anecdotal and flattering.

Lafourcade, Georges. **Swinburne; a Literary Biography.** New York: W. Morrow, 1932. 314 p.
PR5513.L34 1932

This corrects some of the inaccuracies of the Gosse book but has also been superseded by more recent biographical data. However, despite these criticisms it is a notable depiction of Swinburne's world and a fine characterization of the man.

Henderson, Philip. **Swinburne: Portrait of a Poet.** New York: Macmillan, 1974. 305 p.
PR5513.H38

This most recent significant biography was assiduously investigated using the Swinburne letters. Of importance is his depicting the years after the death of his father before he was "rescued" from his debauchery.

SYNGE, J.M. (John Millington) (1871-1909), Irish poet; playwright

Although Synge wrote only six plays, he is considered the greatest playwright of modern Irish theater. He attended Trinity College, Dublin, and lived briefly in Germany and Paris. William Butler Yeats suggested that he return to Ireland, more specifically the Aran Islands, to write about his fellow countryfolk—which he did, resulting in **The Playboy of the Western World** (1907), a travesty of Irish life. His earlier shorter play **Riders to the Sea** is one of the most poignant dramas in modern theater. His death left **Deidre of the Sorrows** incomplete, and it was finished by Yeats and Synge's fiancée.

Greene, David H. (Herbert) and Edward M. Stephens. **J.M. Synge: 1871-1909.** New York: Macmillan, 1959. 321 p.
PR5533.G7

The second author was the nephew of the playwright and inherited his papers. He died suddenly and his widow asked Greene to write this articulate, illustrative, credible account of Synge.

TAGORE, Rabindranath (1861-1941), Indian poet; novelist; playwright

Tagore was a prolific writer who won the Nobel Prize in 1913 for his most well-known collection **Song Offering** (1910). His more than three thousand poems, two thousand songs, eight novels,

forty volumes of essays and short stories and fifty plays drew
their inspiration from India and the English literary tradition.
The major theme of these works was the universal search for God
and truth. He studied law in England but returned to India to
work at agricultural development. There he experienced first hand
the life of the indigent. Besides his extensive literary output
he was also a musician, painter, actor and choreographer.

Kripalani, Krishna. **Rabindranath Tagore; a Biography.** New
York: Oxford University Press, 1962. 417 p.
PK1725.K7

Kripalani knew the influential Tagore family, which greatly
facilitated the writing of this insightful biography, which is at
once authentic and understandable. He assists the reader in
understanding Bengali life with an in-depth picture of the
political and societal atmosphere of the times.

TARKINGTON, Booth (1869-1946), American novelist

Booth Tarkington is known for his novels with adolescent
themes, **Penrod** (1914) and **Seventeen,** two years later. The
insights gained from his brief political career brought novels
based on this experience, **The Magnificent Ambersons** (1918) and
Alice Adams (1921) Pulitzer Prizes. He was also a playwright and
an art collector.

Woodress, James. **Booth Tarkington, Gentleman from Indiana.**
Philadelphia: Lippincott, 1955. 350 p.
PS2973.W6

This is a comprehensive biography of a likable and very
human person. This chronology brings to life the man who despite
losing his sight continued his writing.

TATE, Allen (1899-1979), American poet

Allen Tate was a literary critic as well as a poet. His
background in Latin literature is the structural basis for his
complex poetry. He won the Bollingen Prize for his poetry in
1956. Collections of his poems include **Poems** (1960) and **The
Swimmers and Other Selected Poems** (1970). His literary statement
"Tension in Poetry" is a significant contribution to the new
criticism movement.

Squires, Radcliffe. **Allen Tate; a Literary Biography.** New
York: Pegasus, 1971. 231 p.
PS3539.A74.Z86

This was written before the death of Tate. More must come to the fore such as his marital record and his conversion to Catholicism, important issues for an understanding of the man. However, this is excellent in presenting the early life of Tate.

TCHAIKOVSKY, Peter Ilich (1840-93), Russian composer

Tchaikovsky's musical compositions are among the most accessible in all classical music. His "Nutcracker Suite", which he composed in 1892, is an annual favorite among ballet fans at Christmastime. The music for the ballets, "Swan Lake" (1876) and "Sleeping Beauty" (1889), is part of the standard repertoire. He had a formal music education and was among the first faculty of the famed Moscow Conservatory. He also composed operas, symphonies and smaller works. Much of his lyrical music is based on the Russian song. His marriage brought him to the brink of suicide as it forced him to confront his sexual orientation. Tchaikovsky traveled extensively including a tour in the United States in 1891. He died of cholera in St. Petersburg.

Brown, David. **Tchaikovsky: A Biographical and Critical Study.** 3 vols. New York: Norton, 1978-1986. ML410.C4.B74

This projected four-volume set is the definitive biographical study of Tchaikovsky. Brown has access to primary documentation previously suppressed by Soviet authorities. Despite its scholarship and length, it is a readable record of the life and works of this most popular composer.

TEASDALE, Sara (1884-1933), American poet

Sara Teasdale was one of the finest poets of her generation. Her poetry is marked by simplicity and clarity as in her **Love Songs** (1917). Her later works in **Dark of the Moon** (1926) and **Strange Victory** (1933) are haunted by suffering. She ended her own life.

Carpenter, Margaret Haley. **Sara Teasdale, a Biography.** New York: Schulte Pub., 1960. 377 p. PS3539.E15.Z6

Margaret Carpenter's life of Teasdale is the first major biographical study based on Teasdale's diaries, letters and interviews with her acquaintances. The result is an erudite, candid chronology of the poet.

Drake, William. **Sara Teasdale, Woman and Poet.** San Francisco: Harper & Row, 1979. 304 p.
PS3539.E15.Z64 1979

Drake's book reveals the tormented soul of Teasdale and how this was reflected in her poetry. He also reflects upon the plight of the woman writer and modern American poetry.

TENNYSON, Alfred Tennyson, Baron (1809-92), English poet

This poet was the spokesman for the Victorian age. He was honored as poet laureate in 1850 for "In Memoriam", one of the finest elegies in English literature. He was made a peer of the realm in 1883. His most significant work is the twelve-part **Idylls of the King,** written over nearly a thirty-year period, ending in 1888. After being designated poet laureate, he wanted his poetry to be involved with the times and wrote, for example, his popular "The Charge of the Light Brigade".

Martin, Robert Bernard. **Tennyson, the Unquiet Heart.** New York: Oxford University Press, 1980. 643 p.
PR5581.M3 1980

Robert Martin goes beneath the facade of the benevolent poet to reveal an unstable personality which affected his life and poetry. This is a reaction to the "authorized" but distorted biography of Tennyson's son's **Memoirs.**

Tennyson, Charles. **Alfred Tennyson.** New York: Macmillan, 1949. 579 p.
PR5581.T38

Charles Tennyson draws a fine portrait of his grandfather that corrects the inaccurate perceptions of the **Memoirs.** He looks at Tennyson's family life and how he went from a seeming recluse to a national figure, how his life shaped his art.

THACKERAY, William Makepeace (1811-63), English novelist

Thackeray was born in Calcutta, India, educated in England, traveled on the continent, settled in Paris for awhile and returned to live in London. He began his literary career by writing satirical magazine pieces. His masterpiece **Vanity Fair** (1847-48) portrays a society "living without God in the world." He illustrated many of his own works. His satirical essays are in his **Roundabout Papers** (1860-63). His reputation went into decline at the beginning of the twentieth century.

Ray, Gordon Norton. **Thackeray.** 2 vols. New York: McGraw-Hill, 1955-58.
PR5631.R33

This is not only a thorough two-volume biographical monograph but also contains essays on his writings.

Stevenson, Lionel. **The Showman of Vanity Fair; the Life of William Makepeace Thackeray.** New York: Scribner, 1947. 405 p.
PR5631.S73

This is a good biography for the general reader unacquainted with Thackeray. It is scholarly, based on newly available primary documents.

THOMAS, Dylan (1914-53), Welsh poet

His most popular work is his radio play "Under Milk Wood," published posthumously. His most ambitious works are his complex poems as in **18 Poems** (1934) and two years later a second volume, **Twenty-Five Poems.** He and his wife lived in near poverty until he went back to writing radio scripts. Dylan Thomas traveled in the United States for poetry readings on college campuses as a kind of cult figure. He died in New York City of heavy drinking and depression. His colorful lifestyle and his college campus touring made him the subject of many biographies of varying degrees of quality.

FitzGibbons, Constantine. **The Life of Dylan Thomas.** Boston: Little, Brown, 1965. 370 p.
PR6039.H52.Z643 1965

FitzGibbons was a writer and friend of his subject. Despite his closeness to Dylan Thomas he brings a dispassionate touch and a balanced critical facility to him and his art.

THOMPSON, Francis (1859-1907), English poet

Thompson is considered a "Catholic" poet in terms of his subjects such as the popular "The Hound of Heaven" (1890). He wrote nearly 500 literary reviews and critical essays. Despite the support of friends and a drug rehabilitation program, he continued in his opium habit. He died of tuberculosis after writing the lives of two Catholic saints.

Boardman, Brigid M. **Between Heaven and Charing Cross: The Life of Francis Thompson.** New Haven: Yale University Press, 1989. 410 p.
PR5651.B64 1988

A truly fascinating biography of a pitiful soul whose
literary potential was never truly reached because of his
addiction to opium. The research is exemplary.

TIECK, Ludwig (1773-1853), German prose writer; poet

Ludwig Tieck was a most versatile and prolific writer of the
German romantic period. He wrote novels and plays and is best
known for his stories, some based on medieval legends, others,
forerunners of the supernatural horror stories of Poe and
Hoffmann. Among his plays, the satirical comedy Puss-in Boots
(1797) is noteworthy. Among his very inventive stories is "Blond
Eckbert" written the same year.

Paulin, Roger. Ludwig Tieck, a Literary Biography. New York:
Oxford University Press, 1985. 434 p.
PT2539.P3 1985

A thoroughly readable biography of this long-lived writer
with all the events and people that fill his life, art and times.
It is the best life of him in any language.

TOLSTOY, Leo, graf (1828-1910), Russian novelist

Tolstoy is considered the greatest of Russian novelists.
Masterpieces of world literature are his War and Peace (1862-69)
and Anna Karenina (1873-76). He wrote these novels after
retiring from the army, traveling in Europe, returning to his
estate, founding a school for peasant children on it and
marrying. His moral philosophy, based on nonresistance and
nonparticipation, had a significant influence beyond Russia, on
such persons as Mahatma Gandhi. His estate became something of a
pilgrimage site because of his philosophy. This philosophy
temporarily halted his own creative writing and caused him to
renounce his early writing. However, he did return to writing
fiction. His long, fascinating life has been the subject of many
biographies.

Courcel, Martine de. Tolstoy: The Ultimate Reconciliation.
Translated by Peter Levi. New York: C. Scribner's Sons, 1988.
458 p.
PG3385.C6513 1988

This is one of two biographies on Tolstoy to come out in
1988. Martine de Courcel's thrust is toward the turmoil that
Tolstoy and his wife experienced throughout their long life
together and how this affected his art.

Wilson, A.N. **Tolstoy**. New York: Norton, 1988. 572 p.
PG3385.W48 1988

Wilson is an English biographer of note, who is successful at looking at the genesis of the writer, Tolstoy, but less proficient as a chronicler of the aged Tolstoy.

Simmons, Ernest Joseph. **Leo Tolstoy**. Boston: Little, Brown, 1946. 852 p.
PG3385.S5 1946

Despite more recent attempts at the life of Tolstoy this may still be considered the definitive work. It is extremely readable, impeccably researched and looks at the great impact his marriage and his philosophical meanderings had on the man and his work.

TOOMER, Jean (1894-1967), African-American writer

Jean Toomer's major work is **Cane** (1923). It is a multi-genre work of short fiction, poetry and drama thematically juxtaposing the lives of Southern blacks with their Northern counterparts. Its poor reception moved him away from writing to studying and spreading the teachings of Gurdjieff.

McKay, Nellie Y. **Jean Toomer, Artist: A Study of His Literary Life and Work, 1894-1936**. Chapel Hill: University of North Carolina Press, 1984. 262 p.
PS3539.O478.Z78 1984

This work looks at the life of Toomer until he moved with his wife to Pennsylvania after his last literary publication, the poem "Blue Meridian." McKay, using his autobiographical writings, looks at his ambivalence about his African-American heritage as well as his family relationships.

Kerman, Cynthia Earl, and Richard Eldridge. **The Lives of Jean Toomer: A Hunger for Wholeness**. Baton Rouge: Louisiana State University Press, 1987. 411 p.
PS3539.O478.Z7 1987

Jean Toomer's lifelong quest was for authenticity. He was a writer, a teacher of a form of mysticism and involved with the Quakers. This is quite psychoanalytical in its approach and a good study of the man.

TROLLOPE, Anthony (1815-82), English novelist

Anthony Trollope's mother, Frances, was a prolific writer of
novels, travel books and other writings. Anthony Trollope wrote
series of novels, one such on a fictitious cathedral town,
Barsetshire. He was forty when he had his first novel published
and he continued to work at his job as a civil servant while
writing a certain quota of words every day. His social satire
The Way We Live Now was written in 1875 and is considered to be
his most penetrating look at English society.

Pope-Hennessy, James. **Anthony Trollope.** Boston: Little,
Brown, 1971. 400 p.
PR5686.P63 1971b

This is a very descriptive view of Trollope's life by a
person who trod the same part of the English countryside as did
his subject. The emphasis in this work, considered the most
complete biography of Trollope at the time of its publication, is
on the man and his individuality.

Super, R.H. (Robert Henry) **The Chronicler of Barsetshire; a
Life of Anthony Trollope.** Ann Arbor: University of Michigan Press,
1988. 528 p.
PR5686.S88 1988

This is a biography of facts based on the autobiographical
writings of Trollope. Super also details the background for his
novels. What emerges is an very methodical almost obsessive but
humane person.

TURGENEV, Ivan Sergeevich (1818-83), Russian fiction writer;
playwright

Turgenev's best known play is **A Month in the Country** (1855).
His fiction had great impact upon Russian society, so powerful
was his pen. Considered his masterpiece is the novel **Fathers and
Sons** (1862). Because of his travels in Europe, in pursuit of the
married singer Pauline Viardot, he helped popularize Russian
literature in Western Europe.

Magarshack, David. **Turgenev: A Life.** New York: Grove Press,
1954. 328 p.
PG3435.M2 1954

This is a readable account of the writer's life and its
integration with his art. His dramatic writings are examined in
this book more closely than in other biographies.

Pritchett, V.S. (Victor Sawdon). **The Gentle Barbarian: The Life and Work of Turgenev.** New York: Random House, 1977. 243 p.
PG3435.P7

This is a model of a biography as a literary genre. V.S. Pritchett is a noted writer and his lucid prose lends an accessible reflection upon Turgenev, whom he sees as an autobiographical writer.

Schapiro, Leonard Bertram. **Turgenev: His Life and Times.** New York: Random House, 1978. 382 p.
PG3435.S3 1978

This is a study of the life of Turgenev using material previously unavailable. He pursues more thoroughly the phenomenon of Pauline Viardot, whom Turgenev obsessively pursued.

Yarmolinsky, Avrahm. **Turgenev, the Man, His Art and His Age.** rev. ed. New York: Orion Press, 1959. 406 p.
PG3435.Y3 1959

At the time of its publication it was considered the authoritative biography. It is a full life as well as a discussion of his intellectual and artistic evolution.

Troyat, Henri. **Turgenev.** Translated by Nancy Amphoux. New York: E.P. Dutton, 1988. 184 p.
PG3435.T7613 1988

Henri Troyat, a well-known biographer, picks up the theme of his life, pursued but unfulfilled love. That there are many Pauline Viardots in his writings is one of the theses of Troyat.

TURNER, J.M.W. (Joseph Mallord Williams) (1775-1851), British painter

Turner is often regarded as the greatest landscape painter of all time. He was an industrious artist, with more than 19,000 extant watercolors, drawings and oils at the time of his death. He exhibited at the age of sixteen. Early in his career he traveled almost constantly, which influenced the evolution of his style. He then became more reclusive, painting and operating a gallery displaying his works. His style became more abstract and freer, provoking some negative criticism. In 1987 a new wing was added to the Tate Gallery in London dedicated to his art. Among his many well known works are "Buttermilk Lake" (1798), "Calais Pier" (1803) from his French period, epic scenes such as "The Wreck of a Transport Ship" (c.1805-10), "Fighting Téméraire" (1838) and from his later period "Rain, Steam, and Speed—the Great Western Railway" (1844).

Lindsay, Jack. **Turner, the Man and His Art.** New York:
F. Watts, 1985. 179 p.
ND497.T8.L53 1985

This is a popular introduction to the life of Turner,
written by an author of other biographies of visual artists. It
concentrates on his creativity and artistic development.

TWAIN, Mark (1835-1910), American novelist

Until recently one had to know his "real name", Samuel
Langhorne Clemens. Now the Library of Congress has authorized
his being entered under his pseudonym. Mark Twain began his
career in journalism. He married in 1870 and then made Hartford,
Connecticut his home base, there to write his best known works,
Tom Sawyer, (1875) and, after establishing his own publishing
firm, **Adventures of Huckleberry Finn** (1884). This publishing
venture proved unsuccessful, so Twain went to Europe to
regain some financial stability by doing more writing and a
worldwide lecture tour. The death of his daughter and wife
during this time influenced less well-crafted works penetrated
with pessimism, such as **What is Man?** (1906). His varied life
experiences lend themselves to numerous biographical studies.

Lauber, John. **The Making of Mark Twain; a Biography.** New
York: American Heritage Press, 1985. 298 p.
PS1331.L38 1985

This wonderful book takes us through the first thirty-five
years of Mark Twain's life. John Lauber, in the telling,
effectively foreshadows the later Twain. A lively book written
by a sympathetic biographer.

Emerson, Everett H. **The Authentic Mark Twain: A Literary
Biography of Samuel L. Clemens.** Philadelphia: University of
Pennsylvania Press, 1984. 330 p.
PS1331.E47 1984

The emphasis in this biography is on Twain as writer.
Twain, dominated by his wife, was also subject to manic-
depressive tendencies, and was surrounded by unfinished projects.
It is a thorough chronology that lacks the humor of the subject,
but it is important to an understanding of Mark Twain.

Kaplan, Justin. **Mr. Clemens and Mark Twain: A Biography.** New
York: Simon & Schuster, 1966. 424 p.
PS1331.K33

This book won both a Pulitzer and a National Book Award for
its popular approach to the public face and private person and

the impact that his seemingly split personality had upon his career. It is a lively rendition of a lively life.

VARESE, Edgard (1885-1965), French-American composer

Edgard Varèse was one of the early electronic composers. He moved from France, after studying with or befriending significant composers in Europe, to New York City, where he played a leading role in the avant-garde movement, helping to found important organizations of experimental music. He was among the most innovative composers of this century, eschewing traditional forms in favor of "organized sound." Examples of such are his "Déserts" (1949-53), alternating instruments with taped electronic sound and his "Poème électronique" (1957-58), employing 425 loudspeakers.

Ouelette, Fernand. **Edgard Varèse.** Translated by Derek Coltman. New York: Orion Press, 1968. 270 p. ML410.V27.O83

This is a fine biography of a composer whose approach to music seems to remain accessible only to the illuminati. Despite his music's rather narrow appeal, Ouelette gives us a readable biography unfettered with the intricacies of his music.

VERDI, Giuseppe (1813-1901), Italian composer

Verdi was the foremost composer of Italian opera. Many of his works remain in the contemporary repertoire. His operas are noted for their dramatic ardor, melodious passages and interesting characterizations. He began musical studies with an organist, was refused admission into the Milan Conservatory and started a career as an organist. His wife and both his children died within a two-year period, which temporarily interrupted his budding operatic composing career. In 1842 **Nabucco** brought him his first success. Eighteen operas in fifteen years included **Rigoletto** (1851), **Il Travadore** (1853) and **La Traviata** the same year. His popularity brought him political success as well, as a member of the newly formed Italian parliament. **Otello** (1887) and **Falstaff** (1893) were the climax of his later years.

Toye, Francis. **Guiseppe Verdi, His Life and Works.** New York: A.A. Knopf, 1946. 414 p. ML410.V4.T7 1946

Reviewers found this book to be an absorbing life of an emotional man so involved with music and life. It is an authoritative life, putting Verdi on his stage with a colorful backdrop.

Osborne, Charles. **Verdi; a Life in the Theatre.** New York:
Knopf, 1987. 360 p.
ML410.V4.O66 1987

This book offers nothing new about the life of Verdi but is
a good, contemporary biography, carefully written and useful as a
popular introduction to his life.

VERLAINE, Paul Marie (1844-96), French poet

Paul Verlaine was one of the great symbolist poets of the
nineteenth century. His poetry possessed an uncommon musicality.
The complexity of his life at times overshadows his poetry: in
his youth he exhibited signs of instability, then married,
separated, had a liaison with the poet Arthur Rimbaud, whom he
injured by shooting and was imprisoned for this. He returned to
his Catholic faith and wrote beautiful religious poetry. His
later life and poetry lost the beauty of his middle period. Of
importance was his first volume of poetry of 1866, **Poèmes
saturniens.** **La Bonne Chanson** (1870) and succeeding volumes
during the middle period contain his most exquisite works.

Hanson, Lawrence and Elizabeth Hanson. **Verlaine: Fool of
God.** New York: Random House, 1957. 394 p.
PQ2464.H3

This is a very discreetly written biography of a not-so-
discreet man. All the facts are there in a very organized
fashion. Choice bits are extracted from his diaries without
reducing his life to a tabloid story.

WAGNER, Richard (1813-83), German composer

Richard Wagner was the greatest composer of German romantic
opera. Most of his operas still remain in the repertoire today
and his "Ring cycle" may be the greatest group of operas ever
written. He began at an early age to write drama. Wagner felt
that words alone did not express his creative soul. He studied
music formally briefly and then continued on his own. His **The
Flying Dutchman, Tannhäuser,** and **Lohengrin** of the 1840's brought
German opera to new heights then to the great climax of the "Ring
cycle" of 1853-74. His political activities during the
Revolution of 1848 forced him to flee to Switzerland. He
returned to Beyreuth, Bavaria, to complete the "Ring cycle" and
build a theater for performances of his works. His wife, Cosima,
daughter of Liszt, continued the Beyreuth tradition.

Gregor-Dellin, Martin. **Richard Wagner, His Life, His Work, His Century**. Translated by J. Maxwell Brownjohn. San Diego: Harcourt Brace Jovanovich, 1983. 575 p.
ML410.W1.G73413 1983

This biography is an objective, accurate life of a man subject to hyperbolic adulation. It reads well and what is lost in translation may not be missed by those who did not read the original.

Newman, Ernest. **The Life of Richard Wagner**. 4 vols. New York: A.A. Knopf, 1933-46.
ML410.W1.N53

Richard Wagner's life lends itself to a multi-volume study and Ernest Newman leaves few stones unturned. He looks at the creative life of Wagner as well as Wagner the more pragmatic salesman and producer of his own operas. Certainly exhaustive for the time but not every primary source was available to Ernest Newman.

Watson, Derek. **Richard Wagner: A Biography**. New York: Schirmer Books, 1981, c1979. 352 p.
ML410.W1.W38 1981

This is a good chronology of the circumstances, the people and their impact upon the artist, Richard Wagner. Derek Watson had access to the papers of his wife, Cosima, which had just recently become available. Although the style is somewhat labored it is an important short survey of Wagner's life.

WAUGH, Evelyn (1903-66), English novelist

Evelyn Waugh was noted as the leading social satirist of his generation with such novels as **Decline and Fall** (1928), **Vile Bodies** (1930) and **Black Mischief**, two years later. His best known work, made into a television series, **Brideshead Revisited**, (1945) showed his increasingly conservative, pessimistic view of life as did **The Loved One**, written in 1948, mocking Hollywood mortuary mores.

Sykes, Christopher. **Evelyn Waugh: A Biography**. Boston: Little, Brown, 1975. 462 p.
PR6045.A97.Z83 1975

This is a significant full-length biography of Waugh. It is not a truly balanced view as Sykes was a friend of Waugh's and tended to gloss over the less pleasant aspects of his personality. However, despite that weakness and some problems in the organization of the book, Waugh comes through as a real person.

Stannard, Martin. **Evelyn Waugh; vol. 1, The Early Years,**
1903-1939. New York: Norton, 1987, c1986-
PR6045.A97.Z79 1987

This first volume presents a more balanced view of Waugh
than does the Sykes' biography but Waugh does not come alive.
However Stannard does explore Waugh's unique creative processes.
This project is based upon careful research of primary
documentation and is a significant contribution to the
understanding of Waugh as man and writer.

WELLS, H.G. (Herbert George) (1866-1946), English novelist

Along with Jules Verne, H.G. Wells is one of the founders of
the science fiction genre. From the end of the nineteenth
century until the 1920's, Wells was one of the world's most
famous literary personalities. His studies in biology and other
areas of human endeavor prepared him for his varied and
significant literary output, which covered not only the
scientific area but also insightful social and historical
exploration as well as humor. Of importance are his science
fiction novels, **The Time Machine** (1895) and **The War of the Worlds**
(1898). Of his comic novels, **Kipps: The Story of a Simple Soul**
(1905) and **The History of Mr. Polly** (1910) are minor classics.
In the area of nonfiction his **Outline of History** is considered
the best one-volume history of mankind by a single author.

Dickson, Lovat. **H.G. Wells; his Turbulent Life and Times.**
New York: Atheneum, 1969. 330 p.
PR5776.D5

This is a fine introduction to Wells by Dickson, who knew
Wells in his later years, the period of the book. Despite his
friendship with Wells, Dickson provides an objective and
absorbing biographical sketch with Wells' looming personality
ever present.

Mackenzie, Norman Ian, and Jeanne Mackenzie. **H.G. Wells: A
Biography.** New York: Simon & Schuster, 1973. 487 p.
PR5776.M3

This may still be the most definitive biography of Wells
available. It complements the Dickson one with its emphasis on
Wells' early years and his intellectual development.

WEST, Nathanael (1903-40), American novelist

Nathanael West is best known as the satiric writer of the
novel **Miss Lonelyhearts,** published in 1933 and made into a movie
in 1959. His writings are influenced by French surrealism, which

foreshadowed the schools of black comedy and absurdism. His experience in Hollywood brought him to write another novel to be made into a movie, **The Day of the Locust** (1939).

Martin, Jay. **Nathanael West; the Art of His Life**. New York: Farrar, Straus & Giroux, 1970. 435 p.
PS3545.E8334.Z8

Jay Martin, although not the greatest stylist, does an incredible piece of work pulling together all of the primary documentation about West and exploring the background of his four novels as well as his literary influences. His complex personality is dealt with somewhat more superficially than it could be.

WEST, Rebecca, Dame (1892-1983), English novelist

Rebecca West is better known as an historian, critic and political essayist. Despite her speaking as a feminist her life was not "liberated." Many of her intimate relationships were tragically unfulfilling. She was a prolific writer though and among her psychological novels are **The Return of the Soldier** (1918), **The Judge** (1922) and **The Birds Fall Down** (1966).

Glendinning, Victoria. **Rebecca West; a Life**. New York: Knopf, 1987. 300 p.
PR6045.E8.Z65 1987

A more complete biography needs to be written. Yet we do get an insight into an untidy life contrasted with her organized body of work. In this biography, Glendinning, who has written other biographies, is both thorough and succinct.

WHARTON, Edith (1862-1937), American novelist; short story writer

Edith Wharton belonged to the old New York society of which she frequently wrote. Her first literary success was **The House of Mirth** (1905). In 1920 she won the Pulitzer Prize for **The Age of Innocence**. Her best known work, very different in subject, was **Ethan Frome** (1911). Shortly after her divorce she settled in France, where she wrote of that country and the United States. She was also a poet and a nonfiction writer.

Lewis, R.W.B. (Richard Warrington Baldwin) **Edith Wharton: A Biography**. New York: Harper, 1975. 592 p.
PS3545.H16.Z696

This biography, which won the Pulitzer Prize in 1976, is a scholarly portrait of a captivating woman who pursued her writing career with great seriousness.

Wolff, Cynthia Griffin. **A Feast of Words: The Triumph of Edith Wharton.** New York: Oxford Press, 1977. 453 p.
PS3545.H16.Z94

This book was written with the assistance of Lewis, who gave Cynthia Wolff access to the papers and manuscripts that he used for his work a few years earlier. Her strength lies in her ability to look within the woman, Edith Wharton. And what flows from this is an insightful scholarly biography.

WHISTLER, James McNeill (1834-1903), American painter

Its official title is "Arrangement in Gray and Black, No. 1, Portrait of the Artist's Mother" (1872), but it is better known by its more familiar "Whistler's Mother" as it hangs in the Louvre. Whistler settled in London after studying Velazquez and Japanese prints in Paris, both of which influenced his art. He mounted elaborate exhibits in that city and engaged in other publicity endeavors to call attention to his art for art's sake credo. Toward the end of his life his seriousness of purpose and artistry drew authentic respect for him. He was also a lifelong etcher with a superb technique.

Weintraub, Stanley. **Whistler; a Biography.** New York: Weybright & Talley, 1974. 498 p.
ND237.W6.W44

This is as lively as the Victorian dandy it portrays. As is the case with many artists, Whistler was well traveled and had a large circle of acquaintances, also varied in their backgrounds. Weintraub does a wonderful piece of work pulling this world together.

WHITE, E.B. (Elwyn Brooks) (1899-1985), American prose writer

E.B. White, who is best known for his children's fiction, won a special Pulitzer Prize in 1978 for his lifetime of writing. He wrote for the **New Yorker** and **Harper's** magazines as well as the standard manual for writers, **The Elements of Style.** His famous children's books include the ever-popular **Charlotte's Web** (1952) and **The Trumpet of the Swan** (1970). His wife Katharine Angell White was an editor at the **New Yorker.**

Elledge, Scott. **E.B. White: A Biography.** New York: Norton, 1984. 400 p.
PS3545.H5187.Z64 1984

This is an unpretentious, methodic, birth-to-death narrative of the life of a writer who may or may not be known beyond his lifetime except as the author of children's classics.

WHITMAN, Walt (1819-92), American poet

Walt Whitman's early life was that of a drifter, a
journalist until his political views clashed with the powers that
be. He published his first edition of **Leaves of Grass**
himself. He continued to revise it but had to support himself as
a free-lance journalist while doing so. Now it is considered one
of the seminal books in all American literature. He was ahead of
his time in his poetic structure and subject matter. He was a
Civil War nurse and used this experience in his renowned
"When Lilacs Last in the Dooryard Bloom'd" and "O Captain, My
Captain." He lived his last years, crippled by a stroke, in his
Camden, New Jersey, home that became a kind of shrine even during
his lifetime. Despite his disability he continued to revise
Leaves of Grass and is celebrated as a literary emancipator.

Allen, Gay Wilson. **The Solitary Singer**. rev ed. New York:
New York University Press, 1967. 616 p.
PS3231.A69 1967

This is a detailed biography that gives a full portrait of
the milieu in which Whitman lived and worked. It has been
considered a definitive biography.

Asselineau, Roger. **The Evolution of Walt Whitman**. 2 vols.
Translated by Richard P. Adams and the author. Cambridge: Belknap
Press of Harvard University Press, 1960-1962.
PS3231.A833

The first of this two-volume set is subtitled **The Creation
of a Personality** and looks at the struggle of sexual orientation
that Whitman experienced in his life. The second volume analyzes
his work. Both volumes are copiously documented.

Kaplan, Justin. **Walt Whitman, a Life**. New York: Simon &
Schuster, 1980. 429 p.
PS3231.K3

This reads like a novel but is a serious study of Whitman's
life using the usual primary sources for his narrative and
interpretations.

Zweig, Paul. **Walt Whitman: The Making of the Poet**.
Basic Books, 1984. 372 p.
PS3231.Z87 1984

The emphasis in this biography is on the middle years of the
poet. Because of the limited span of time, Zweig is able to go
into more depth about Whitman's creative evolution from a roving
journalist to his ever-evolving **Leaves of Grass**.

WILDE, Oscar (1854-1900), Irish writer

Wilde's ambition was to be one of the greatest poets but his play, **The Importance of Being Earnest** (1895), and his earlier novel, **The Picture of Dorian Gray** (1890), upstaged his poetic attempts. His real fame may lie in his rather scandalous lifestyle, his brilliant conversation and his aesthetic posture. His way with words may have come from his parents who were both involved in literary pursuits. Wilde was a promising classical scholar and poet during his days at Trinity College, Dublin. He was also an essayist and critic of note. His "gross indecency" landed him a two-year stint of hard labor from 1895-97 during which time he continued writing.

Hyde, H. Montgomery. **Oscar Wilde: A Biography.** New York: Farrar, Straus, & Giroux, 1975. 410 p.
PR5823.H88

This is an important biography of Wilde. It is a frank assessment of this "dandy" with special emphasis on his last years, "falling from grace." It is somewhat weak on the years during which he produced his best writing.

Pearson, Hesketh. **Oscar Wilde, His Life and Wit.** New York: Harper & Brothers, 1946. 345 p.
PR5823.P4

Pearson is a biographer of note who has written a thorough and readable life, well balanced and accurate.

Ellmann, Richard. **Oscar Wilde.** New York: Vintage Books, 1988, c1987. 680 p.
PR5823.E38 1988b

Richard Ellmann was one of the pre-eminent biographers of the present time. He illuminates a life. The style is accessible and it will appeal to all audiences.

WILDER, Thornton (1897-1975), American playwright; novelist

Three-time Pulitzer Prize winner, Thornton Wilder was a novelist and dramatist. One of his prize-winning plays, **Our Town** (1938), has become one of the most frequently dramatized works of the American stage. Although his works are considered "popular" they all contain an exceptionally penetrating intellectual grasp of life. His early novel, **The Bridge of San Luis Rey** (1927), is set in Peru. **The Skin of Our Teeth** (1942) is a drama which traces the course of the history of mankind. **Hello, Dolly!** is the musical version of Wilder's **The Matchmaker** (1954). Despite his wide-ranging success he lived an emotionally painful life.

Harrison, Gilbert A. **The Enthusiast: A Life of Thornton Wilder**. New Haven, Conn.: Ticknor & Fields, 1983. 403 p.
PS3545.I345.Z694 1983

Despite his deep emotional pain, Wilder, according to the title of the book, was an essentially enthusiastic person. Although it does not go into detail about his personal travails, the book is well researched and is considered to be the best biography so far.

WILLIAMS, Tennessee (1911-83), American playwright

Tennessee Williams was a major American dramatist. His most effective work is **A Streetcar Named Desire** (1947) in which he seemed to literally get inside his characters. **The Glass Menagerie** (1945), **Cat on a Hot Tin Roof** (1955) and **Night of the Iguana** (1961) as well as **Streetcar** all received the New York Drama Critics' Circle Award. Of his novels, **The Roman Spring of Mrs. Stone** (1950) is best known. His later works, with few exceptions, do not have the power of his earlier ones.

Rader, Dotson. **Tennessee, Cry of the Heart**. Garden City, N.Y.: Doubleday, 1985. 348 p.
PS3545.I5365.Z824 1985

Dotson Rader was a close friend of Tennessee Williams and presents an intimate account of his life. Despite its rather anecdotal structure it is an effective work.

Spoto, Donald. **The Kindness of Strangers: The Life of Tennessee Williams**. Boston: Little, Brown, 1985. 409 p.
PS3545.I5365.Z836 1985

This is an objective, comprehensive life of Williams, based on the standard documentation as well as interviews of his friends and associates.

Tischler, Nancy Marie Patterson. **Tennessee Williams: Rebellious Puritan**. New York: Citadel, 1961. 319 p.
PS3545.I5365.Z85

The research about Williams has increased enormously since Nancy Tischler wrote her biography. However, it remains an important work because of her skills in intertwining his work and life.

WILLIAMS, William Carlos (1883-1963), American poet

William Carlos Williams maintained a large medical practice in pediatrics, spending most of his life in his birthplace in New

Jersey. Despite being in this demanding profession, he is considered one of the most innovative poets of modern American literature. He produced more than most full-time writers, more than forty volumes of poetry, fiction, plays, essays. His poems are his most important writings. He looked at everyday existence from a fresh point of view. Although he was a published poet since 1913, his reputation was not established until close to the end of his life with his epic poem Paterson (1946-58) and his Pulitzer Prize for Pictures from Brueghel (1962).

Mariani, Paul L. **William Carlos Williams: A New World Naked.** New York: McGraw-Hill, 1981. 875 p.
PS3454.I544.Z628

This finely crafted biography is a sympathetic and lengthy account of Williams. His thesis is subject to dispute: Mariani considers Williams to be the most important figure in American poetry in the twentieth century.

WISTER, Owen (1860-1938), American novelist

Owen Wister's claim to literary fame was **The Virginian** (1902), which was well "milked" into three films, a stage play and a television series. Its hero became the model for the contemporary cowboy. He is a minor literary figure, despite the popular spin-offs of his work. However, his life is most interesting as an American patrician who was a lawyer, student of music and friend of some of America's greats.

Payne, Darwin. **Owen Wister, Chronicler of the West, Gentleman of the East.** Dallas, Tex.: Southern Methodist University Press, 1985. 377 p.
PS3346.P39 1985

This work is a labor of love, based on going through the voluminous papers of Wister in the Library of Congress. This exceptional biography will be hard to supersede.

WODEHOUSE, P.G. (Pelham Grenville) (1881-1975), English novelist

Wodehouse wrote more than ninety novels! In his spare time he managed more than thirty plays and the lyrics to musicals. This English humorist may be best known for his Edwardian-English, charmingly inept Bertie Wooster and his butler, Jeeves, as in **The Inimitable Jeeves** (1924). He made political broadcasts in 1941 and was imprisoned by the Germans for them.

Green, Benny. **P.G. Wodehouse; a Literary Biography.** New York: Rutledge Press, 1981. 256 p.
PR6045.O53.Z675 1981

This book was written for the centenary of the birth of Wodehouse. It chronicles his ninety plus years as a writer and is as delightful as Wodehouse and his writings.

Donaldson, Frances Lonsdale. **P.G. Wodehouse, a Biography.** New York: Knopf, 1982. 369 p. PR6045.O53.Z63 1982

Lady Donaldson includes the transcripts of the five broadcasts that caused Wodehouse to be interned during World War II. The book is uneven in its amount of coverage of various parts of his life and a bit sentimental in parts.

WOLFE, Thomas (1900-38), American novelist

Thomas Wolfe wrote "the great American novel(s)." He started out as a writer of short plays in North Carolina, in which genre he continued while pursuing a master's degree in English at Harvard. He taught intermittently at New York University while he began his autobiographical **Look Homeward, Angel** (1929). Overwhelmed by trying to write a series of novels based on the American experience, Wolfe turned to Maxwell Perkins, an editor at Scribner's, who assisted him in finding a novel, **Of Time and the River** (1935), within this mass of material. This action on the part of Wolfe gave him the reputation of needing an editor to write. Wolfe died suddenly, leaving many fragmented works. An editor from Harper & Brothers pulled together his other well-known autobiographical novel, **You Can't Go Home Again.**

Donald, David Herbert. **Look Homeward: A Life of Thomas Wolfe.** Boston: Little, Brown, 1987. 579 p. PS3545.O337.Z674 1987

This is a very full biography written after most anyone the biographer could offend was dead. The issue: Was Wolfe the product of good editors? Draw your own conclusions from the material in this book.

Nowell, Elizabeth. **Thomas Wolfe: A Biography.** Garden City, N. Y.: Doubleday, 1960. 456 p. PS3545.O337.Z82

Elizabeth Nowell was Wolfe's literary agent. It is a sympathetic, balanced life.

Turnbull, Andrew. **Thomas Wolfe.** New York: Scribner, 1968, c1967. 374 p. PS3545.O337.Z865

Turnbull, who has written other biographies, focuses on Maxwell Perkins as the key to the literary life of Thomas Wolfe.

WOOLF, Virginia (1882-1941), English novelist

Virginia Woolf grew up in a household headed by her scholarly father, Sir Leslie Stephen. It was frequented by writers of the day. She began contributing to the **Times Literary Supplement** in her early twenties. Of a delicate constitution she was subject to "nervous breakdowns" and eventually committed suicide. After her father's death she moved with her sister and brother into the Bloomsbury Group. She married another member of that Group, Leonard Woolf, with whom she founded the Hogarth Press, which printed some of the works of T. S. Eliot and Katherine Mansfield. She used the "stream of consciousness" technique and the interior monologue in her famous **To the Lighthouse** (1927) and is considered one of the most distinguished novelists and literary critics of the first half of the twentieth century.

Bell, Quentin. **Virginia Woolf: A Biography.** New York: Harcourt Brace Jovanovich, 1972. 314 p.
PR6045.O72.Z545 1972

This biography by Virginia Woolfe's nephew was authorized and assisted by her husband. Despite his closeness to his subject, Bell presents a carefully written, if a bit informal, study of her life in pleasant prose.

Gordon, Lyndall. **Virginia Woolf, a Writer's Life.** New York: Norton, 1985, c1984. 341 p.
PR6045.O72.Z653 1985

This is not the first book to read about Virginia Woolf. It is written with insight and is readable but does not reach beyond the documentation at hand. The emphasis is on the writer but not without noting her painful personal life.

Rose, Phyllis. **Woman of Letters: A Life of Virginia Woolf.** New York: Oxford University Press, 1978. 298 p.
PR6045.O72.Z867

Phyllis Rose's approach is to look at Woolf not only from her continuing mental health problems but from the more positive feminist voice that she also exhibited in her writing.

WORDSWORTH, William (1770-1850), English poet

William Wordsworth is the giant of English literature who established the major movement, romanticism, of the nineteenth century with the publication of his Lyric Ballads in 1798. He spent most of his life in the Lake District of England. After some traveling around until his early twenties he settled with his sister Dorothy. He best poetry was during the "great decade" of 1797-1807 during which he wrote "Ode," "Intimations of Immortality from Recollections of Early Childhood" and the "Lucy" poems. More contemporary emphasis has been on the dark side of his life and his personal tragedies. His poetry remains among the most influential in all of English literature.

Harper, George McLean. **William Wordsworth: His Life, Works, and Influence.** 3d ed. New York: Scribner, 1929. 621 p.
PR5881.H29w 1929

This is one of the standard biographies of Wordsworth which makes use of the writings of his sister, Dorothy. There may be in this book an overemphasis on his political activities.

Moorman, Mary Trevelyan. **William Wordsworth: a Biography.** 2 vols. Oxford: Clarendon Press, 1957-1966.
PR5881.M6

Mary Moorman used similar but more up-to-date material than in the Harper book. This is also considered a standard biography of a man about whom a massive amount has been written.

Gill, Stephen Charles. **William Wordsworth: A Life.** New York: Oxford University Press, 1989. 525 p.
PR5881.G55 1989

The other two books are considered reputable. This is the definitive biography; it uses the research gathered since the writing of the earlier two works. Although it is acknowledged that Wordsworth had a creative decade early in his life, Gill finds significance in the output of his later years. As a person Wordsworth is brought into a sharper focus.

WRIGHT, Richard (1908-60), African-American novelist; prose writer

Richard Wright is considered to be one of the foremost African-American writers. He portrayed his fellow African-Americans as they struggle to survive in a white culture. His **Native Son** (1940) is considered his best novel and is also as a form of social protest. During the Depression the Federal Writers' Project gave him the chance to write. He joined the Communist Party to alleviate his people's plight, which put him in great disfavor with the government. He broke from the Party and moved to Paris in self-imposed exile, writing several novels and other works. He died suddenly of an apparent heart attack.

Fabre, Michel. **The Unfinished Quest of Richard Wright.**
Translated by Isabel Barzun. New York: Morrow, 1973. 652 p.
PS3545.R815.Z6513

This is a detailed life, showing the clear relationship
between Wright's life and writings. Fabre speculates that
Wright's sudden death was from "pressure engendered by racism."
He proposes Wright as a twentieth century Emerson.

Gayle, Addison. **Richard Wright: Ordeal of a Native Son.**
Garden City, N. Y.: Anchor Press/Doubleday, 1980. 342 p.
PS3545.R815.Z664

This is an absorbing work which looks at the controversy
surrounding Wright's involvement in the Communist Party and his
sudden death. This book raises unanswered questions and is a
tribute to the imperfect but extraordinary life of Richard
Wright.

YEATS, William Butler (1865-1939), Irish poet; playwright

William Butler Yeats had a varied existence. He began to
follow the career path of his father as a painter and lived in
London. He returned to County Sligo, where he became caught up in
the Irish legend and became a leader of the Irish Literary
Renaissance. His poetry and drama of his earlier period focus on
the Irish tradition. His later works are more contemporary in
their themes. He helped found the Irish Literary Theatre where
some of his plays were performed. **The Hour Glass** (1904) and
Deidre (1907) appeared on the Abbey Theatre stage. Despite his
infirmities some of his best poetry was written toward the end of
his life in **The Tower** (1928), and **Last Poems** published
posthumously. He received the Nobel Prize for Literature in
1923.

Ellmann, Richard. **Yeats: The Man and the Masks.** New York:
Macmillan, 1948. 331 p.
PR5906.E4 1949

This book looks at the influence of outside and inner forces
upon the creative acts of the poetry and plays of Yeats.

Jeffares, A. Norman. **W.B. Yeats; a New Biography.** New York:
Farrar, Straus & Giroux, 1989, c1988. 374 p.
PR5906.J43 1989

Yeats encouraged biographical study as he kept copious
notes. He lived a multi-faceted life as a nationalist, admirer of
the occult, manager of the Abbey Theatre and, most significantly,
man of letters. This is a sparse edition of this full life from

which the real Yeats never emerges. It is useful in its
integration of his life and his writings.

ZOLA, Emile (1840-1902), French novelist

Zola's novels are the stage for his naturalism. These works,
dealing with the working class, are lurid but real. His powerful
Thérèse Raquin (1867) is a study of passion, murder, guilt. The
twenty-novel cycle **Les Rougon-Macquart** (1871-93) contains some
very fine parts such as **The Dram-Shop, Nana** and possibly the
best, **Germinal**. He was involved in the Dreyfus Affair. He was
advised to take refuge and did so in England, where he wrote some
art criticism as a result of a friendship with Cézanne.

Walker, Philip D. **Zola**. Boston: Routledge & Kegan Paul,
1985. 257 p.
PQ2528.W33 1985

Walker has written extensively on Zola. This is not an
exhaustive biography but a reasonable, animated introduction to a
serious thinker and prolific author.

Schom, Alan. **Emile Zola: A Biography**. New York: Holt, 1988,
c1987. 303 p.
PQ2528.S36 1988

This in-depth study of Zola is best on his early years. It
also looks at his failed attempt as a dramatist and the issue of
his involvement in the Dreyfus Affair and his unsettling death.

Hemmings, F.W.J. (Frederick William John). **The Life and
Times of Emile Zola**. New York: Scribner, 1977. 192 p.
PQ2528.H44 1977b

The more recent books noted supersede some of the
information in this biography. It is a brief introduction
containing illustrations and photographs that enhance the
succinct narrative.

Art Form Index

LITERARY ARTISTS

POETS

American

AIKEN, Conrad (1889-1973), American poet
AUDEN, W.H. (Wystan Hugh) (1907-73), Anglo-American poet
BENET, Stephen Vincent (1898-1943), American poet; short story writer
BOGAN, Louise (1897-1970), American poet
BRADSTREET, Anne (1612?-72), American poet
BROOKS, Gwendolyn (1917-   ), African-American poet
BRYANT, William Cullen (1794-1878), American poet
CRANE, Hart (1899-1932), American poet
CUMMINGS, E.E. (Edward Estlin) (1894-1962), American poet
DICKINSON, Emily (1830-86), American poet
FROST, Robert (1874-1963), American poet
H.D. (Hilda Doolittle) (1886-1961), American poet
HARTE, Bret (1836-1902), American short story writer; poet
HUGHES, Langston (1902-67), African-American poet
JEFFERS, Robinson (1887-1962), American poet
LONGFELLOW, Henry Wadsworth (1807-82), American poet
LOWELL, Amy (1874-1925), American poet
MILLAY, Edna St. Vincent (1892-1950), American poet
PLATH, Sylvia (1932-63), American poet
POUND, Ezra (1885-1972), American poet
RANSOM, John Crowe (1888-1974), American poet
SANDBURG, Carl (1878-1967), American poet
SCHWARTZ, Delmore (1913-66), American poet
TATE, Allen (1899-1979), American poet
TEASDALE, Sara (1884-1933), American poet
WHITMAN, Walt (1819-92), American poet
WILLIAMS, William Carlos (1883-1963), American poet

POETS

English

ARNOLD, Matthew (1822-88), English poet
BELLOC, Hilaire (1870-1953), English poet; writer
BLAKE, William (1757-1827), English poet; artist
BRONTE, Charlotte (1816-55), English novelist; poet
BRONTE, Emily (1818-48), English novelist; poet
BROOKE, Rupert (1887-1915), English poet
BROWNING, Elizabeth Barrett (1806-61), English poet
BROWNING, Robert (1812-89), English poet
BURNS, Robert (1759-96), Scottish poet
BYRON, George Gordon Byron (1788-1824), English poet
CLARE, John (1763-1864), English poet
CLOUGH, Arthur Hugh (1819-61), English poet
COLERIDGE, Samuel (1772-1834), English poet
COWPER, William (1731-1800), English poet
DEFOE, Daniel (1661-1731), English novelist; poet
DONNE, John (1572-1631), English poet
DRYDEN, John (1631-1700), English poet
ELIOT, T.S. (Thomas Sterns) (1888-1965), English poet
GILBERT, W.S. (William Schwenck) (1836-1911), English
    playwright; poet
GRAVES, Robert (1895-1985), English poet
GRAY, Thomas (1716-71), English poet
HARDY, Thomas (1840-1928), English novelist; poet
HOUSMAN, A.E. (Alfred Edward) (1859-1936), English poet
JONSON, Ben (1573?-1637), English playwright; poet
KEATS, John (1795-1821), English poet
KIPLING, Rudyard (1865-1936), English poet; fiction writer
MEREDITH, George (1828-1909), English novelist; poet
MILTON, John (1608-74), English poet
MORRIS, William (1834-96), English poet; artist
OWEN, Wilfred (1893-1918), English poet
POPE, Alexander (1688-1744), English poet
ROSSETTI, Christine Georgina (1830-94), English poet
SACKVILLE-WEST, V. (Victoria) (1892-1962), English novelist; poet
SCOTT, Walter (1771-1832), Scottish novelist; poet
SHELLEY, Percy Bysshe (1792-1822), English poet
SITWELL, Edith (1887-1964), English poet
STEVENSON, Robert Louis (1850-94), Scottish novelist; poet
SWINBURNE, Algernon Charles (1837-1909), English poet
TENNYSON, Alfred (1809-92), English poet
THOMAS, Dylan (1914-53), Welsh poet
THOMPSON, Francis (1859-1907), English poet
WORDSWORTH, William (1770-1850), English poet

POETS

Other than American or English

APOLLINAIRE, Guillaume (1880-1918), French poet
BAUDELAIRE, Charles (1821-67), French poet
BLOK, Aleksandr Aleksandrovich (1880-1921), Russian poet
BRECHT, Bertolt (1898-1956), German playwright; poet
CLAUDEL, Paul (1868-1955), French playwright; poet
COCTEAU, Jean (1889-1963), French poet; fiction writer
D'ANNUNZIO, Gabriele (1863-1938), Italian poet; novelist; playwright
ESENIN, Sergei Aleksandrovich (1895-1925), Russian poet
GARCIA LORCA, Federico (1898-1936), Spanish poet; playwright
GOETHE, Johann Wolfgang von (1749-1832), German poet; playwright; novelist
HEINE, Heinrich (1797-1856), German poet
HUGO, Victor Marie (1802-85), French poet; novelist; playwright
PASTERNAK, Boris Leonidovich (1890-1960), Russian poet; novelist
PUSHKIN, Aleksandr Sergeevich (1799-1837), Russian poet; prose writer
RILKE, Rainer Maria (1875-1926), German poet
RIMBAUD, Arthur (1854-91), French poet
STRINDBERG, August (1849-1912), Swedish novelist; playwright; poet
SYNGE, J.M. (John Millington) (1871-1909), Irish poet; playwright
TAGORE, Rabindranath (1861-1941), Indian poet; novelist; playwright
TIECK, Ludwig (1773-1853), German prose writer; poet
VERLAINE, Paul Marie (1844-96), French poet
YEATS, William Butler (1865-1939), Irish poet; playwright

PLAYWRIGHTS

English language

ANDERSON, Maxwell (1888-1959), American playwright
BARRIE, J.M. (James Matthew) (1860-1937), Scottish playwright;
    novelist
BEHN, Aphra Amis (1640-89), English playwright; novelist
BENNETT, Arnold (1867-1931), English novelist; playwright
DRYDEN, John (1631-1700), English poet; playwright
FIELDING, Henry (1707-54), English novelist; playwright
GILBERT, W.S. (William Schwenck) (1836-1911), English playwright; poet
GOLDSMITH, Oliver (1728-74), Anglo-Irish novelist; playwright
HELLMAN, Lillian (1906-84), American playwright
JONSON, Ben (1573?-1637), English playwright; poet
MAUGHAM, William Somerset (1874-1965), English novelist; playwright; short
    story writer
O'CASEY, Sean (1884-1964), Irish playwright
ODETS, Clifford (1906-63), American playwright
O'NEILL, Eugene Gladstone (1888-1953), American playwright
SHAW, George Bernard (1856-1950), Irish playwright
SYNGE, J.M. (John Millington) (1871-1909), Irish poet; playwright
WILDER, Thornton (1897-1975), American playwright; novelist

182

WILLIAMS, Tennessee (1911-1983), American playwright
YEATS, William Butler (1865-1939), Irish poet; playwright

PLAYWRIGHTS

Non-English Language

BEAUMARCHAIS, Pierre Augustin Caron de (1732-99), French playwright
BECKETT, Samuel (1906-89), Irish-French novelist; playwright
BRECHT, Bertolt (1898-1956), German playwright; poet
BULGAKOV, Mikhail Afanasevich (1891-1940), Russian novelist; playwright
CAMUS, Albert (1913-60), French novelist; playwright
CHEKHOV, Anton Pavlovich (1860-1904), Russian playwright; short story writer
CLAUDEL, Paul (1868-1955), French playwright; poet
D'ANNUNZIO, Gabriele (1863-1938), Italian poet; novelist; playwright
DUMAS, Alexandre (1802-70), French playwright; novelist
GARCIA LORCA, Federico (1898-1936), Spanish poet; playwright
GIRAUDOUX, Jean (1882-1944), French playwright; novelist
GOETHE, Johann Wolfgang von (1749-1832), German poet; playwright; novelist
GORKY, Maksim (1868-1936), Russian novelist; short story writer; playwright
HEBBEL, Friedrich (1813-63), German playwright
IBSEN, Henrik (1828-1906), Norwegian playwright
KLEIST, Heinrich von (1777-1811), German poet; playwright
MAUPASSANT, Guy de (1850-93), French fiction writer; playwright
MOLIERE, Jean Baptiste Poquelin (1622-73), French playwright
SCHILLER, Friedrich (1759-1805), German playwright; poet
STRINDBERG, August (1849-1912), Swedish novelist; playwright; poet
TAGORE, Rabindranath (1861-1941), Indian poet; novelist; playwright

NOVELISTS

American

ALCOTT, Louisa May (1832-88), American novelist
ANDERSON, Sherwood (1876-1941), American novelist
BUCK, Pearl S. (1892-1973), American novelist
CAIN, James M. (James Mallahan) (1892-1977), American novelist
CATHER, Willa (1873-1947), American novelist
CHESTNUTT, Charles Waddell (1858-1932), African-American novelist
CHOPIN, Kate (1851-1904), American novelist
COZZENS, John Gould (1903-78), American novelist
CRANE, Stephen (1871-1900), American novelist
DOS PASSOS, John (1896-1970), American novelist
DREISER, Theodore (1871-1945), American novelist
FAULKNER, William (1897-1962), American novelist
FISHER, Dorothy Canfield (1879-1958), American novelist
FITZGERALD, Francis Scott Key (1896-1940), American novelist; short story
    writer
GLASGOW, Ellen Anderson Gholson (1873-1945), American novelist

HEMINGWAY, Ernest (1889-1961), American novelist; short story
    writer
HOWELLS, William Dean (1837-1920), American novelist
JAMES, Henry (1843-1916), American novelist
LEWIS, Sinclair (1885-1951), American novelist
McCULLERS, Carson (1917-67), American novelist; short story writer
MARQUAND, John P. (Phillips) (1893-1960), American novelist
MELVILLE, Herman (1819-91), American novelist
NORRIS, Frank (1870-1902), American novelist
O'HARA, John (1905-70), American novelist; short story writer
PORTER, Katherine Anne (1890-1980), American short story writer; novelist
TARKINGTON, Booth (1869-1946), American novelist
TWAIN, Mark (1835-1910), American novelist
WEST, Nathanael (1903-40), American novelist
WHARTON, Edith (1862-1937), American novelist
WILDER, Thornton (1897-1975), American playwright; novelist
WISTER, Owen (1860-1938), American novelist
WOLFE, Thomas (1900-38), American novelist
WRIGHT, Richard (1908-60), African-American novelist; prose writer

NOVELISTS

English

ASHTON-WARNER, Sylvia (1908-84), New Zealand novelist
AUSTEN, Jane (1775-1817), English novelist
BARRIE, J.M. (James Matthew) (1860-1937), Scottish playwright;
    novelist
BEHN, Aphra Amis (1640-89), English playwright; novelist
BENNETT, Arnold (1867-1931), English novelist; playwright
BRONTE, Charlotte (1816-55), English novelist; poet
BRONTE, Emily (1818-48), English novelist; poet
BURNEY, Fanny (1752-1840), English novelist
BUTLER, Samuel (1835-1902), English novelist
CARY, Joyce (1888-1957), Anglo-Irish fiction writer
CHESTERTON, G.K. (Gilbert Keith) (1874-1936), English novelist
CHRISTIE, Agatha (1891-1976), English novelist
COMPTON-BURNETT, I. (Ivy) (1884-1969), English novelist
CONRAD, Joseph (1857-1924), English novelist
DEFOE, Daniel (1661-1731), English novelist; poet
DICKENS, Charles (1812-70), English novelist
DOYLE, Arthur Conan, Sir (1859-1930), English novelist
ELIOT, George (1819-80), English novelist
FIELDING, Henry (1707-54), English novelist; playwright
FORSTER, E.M. (Edward Morgan) (1879-1970), English novelist
GASKELL, Elizabeth Gleghorn (1810-65), English novelist
GOLDSMITH, Oliver (1728-74), Anglo-Irish novelist; playwright
GREENE, Graham (1904-   ), English novelist
HARDY, Thomas (1840-1928), English novelist; poet
ISHERWOOD, Christopher (1904-84), English novelist

JOYCE, James (1882-1941), Irish novelist
LAWRENCE, D.H. (David Herbert) (1885-1930), English novelist
LEWIS, Wyndham (1886-1957), English painter; novelist
MAUGHAM, William Somerset (1874-1965), English novelist; playwright; short
    story writer
MEREDITH, George (1828-1909), English novelist; poet
O'CONNOR, Frank (1903-66), Irish short-story writer
RICHARDSON, Samuel (1689-1761), English novelist
SACKVILLE-WEST, V. (Victoria) (1892-1962), English novelist; poet
SCOTT, Walter (1771-1832), Scottish novelist; poet
SHELLEY, Mary Wollstonecraft (1797-1851), English novelist
STEVENSON, Robert Louis (1850-94), Scottish novelist; poet
THACKERAY, William Makepeace (1811-63), English novelist
TROLLOPE, Anthony (1815-82), English novelist
WAUGH, Evelyn (1903-66), English novelist
WELLS, H.G. (Herbert George) (1866-1946), English novelist
WEST, Rebecca (1892-1983), English novelist
WODEHOUSE, P.G. (Pelham Grenville) (1881-1975), English novelist
WOOLF, Virginia (1882-1941), English novelist

NOVELISTS

Other than American or English

ALAIN-FOURNIER (1886-1914), French novelist
BALZAC, Honoré de (1799-1850), French novelist
BERNANOS, Georges (1888-1948), French novelist
BULGAKOV, Mikhail Afanasevich (1891-1940), Russian novelist; playwright
CAMUS, Albert (1913-60), French novelist; playwright
CERVANTES SAAVEDRA, Miguel de (1547-1616), Spanish novelist
COLETTE (1873-1954), French novelist
D'ANNUNZIO, Gabriele (1863-1938), Italian poet; novelist; playwright
DOSTOYEVSKY, Fyodor (1821-81), Russian novelist
DUMAS, Alexandre (1802-70), French playwright; novelist
FLAUBERT, Gustave (1821-80), French novelist
FRANCE, Anatole (1844-1924), French novelist
GIDE, André (1869-1951), French novelist
GIRAUDOUX, Jean (1882-1944), French playwright; novelist
GOETHE, Johann Wolfgang von (1749-1832), German poet; playwright; novelist
GORKY, Maksim (1868-1936), Russian novelist; short story writer; playwright
HESSE, Hermann (1877-1962), German novelist
HUGO, Victor Marie (1802-85), French poet; novelist; playwright
KAFKA, Franz (1883-1924), German novelist; short story writer
MALRAUX, André (1901-76), French novelist; writer
MANN, Heinrich (1871-1950), German novelist
MANN, Thomas (1875-1955), German novelist
PASTERNAK, Boris Leonidovich (1890-1960), Russian poet; novelist
PROUST, Marcel (1871-1922), French novelist
SAND, George (1804-76), French novelist
SOLZHENITSYN, Aleksandr Isaevich (1918-   ), Russian novelist

STRINDBERG, August (1849-1912), Swedish novelist; playwright; poet
TAGORE, Rabindranath (1861-1941), Indian poet; novelist; playwright
TOLSTOY, Leo (1828-1910), Russian novelist
TURGENEV, Ivan Sergeevich (1818-83), Russian novelist
VERNE, Jules (1828-1905), French novelist
ZOLA, Emile (1840-1902), French novelist

OTHER LITERARY GENRES

American

AGEE, James (1909-55), American writer
ANDERSON, Sherwood (1876-1941), American writer
BENET, Stephen Vincent (1898-1934), American poet; short story writer
BIERCE, Ambrose (1842-1914?), American short story writer
CABLE, George Washington (1844-1925), American fiction writer
CHEEVER, John (1912-82), American fiction writer
FITZGERALD, Francis Scott Key (1896-1940), American novelist; short story
    writer
FREEMAN, Mary Eleanor Wilkins (1852-1930), American fiction writer
HARRIS, Joel Chandler (1848-1908), American fiction writer
HARTE, Bret (1836-1902), American short story writer; poet
HAWTHORNE, Nathaniel (1804-64), American fiction writer
HEMINGWAY, Ernest (1889-1961), American novelist; short story writer
HENRY, O. (1862-1910), American short story writer
HURSTON, Zora Neale (1901-60), African-American writer
IRVING, Washington (1783-1859), American fiction writer
McCULLERS, Carson (1917-67), American novelist; short story writer
O'HARA, John (1905-70), American novelist; short story writer
POE, Edgar Allan (1909-49), American short story writer
PORTER, Katherine Anne (1890-1980), American short story writer; novelist
STEIN, Gertrude (1874-1946), American fiction writer
STEINBECK, John (1902-68), American fiction writer
TOOMER, Jean (1894-1967), African-American writer
WHITE, E.B. (Elwyn Brooks) (1899-1985), American prose writer
WRIGHT, Richard (1908-60), African-American novelist; prose writer

OTHER LITERARY GENRES

English

BELLOC, Hilaire (1870-1953), English poet; writer
CARY, Joyce (1888-1957), Anglo-Irish fiction writer
KIPLING, Rudyard (1865-1936), English poet; fiction writer
MANSFIELD, Katherine (1888-1923), English short story writer
MAUGHAM, William Somerset (1874-1965), English novelist; playwright; short
    story writer
O'CONNOR, Frank (1903-66), Irish short story writer
OLIPHANT, Margaret (1828-97), English fiction writer

ORWELL, George (1903-50), English fiction writer
POTTER, Beatrix (1866-1943), English children's author
SAYERS, Dorothy L. (Dorothy Leigh) (1893-1957), English story writer
SWIFT, Jonathon (1667-1745), Anglo-Irish satirist
WILDE, Oscar (1854-1900), Irish writer

OTHER LITERARY GENRES

Other than American or English

BRETON, André (1896-1966), French writer
CHEKHOV, Anton Pavlovich (1860-1904), Russian playwright; short story writer
COCTEAU, Jean (1889-1963), French poet; fiction writer
DINESEN, Isak (1885-1962), Danish fiction writer
GOGOL, Nickolai Vasilevich (1809-52), Russian fiction writer
KAFKA, Franz (1883-1924), German novelist; short story writer
KOKOSCHKA, Oskar (1886-1980), Austrian painter; author
MALRAUX, André (1901-76), French novelist; writer
MAUPASSANT, Guy de (1850-93), French fiction writer; playwright
PUSHKIN, Aleksandr Sergeevich (1799-1837), Russian poet; prose writer
SAINT-EXUPERY, Antoine de (1900-44), French prose writer
TIECK, Ludwig (1773-1853), German prose writer; poet

VISUAL ARTISTS

ADAMS, Ansel (1902-84), American photographer
AVERY, Milton (1885-1965), American painter
BELL, Vanessa (1879-1961), English painter
BELLOWS, George (1882-1925), American painter
BENTON, Thomas Hart (1889-1975), American painter
BINGHAM, George Caleb (1811-79), American painter
BLAKE, William (1757-1827), English poet; artist
BONINGTON, Richard Parkes (1801-28), English painter
BURCHFIELD, Charles Ephraim (1893-1967), American painter
BURNE-JONES, Edward Coley (1833-98), English painter
CARPEAUX, Jean-Baptiste (1827-75), French sculptor; painter
CASSATT, Mary (1844-1926), American painter
CELLINI, Benvenuto (1500-71), Italian sculptor
CEZANNE, Paul (1839-1906), French painter
CHAGALL, Marc (1889-1985), Russian painter
CONNELL, Clyde (1901-   ), American sculptor
COURBET, Gustave (1819-77), French painter
DALI, Salvador (1904-89), Spanish painter
DAUMIER, Honoré (1808-79), French painter; sculptor; caricaturist
DEGAS, Edgar (1834-1917), French painter
DELACROIX, Eugène (1798-1863), French painter
DEMUTH, Charles (1883-1935), American painter
DUCHAMP, Marcel (1887-1968), French painter
ERNST, Max (1891-1976), German painter

187

FEININGER, Lyonel (1871-1956), American painter
FRENCH, Daniel Chester (1850-1931), American sculptor
GAINSBOROUGH, Thomas (1727-88), English painter
GAUGUIN, Paul (1848-1903), French painter; woodcut artist
GIACOMETTI, Alberto (1901-66), Swiss sculptor; painter
GOGH, Vincent van (1853-90), Dutch painter
GRECO (1541?-1614), Greek-Spanish painter
GREENAWAY, Kate (1846-1901), English illustrator
HICKS, Edward (1780-1849), American painter
HOGARTH, William (1697-1764), English painter
KAHLO, Frida (1907-54), Mexican painter
KLEE, Paul (1879-1940), Swiss painter; graphic artist
KOKOSCHKA, Oskar (1886-1980), Austrian painter; author
KOLLWITZ, Käthe (1867-1945), German graphic artist; sculptor
LEWIS, Wyndham (1886-1957), English painter; novelist
MATISSE, Henri (1869-1954), French painter; sculptor
MODIGLIANI, Amedeo (1884-1920), Italian painter
MORRIS, William (1834-96), English poet; artist
O'KEEFFE, Georgia (1887-1986), American painter
ORPEN, William (1878-1931), English painter
PICASSO, Pablo (1881-1973), Spanish sculptor; painter; graphic artist
POLLOCK, Jackson (1912-56), American painter
RAY, Man (1890-1976), American painter; photographer
REMBRANDT HARMENSZOON van RIJN (1606-69), Dutch painter
REYNOLDS, Joshua (1723-92), English painter
RODIN, Auguste (1840-1917), French sculptor
RUBENS, Peter Paul (1577-1640), Flemish painter
SAINT GAUDENS, Augustus (1848-1907), American sculptor
SARGENT, John Singer (1856-1925), American painter
SLOAN, John (1871-1951), American painter
STUART, Gilbert (1755-1828), American painter
SUTHERLAND, Graham Vivian (1903-80), English painter
TURNER, J.M.W. (Joseph Mallord William) (1775-1851), English
     painter
WHISTLER, James McNeill (1834-1903), American painter

COMPOSERS AND MUSICIANS

ANTHEIL, George (1900-59), American composer
BACH, Johann Christian (1735-82), German composer
BARTOK, Béla (1881-1945), Hungarian composer
BEETHOVEN, Ludwig van (1770-1827), German composer
BERNSTEIN, Leonard (1918-90), American composer; musician
BRAHMS, Johannes (1833-97), German composer
BRITTEN, Benjamin (1913-76), English composer
BRUCKNER, Anton (1824-96), Austrian composer
CHOPIN, Frédéric (1810-49), Polish-French composer
DEBUSSY, Claude (1862-1918), French composer
ELGAR, Edward (1857-1934), English composer
FRANCK, César (1822-90), Belgian-French composer

GERSHWIN, George (1898-1937), American composer
GRIFFES, Charles Tomlinson (1884-1920), American composer
HANDEL, George Friederich (1685-1759), English composer
HAYDN, Joseph (1732-1809), Austrian composer
HINDEMITH, Paul (1895-1963), German-American composer
IVES, Charles (1874-1954), American composer
JANACEK, Leos (1854-1928), Czech composer
KLEMPERER, Otto (1885-1973), German musician
KODALY, Zoltán (1882-1967), Hungarian composer
LISZT, Franz (1811-86), Hungarian composer
MAHLER, Gustave (1860-1911), Austrian composer
MENDELSSOHN-BARTHOLDY, Felix (1809-47), German composer
MOZART, Wolfgang Amadeus (1756-91), Austrian composer
PROKOFIEV, Sergey (1891-1953), Russian composer
RAVEL, Maurice (1875-1937), French composer
ROSSINI, Gioacchino (1792-1868), Italian composer
SATIE, Erik (1866-1925), French composer
SCHOENBERG, Arnold (1874-1951), Austrian composer
SCHUBERT, Franz (1797-1828), German composer
SCHUMANN, Robert (1810-56), German composer
SMETANA, Bedrich (1824-84), Czech composer
STRAUSS, Richard (1864-1949), German composer
SULLIVAN, Arthur (1842-1900), English composer
TCHAIKOVSKY, Peter Ilich (1840-93), Russian composer
VARESE, Edgard (1885-1965), French-American composer
VERDI, Giuseppe (1813-1901), Italian composer
WAGNER, Richard (1813-83), German composer

THEATER, DANCE, NOT PLAYWRIGHTS

BALANCHINE, George (1904-83), Russian-American choreographer
CRANKO, John (1927-73), English choreographer
GRAHAM, Martha (1894-   ), American choreographer
LUNT, Alfred (1892-1977), American actor
(LUNT) FONTANNE Lynn (1887-1983), American actress
PAVLOVA, Anna (1881-1931), Russian dancer
PERROT, Jules (1810-92), French choreographer
RICHARDSON, Ralph, Sir (1902-83), English actor

Country of Origin Index
arranged chronologically

AMERICAN

BRADSTREET, Anne (1612?-72), American poet
STUART, Gilbert (1755-1828), American painter
HICKS, Edward (1780-1849), American painter
IRVING, Washington (1783-1859), American fiction writer
BRYANT, William Cullen (1794-1878), American poet
HAWTHORNE, Nathaniel (1804-64), American fiction writer
LONGFELLOW, Henry Wadsworth (1807-82), American poet
POE, Edgar Allan (1809-49), American short story writer
BINGHAM, George Caleb (1811-79), American painter
MELVILLE, Herman (1819-91), American novelist
WHITMAN, Walt (1819-92), American poet
DICKINSON, Emily (1830-86), American poet
ALCOTT, Louisa May (1832-88), American novelist
WHISTLER, James McNeill (1834-1903), American painter
TWAIN, Mark (1835-1910), American novelist
HARTE, Bret (1836-1902), American short story writer; poet
HOWELLS, William Dean (1837-1920), American novelist
BIERCE, Ambrose (1842-1914?), American short story writer
JAMES, Henry (1843-1916), American novelist
CABLE, George Washington (1844-1925), American fiction writer
CASSATT, Mary (1844-1926), American painter
HARRIS, Joel Chandler (1848-1908), American fiction writer
SAINT GAUDENS, Augustus (1848-1907), American sculptor
FRENCH, Daniel Chester (1850-1931), American sculptor
CHOPIN, Kate (1851-1904), American novelist
FREEMAN, Mary Eleanor Wilkins (1852-1930), American fiction writer
SARGENT, John Singer (1856-1925), American painter
CHESTNUTT, Charles Waddell (1858-1932), African-American novelist
WISTER, Owen (1860-1938), American novelist
HENRY, O. (1862-1910), American short story writer
WHARTON, Edith (1862-1937), American novelist
TARKINGTON, Booth (1869-1946), American novelist
NORRIS, Frank (1870-1902), American novelist
CRANE, Stephen (1871-1900), American novelist
DREISER, Theodore (1871-1945), American novelist
FEININGER, Lyonel (1871-1956), American painter
SLOAN, John (1871-1951), American painter

CATHER, Willa (1873-1947), American novelist
GLASGOW, Ellen Anderson Gholson (1873-1945), American novelist
FROST, Robert (1874-1963), American poet
IVES, Charles (1874-1954), American composer
LOWELL, Amy (1874-1925), American poet
STEIN, Gertrude (1874-1946), American fiction writer
ANDERSON, Sherwood (1876-1941), American writer
SANDBURG, Carl (1878-1967), American poet
FISHER, Dorothy Canfield (1879-1958), American novelist
BELLOWS, George (1882-1925), American painter
DEMUTH, Charles (1883-1935), American painter
WILLIAMS, William Carlos (1883-1963), American poet
GRIFFES, Charles Tomlinson (1884-1920), American composer
TEASDALE, Sara (1884-1933), American poet
AVERY, Milton (1885-1965), American painter
LEWIS, Sinclair (1885-1951), American novelist
POUND, Ezra (1885-1972), American poet
VARESE, Edgard (1885-1965), French-American composer
H.D. (Hilda Doolittle) (1886-1961), American poet
JEFFERS, Robinson (1887-1962), American poet
(LUNT) FONTANNE, Lynn (1887-1983), American actress
O'KEEFFE, Georgia (1887-1986), American painter
ANDERSON, Maxwell (1888-1959), American playwright
O'NEILL, Eugene Gladstone (1888-1953), American playwright
RANSOM, John Crowe (1888-1974), American poet
AIKEN, Conrad (1889-1973), American poet
BENTON, Thomas Hart (1889-1975), American painter
HEMINGWAY, Ernest (1889-1961), American novelist; short story writer
PORTER, Katherine Anne (1890-1980), American short story writer; novelist
RAY, Man (1890-1976), American painter; photographer
BUCK, Pearl S. (1892-1973), American novelist
CAIN, James M. (James Mallahan) (1892-1977), American novelist
LUNT, Alfred (1892-1977), American actor
MILLAY, Edna St. Vincent (1892-1950), American poet
BURCHFIELD, Charles Ephraim (1893-1967), American painter
MARQUAND, John P. (Phillips) (1893-1960), American novelist
CUMMINGS, E.E. (Edward Estlin) (1894-1962), American poet
GRAHAM, Martha (1894-   ), American choreographer
TOOMER, Jean (1894-1967), Afro-American writer
HINDEMITH, Paul (1895-1963), German-American composer
DOS PASSOS, John (1896-1970), American novelist
FITZGERALD, Francis Scott Key (1896-1940), American novelist; short story
     writer
BOGAN, Louise (1897-1970), American poet
FAULKNER, William (1897-1962), American novelist
WILDER, Thornton (1897-1975), American playwright; novelist
BENET, Stephen Vincent (1898-1943), American poet; short story writer
GERSHWIN, George (1898-1937), American composer
CRANE, Hart (1899-1932), American poet
NABOKOV, Vladimir Vladimirovich (1899-1977), Russian-American novelist
TATE, Allen (1899-1979), American poet

WHITE, E.B. (Elwyn Brooks) (1899-1985), American prose writer
ANTHEIL, George (1900-59), American composer
WOLFE, Thomas (1900-38), American novelist
HURSTON, Zora Neale (1901-60), African-American writer
ADAMS, Ansel (1902-84), American photographer
CONNELL, Clyde (1901-   ), American sculptor
HUGHES, Langston (1902-67), African-American poet
STEINBECK, John (1902-68), American fiction writer
COZZENS, John Gould (1903-78), American novelist
WEST, Nathanael (1903-40), American novelist
BALANCHINE, George (1904-83), Russian-American choreographer
GORKY, Arshile (1904-48), American painter
O'HARA, John (1905-70), American novelist
HELLMAN, Lillian (1906-84), American playwright
ODETS, Clifford (1906-63), American playwright
AUDEN, W.H. (Wystan Hugh) (1907-73), Anglo-American poet
WRIGHT, Richard (1908-60), African-American novelist; prose writer
AGEE, James (1909-55), American writer
WILLIAMS, Tennessee (1911-83), American playwright
CHEEVER, John (1912-82), American fiction writer
POLLOCK, Jackson (1912-56), American painter
SCHWARTZ, Delmore (1913-66), American poet
BROOKS, Gwendolyn (1917-   ), African-American poet
McCULLERS, Carson (1917-67), American novelist; short story writer
BERNSTEIN, Leonard (1918-90), American composer; musician
PLATH, Sylvia (1932-63), American poet

AUSTRIAN

HAYDN, Joseph (1732-1809), Austrian composer
MOZART, Wolfgang Amadeus (1756-91), Austrian composer
BRUCKNER, Anton (1824-96), Austrian composer
MAHLER, Gustave (1860-1911), Austrian composer; conductor
SCHOENBERG, Arnold (1874-1951), Austrian composer
KOKOSCHKA, Oskar (1886-1980), Austrian painter; author

BELGIAN

FRANCK, César (1822-90), Belgian-French composer

CZECH

JANACEK, Leos (1854-1928), Czech composer

192

DUTCH

REMBRANDT HARMENSZOON van RIJN (1606-69), Dutch painter
GOGH, Vincent van (1853-90), Dutch painter

ENGLISH

DONNE, John (1572-1631), English poet
JONSON, Ben (1573?-1637), English playwright; poet
MILTON, John (1608-74), English poet
DRYDEN, John (1631-1700), English poet; playwright
BEHN, Aphra Amis (1640-89), English playwright; novelist
DEFOE, Daniel (1661-1731), English novelist; poet
SWIFT, Jonathan (1667-1745), Anglo-Irish satirist
HANDEL, George Friederich (1685-1759), English composer
POPE, Alexander (1688-1744), English poet
RICHARDSON, Samuel (1689-1761), English novelist
HOGARTH, William (1697-1764), English painter
FIELDING, Henry (1707-54), English novelist; playwright
JOHNSON, Samuel (1709-84), English man of letters
GRAY, Thomas (1716-71), English poet
REYNOLDS, Joshua (1723-92), English painter
GAINSBOROUGH, Thomas (1727-88), English painter
COWPER, William (1731-1800), English poet
BURNEY, Fanny (1752-1840), English novelist
BLAKE, William (1757-1827), English poet; artist
BURNS, Robert (1759-96), Scottish poet
CLARE, John (1763-1864), English poet
WORDSWORTH, William (1770-1850), English poet
SCOTT, Walter (1771-1832), Scottish novelist; poet
COLERIDGE, Samuel (1772-1834), English poet
AUSTEN, Jane (1775-1817), English novelist
TURNER, J.M.W. (Joseph Mallord William) (1775-1851), English painter
BYRON, George Gordon Byron, Baron (1788-1824), English poet
SHELLEY, Percy Bysshe (1792-1822), English poet
KEATS, John (1795-1821), English poet
SHELLEY, Mary Wollstonecraft (1797-1851), English novelist
BONINGTON, Richard Parkes (1801-28), English painter
BROWNING, Elizabeth Barrett (1806-61), English poet
TENNYSON, Alfred Tennyson (1809-92), English poet
GASKELL, Elizabeth Gleghorn (1810-65), English novelist
THACKERAY, William Makepeace (1811-63), English novelist
BROWNING, Robert (1812-89), English poet
DICKENS, Charles (1812-70), English novelist
TROLLOPE, Anthony (1815-82), English novelist
BRONTE, Charlotte (1816-55), English novelist; poet
BRONTE, Emily (1818-48), English novelist; poet
CLOUGH, Arthur Hugh (1819-61), English poet
ELIOT, George (1819-80), English novelist
ARNOLD, Matthew (1822-88), English poet

MEREDITH, George (1828-1909), English novelist; poet
OLIPHANT, Margaret (1828-97), English fiction writer
ROSSETTI, Christina Georgina (1830-94), English poet
BURNE-JONES, Edward Coley (1833-98), English painter
MORRIS, William (1834-96), English poet; artist
BUTLER, Samuel (1835-1902), English novelist
GILBERT, W.S. (William Schwenck) (1836-1911), English playwright; poet
SWINBURNE, Algernon Charles (1837-1909), English poet
HARDY, Thomas (1840-1928), English novelist; poet
SULLIVAN, Arthur (1842-1900), English composer
GREENAWAY, Kate (1846-1901), English illustrator
STEVENSON, Robert Louis (1850-94), Scottish novelist; poet
WILDE, Oscar (1854-1900), Irish writer
SHAW, George Bernard (1856-1950), Irish playwright
CONRAD, Joseph (1857-1924), English novelist
ELGAR, Edward (1857-1934), English composer
DOYLE, Arthur Conan (1859-1930), English novelist
HOUSMAN, A.E. (Alfred Edward) (1859-1936), English poet
THOMPSON, Francis (1859-1907), English poet
BARRIE, J.M. (James Matthew) (1860-1937), Scottish playwright;
    novelist
KIPLING, Rudyard (1865-1936), English poet; fiction writer
YEATS, William Butler (1865-1939), Irish poet; playwright
POTTER, Beatrix (1866-1943), English children's author
WELLS, H.G. (Herbert George) (1866-1946), English novelist
BENNETT, Arnold (1867-1931), English novelist; playwright
BELLOC, Hilaire (1870-1953), English poet; writer
SYNGE, J.M. (John Millington) (1871-1909), Irish poet; playwright
CHESTERTON, G.K. (Gilbert Keith) (1874-1936), English novelist
MAUGHAM, William Somerset (1874-1965), English novelist; playwright; short
    story writer
ORPEN, William (1878-1931), English painter
BELL, Vanessa (1879-1961), English painter
FORSTER, E.M. (Edward Morgan) (1879-1970), English novelist
WODEHOUSE, P.G. (Pelham Grenville) (1881-1975), English novelist
JOYCE, James (1882-1941), Irish novelist
WOOLF, Virginia (1882-1941), English novelist
COMPTON-BURNETT, I. (Ivy) (1884-1969), English novelist
O'CASEY, Sean (1884-1964), Irish playwright
LAWRENCE, D.H. (David Herbert) (1885-1930), English novelist
LEWIS, Wyndham (1886-1957), English painter; novelist
BROOKE, Rupert (1887-1915), English poet
SITWELL, Edith (1887-1964), English poet
ELIOT, T.S. (Thomas Sterns) (1888-1965), English poet
MANSFIELD, Katherine (1888-1923), English short story writer
CHRISTIE, Agatha (1891-1976), English novelist
SACKVILLE-WEST, V. (Victoria) (1892-1962), English novelist; poet
WEST, Rebecca (1892-1983), English novelist
OWEN, Wilfred (1893-1918), English poet
SAYERS, Dorothy L. (Dorothy Leigh) (1893-1957), English story writer
GRAVES, Robert (1895-1985), English poet

RICHARDSON, Ralph, Sir (1902-83), English actor
O'CONNOR, Frank (1903-66), Irish short story writer
ORWELL, George (1903-50), English fiction writer
SUTHERLAND, Graham Vivian (1903-80), English painter
WAUGH, Evelyn (1903-66), English novelist
GREENE, Graham (1904-   ), English novelist
ISHERWOOD, Christopher (1904-84), English novelist
BRITTEN, Benjamin (1913-76), English composer
THOMAS, Dylan (1914-53), Welsh poet
CRANKO, John (1927-73), English choreographer

ENGLISH OTHER THAN ENGLAND

SWIFT, Jonathan (1667-1745), Anglo-Irish satirist
SCOTT, Walter (1771-1832), Scottish novelist; poet
STEVENSON, Robert Louis (1850-94), Scottish novelist; poet
WILDE, Oscar (1854-1900), Irish writer
YEATS, William Butler (1865-1939), Irish poet; playwright
SYNGE, J.M. (John Millington) (1871-1909), Irish poet; playwright
JOYCE, James (1882-1941), Irish novelist
BECKETT, Samuel (1906-89), Irish-French novelist; playwright
ASHTON-WARNER, Sylvia (1908-84), New Zealand novelist
THOMAS, Dylan (1914-53), Welsh poet

FLEMISH

RUBENS, Peter Paul, Sir (1577-1640), Flemish painter

FRENCH

MOLIERE, Jean Baptiste Poquelin (1622-73), French playwright
BEAUMARCHAIS, Pierre Augustin Caron de (1732-99), French playwright
DELACROIX, Eugène (1798-1863), French painter
BALZAC, Honoré de (1799-1850), French novelist
DUMAS, Alexandre (1802-70), French playwright; novelist
HUGO, Victor Marie (1802-85), French poet; novelist; playwright
SAND, George (1804-76), French novelist
DAUMIER, Honoré (1808-79), French painter; sculptor; caricaturist
CHOPIN, Frédéric (1810-49), Polish-French composer
PERROT, Jules (1810-92), French choreographer
COURBET, Gustave (1819-77), French painter
BAUDELAIRE, Charles (1821-67), French poet
FLAUBERT, Gustave (1821-80), French novelist
FRANCK, César (1822-90), Belgian-French composer
CARPEAUX, Jean-Baptiste (1827-75), French sculptor; painter
VERNE, Jules (1828-1905), French novelist
DEGAS, Edgar (1834-1917), French painter
CEZANNE, Paul (1839-1906), French painter

RODIN, Auguste (1840-1917), French sculptor
ZOLA, Emile (1840-1902), French novelist
FRANCE, Anatole (1844-1924), French novelist
VERLAINE, Paul (1844-96), French poet
GAUGUIN, Paul (1848-1903), French painter; woodcut artist
MAUPASSANT, Guy de (1850-93), French fiction writer; playwright
RIMBAUD, Arthur (1854-91), French poet
DEBUSSY, Claude (1862-1918), French composer
SATIE, Erik (1866-1925), French composer
CLAUDEL, Paul (1868-1955), French playwright; poet
GIDE, André (1869-1951), French novelist
MATISSE, Henri (1869-1954), French painter; sculptor
PROUST, Marcel (1871-1922), French novelist
COLETTE (1873-1954), French novelist
RAVEL, Maurice (1875-1937), French composer
APOLLINAIRE, Guillaume (1880-1918), French poet
GIRAUDOUX, Jean (1882-1944), French playwright; novelist
ALAIN-FOURNIER (1886-1914), French writer
DUCHAMP, Marcel (1887-1968), French painter
BERNANOS, Georges (1888-1948), French novelist
COCTEAU, Jean (1889-1963), French poet; fiction writer
BRETON, André (1896-1966), French writer
SAINT-EXUPERY, Antoine de (1900-44), French prose writer
MALRAUX, André (1901-76), French novelist; writer
BECKETT, Samuel (1906-89), Irish-French novelist; playwright
CAMUS, Albert (1913-60), French novelist; playwright

GERMAN

BACH, Johann Christian (1735-82), German composer
GOETHE, Johann Wolfgang von (1749-1832), German poet; playwright;
    novelist
BEETHOVEN, Ludwig van (1770-1827), German composer
TIECK, Ludwig (1773-1853), German prose writer; poet
KLEIST, Heinrich von (1777-1811), German poet
HEINE, Heinrich (1797-1856), German poet
SCHUBERT, Franz (1797-1828), German composer
MENDELSSOHN-BARTHOLDY, Felix (1809-47), German composer
SCHUMANN, Robert (1810-56), German composer
HEBBEL, Friedrich (1813-63), German playwright
WAGNER, Richard (1813-83), German composer
BRAHMS, Johannes (1833-97), German composer
STRAUSS, Richard (1864-1949), German composer
KOLLWITZ, Käthe (1867-1945), German graphic artist; sculptor
MANN, Heinrich (1871-1950), German novelist
MANN, Thomas (1875-1955), German novelist
RILKE, Rainer Maria (1875-1926), German poet
HESSE, Hermann (1877-1962), German novelist
KAFKA, Franz (1883-1924), German novelist; short story writer
KLEMPERER, Otto (1885-1973), German musician

ERNST, Max (1891-1976), German painter
BRECHT, Bertolt (1898-1956), German playwright; poet

HUNGARIAN

LISZT, Franz (1811-86), Hungarian composer
BARTOK, Béla (1881-1945), Hungarian composer
KODALY, Zoltán (1882-1967), Hungarian composer

INDIAN

TAGORE, Rabindranath (1861-1941), Indian poet; novelist; playwright

ITALIAN

ROSSINI, Gioacchino (1792-1868), Italian composer
VERDI, Giuseppe (1813-1901), Italian composer
D'ANNUNZIO, Gabriele (1863-1938), Italian poet; novelist; playwright
MODIGLIANI, Amedeo (1884-1920), Italian painter

POLISH

CHOPIN, Frédéric (1810-49), Polish-French composer

RUSSIAN

PUSHKIN, Aleksandr Sergeevich (1799-1837), Russian poet; prose writer
GOGOL, Nikolai Vasilevich (1809-52), Russian fiction writer
TURGENEV, Ivan Sergeevich (1818-83), Russian novelist
DOSTOYEVSKY, Fyodor (1821-81), Russian novelist
TOLSTOY, Leo (1828-1910), Russian novelist
TCHAIKOVSKY, Peter Ilich (1840-93), Russian composer
CHEKHOV, Anton Pavlovich (1860-1904), Russian playwright; short story writer
GORKY, Maksim (1868-1936), Russian novelist; short story writer; playwright
BLOK, Aleksandr Aleksandrovich (1880-1921), Russian poet
PAVLOVA, Anna (1881-1931), Russian dancer
CHAGALL, Marc (1889-1985), Russian painter
PASTERNAK, Boris Leonidovich (1890-1960), Russian poet; novelist
PROKOFIEV, Sergey (1891-1953), Russian composer
BULGAKOV, Mikhail Afanasevich (1895-1975), Russian novelist; playwright
ESENIN, Sergei Aleksandrovich (1895-1925), Russian poet
SOLZHENITSYN, Aleksandr Isaevich (1918-   ), Russian novelist

SCANDINAVIAN

IBSEN, Henrik (1828-1906), Norwegian playwright
STRINDBERG, August (1849-1912), Swedish novelist; playwright; poet
LAGERLOF, Selma (1858-1940), Swedish prose writer
DINESEN, Isak (1885-1962), Danish fiction writer

SPANISH ORIGIN

GRECO (1541?-1614), Greek-Spanish painter
CERVANTES SAAVEDRA, Miguel de (1547-1616), Spanish novelist
PICASSO, Pablo (1881-1973), Spanish sculptor; painter; graphic artist
GARCIA LORCA, Federico (1898-1936), Spanish poet; playwright
DALI, Salvador (1904-89), Spanish painter
KAHLO, Frida (1907-54), Mexican painter

SWISS

KLEE, Paul (1879-1940), Swiss painter; graphic artist
GIACOMETTI, Alberto (1901-66), Swiss sculptor; painter

Women Creative Artists Index

ALCOTT, Lousia May (1832-88), American novelist
ASHTON-WARNER, Sylvia (1908-84), New Zealand novelist
AUSTEN, Jane (1775-1817), English novelist
BEHN, Aphra Amis (1640-89), English playwright; novelist
BELL, Vanessa (1879-1961), English painter
BOGAN, Louise (1879-1970), American poet
BRADSTREET, Anne (1612?-72), American poet
BRONTE, Charlotte (1816-55), English novelist; poet
BRONTE, Emily (1818-48), English novelist; poet
BROOKS, Gwendolyn (1917-   ), African-American poet
BROWNING, Elizabeth Barrett (1806-61), English poet
BUCK, Pearl S. (Pearl Sydenstricker) (1892-1973), American novelist
BURNEY, Fanny (1752-1840), English novelist
CASSATT, Mary (1844-1926), American painter
CATHER, Willa (1873-1947), American novelist
CHOPIN, Kate (1851-1904), American novelist
CHRISTIE, Agatha (1891-1976), English novelist
COLETTE (1873-1954), French novelist
COMPTON-BURNETT, I. (Ivy) (1884-1969), English novelist
CONNELL, Clyde (1901-   ), American sculptor
DICKINSON, Emily (1830-86), American poet
DINESEN, Isak (1885-1962), Danish fiction writer
ELIOT, George (1819-80), English novelist
FISHER, Dorothy Canfield (1879-1958), American novelist
FONTANNE, Lynn see (LUNT) FONTANNE, Lynn
FREEMAN, Mary Eleanor Wilkins (1852-1930), American fiction writer
GASKELL, Elizabeth Gleghorn (1810-65), English novelist
GLASGOW, Ellen Anderson Gholson (1873-1945), American novelist
GRAHAM, Martha (1894-   ), American choreographer
GREENAWAY, Kate (1846-1901), English illustrator
H.D. (Hilda Doolittle) (1886-1961), American poet
HELLMAN, Lillian (1906-84), American playwright
HURSTON, Zora Neale (1901-60), African-American writer
KAHLO, Frida (1907-54), Mexican painter
KOLLWITZ, Käthe (1867-1945), German graphic artist; sculptor
LOWELL, Amy (1874-1925), American poet
(LUNT) FONTANNE, Lynn (1887-1983), American actress
MANSFIELD, Katherine (1888-1923), English short story writer
MILLAY, Edna St. Vincent (1892-1950), American poet

O'KEEFFE, Georgia (1887-1986), American painter
OLIPHANT, Margaret (1828-97), English fiction writer
PAVLOVA, Anna (1881-1931), Russian dancer
PLATH, Sylvia (1932-63), American poet
PORTER, Katherine Anne (1890-1980), American short story writer
POTTER, Beatrix (1866-1943), English children's author
ROSSETTI, Christina Georgina (1830-94), English poet
SACKVILLE-WEST, V. (Victoria) (1892-1962), English novelist; poet
SAND, George (1804-76), French novelist
SAYERS, Dorothy L. (Dorothy Leigh) (1893-1957), English story writer
SHELLEY, Mary Wollstonecraft (1797-1851), English novelist
SITWELL, Edith (1887-1964), English poet
STEIN, Gertrude (1874-1946), American fiction writer
TEASDALE, Sara (1884-1933), American poet
WEST, Rebecca (1892-1983), English novelist
WHARTON, Edith (1862-1937), American novelist
WOOLF, Virginia (1882-1941), English novelist

Author Index

Ackroyd, Peter. ELIOT, T.
Adams, Ansel. ADAMS, A.
Adams, Henry. BENTON, T.
Adéma, Pierre-Marcel. APOLLINAIRE, G.
Alexander, Doris. O'NEILL, E.
Allen, Gay Wilson. WHITMAN, W.
Allen, Michael. DICKENS, C.
Alpers, Antony. MANSFIELD, K.
Andersen, Wayne V. GAUGUIN, P.
Arnold, Bruce. ORPEN, W.
Asselineau, Roger. WHITMAN, W.
Atlas, James. SCHWARTZ, D.
Baines, Jocelyn. CONRAD, J.
Bair, Deirdre. BECKETT, S.
Baker, Carlos. HEMINGWAY, E.
Balakian, Anna Elizabeth. BRETON, A.
Bald, R.C. DONNE, J.
Baldwin, Neil. RAY, M.
Barker, Dudley. BENNETT, A.
                 CHESTERTON, G.
Barr, Alfred Hamilton. MATISSE, H.
Bart, Benjamin F. FLAUBERT, G.
Bate, Walter Jackson. KEATS, J.
                      JOHNSON, S.
Battiscombe, Georgina. ROSSETTI, C.
Baur, John I.H. BURCHFIELD, C.
Beer, Thomas. CRANE, S.
Bell, Millicent. MARQUAND, J.
Bennett, Melba Berry. JEFFERS, R.
Benson, Jackson J. STEINBECK, J.
Bergreen, Laurence. AGEE, J.
Berryman, John. CRANE, S.
Berthoud, Roger. SUTHERLAND, G.
Bielschowsky, Albert. GOETHE, J.
Birmingham, Stephen. MARQUAND, J.
Biswas, Robindra Kumar. CLOUGH, A.
Blaukopf, Kurt. MAHLER, G.
Bloch, E. Maurice. BINGHAM, G.
Blotner, Joseph Leo. FAULKNER, W.
Blunt, Wilfrid. MENDELSSOHN-BARTHOLDY, F.
Boswell, James. JOHNSON, S.
Brabazon, James. SAYERS, D.

201

Brennan-Gibson, Margaret. ODETS, C.
Brian, Denis. HEMINGWAY, E.
Broadman, Brigid M. THOMPSON, F.
Brooks, Van Wyck. SLOAN, J.
Brown, Charles Henry. BRYANT, W.
Brown, David. TCHAIKOVSKY, P.
Brown, Jared. LUNT, A. and (LUNT) FONTANNE, L.
Brown, Maurice John Edwin. SCHUBERT, F.
Bruccoli, Matthew Joseph. COZZENS, J.
                           FITZGERALD, F.
                           O'HARA, J.
Buchan, John. SCOTT, W.
Burne-Jones, Georgiana (Macdonald). BURNE-JONES, E.
Butler, E.M. HEINE, H.
Butscher, Edward. AIKEN, C.
                  PLATH, S.
Cady, Edwin H. HOWELLS, W.
Calder, Jenni. STEVENSON, R.
Callahan, North. SANDBURG, C.
Carpenter, Humphrey. AUDEN, W.
                     POUND, E.
Carpenter, Margaret Haley. TEASDALE, S.
Carr, John Dickson. DOYLE, A.
Carr, Virginia Spencer. DOS PASSOS, J.
                        McCULLERS, C.
Carrington, Charles Edmund. KIPLING, R.
Cate, Curtis. SAINT-EXUPERY, A.
              SAND, G.
Chaigne, Louis. CLAUDEL, P.
Cheever, Susan. CHEEVER, J.
Chestnutt, Helen M. CHESTNUTT, C.
Chitham, Edward. BRONTE, E.
Chute, Marchette Gaylord. JONSON, B.
Colvert, James. CRANE, S.
Cottrell, Robert D. COLETTE
Courcel, Martine de. TOLSTOY, L.
Cousins, Paul M. HARRIS, J.
Cowell, Henry and Sidney Cowell. IVES, C.
Cox, Cynthia. BEAUMARCHAIS, P.
Cresson, Margaret French. FRENCH, D.
Crick, Bernard. ORWELL, G.
Cross, Wilbur Lucius. FIELDING, H.
Daiches, David. BURNS, R.
Dale, Alzina Stone. CHESTERTON, G.
Damon, S. Foster. LOWELL, A.
Dark, Sidney and Rowland Grey. GILBERT, W.S.
Davies, Margaret. APOLLINAIRE, G.
Delay, Jean. GIDE, A.
Deutsch, Otto Erich. HANDEL, G.
Dickson, Lovat. WELLS, H.

Donaldson, Scott. CHEEVER, J.
FITZGERALD, F.
Doughty, Oswald. COLERIDGE, S.
Drabble, Margaret. BENNETT, A.
Drake, William. TEASDALE, S.
Dudden, F. Homes. FIELDING, H.
Dunbar, Janet. BARRIE, J.
Eaves, T.C. Duncan and Ben D. Kimpel. RICHARDSON, R.
Edel, Leon. JAMES, H.
Edwards, Owen Dudley. DOYLE, A.
Ehrenpreis, Irvin. SWIFT, J.
Elias, Robert Henry. DREISER, T.
Elledge, Scott. WHITE, E.
Ellmann, Richard. JOYCE, J.
WILDE, O.
Emerson, Everett H. TWAIN, M.
Engen, Rodney K. GREENAWAY, K.
Ewen, David. GERSHWIN, G.
Ewen, Frederic. BRECHT, B.
Fairley, Barker. GOETHE, J.
Farnham, Emily. DEMUTH, C.
Fatout, Paul. BIERCE, A.
Fenton, Charles A. BENET, S.
Ffinch, Michael. CHESTERTON, G.
Finney, Brian. ISHERWOOD, C.
Fitzgerald, Penelope. BURNE-JONES, E.
FitzGibbons, Constantine. THOMAS, D.
Fitzhugh, Robert Tyson. BURNS, R.
Ford, Alice. HICKS, E.
Foster, Edward. FREEMAN, M.
Foster, Malcolm. CARY, J.
Fowlie, Wallace. GIDE, A.
Frank, Elizabeth. BOGAN, L.
Frank, Joseph. DOSTOYEVSKY, F.
Freedman, Ralph. HESSE, H.
Friedenthal, Richard. GOETHE, J.
Furbank, Philip Nicholas. FORSTER, E.
Furnas, J.C. STEVENSON, R.
Gaskell, Elizabeth Cleghorn. BRONTE, C.
Gérin, Winifred. BRONTE, C.
BRONTE, E.
Geiringer, Karl. BRAHMS, J.
HAYDN, J.
Gelb, Arthur and Barbara Gelb. O'NEILL, E.
Gibson, Ian. GARCIA LORCA, F.
Gibson, Robert Donald Davidson. ALAIN-FOURNIER
Gittings, Robert. KEATS, J.
Givner, Joan. PORTER, K.
Glendinning, Victoria. SACKVILLE-WEST, V.
SITWELL, E.
WEST, R.

Godbold, E. Stanly. GLASGOW, E.
Goreau, Angeline. BEHN, A.
Gorman, Herbert Sherman. DUMAS, A.
                         JOYCE, J.
Gosse, Edmund. SWINBURNE, A.
Goudeket, Maurice. COLETTE
Gould, Jean. MILLAY, E.
Grant, Elliott Mansfield. HUGO, V.
Graves, Richard Perceval. GRAVES, R.
                          HOUSMAN, A.
Greene, David H. and Edward M. Stephens. SYNGE, J.
Gregor-Dellim, Martin. WAGNER, R.
Grierson, Herbert John Clifford. SCOTT, W.
Grimm, Hermann Friedrich. GOETHE, J.
Grunfield, Frederic V. RODIN, A.
Guest, Barbara. H.D. (Hilda Doolittle)
Guest, Ivor Forbes. PERROT, J.
Haftmann, Werner. KLEE, P.
Haight, Gordon Sherman. ELIOT, G.
Hale, Nancy. CASSATT, M.
Halperin, John. AUSTEN, J.
Hamilton, Nigel. MANN, H. and MANN, T.
Hammacher, Abraham Marie and Renilde Hammacher. GOGH, V.
Hanson, Lawrence and Elizabeth Hanson. VERLAINE, P.
Harding, James. SATIE, E.
Harrison, Gilbert A. WILDER, T.
Haskell, Barbara. AVERY, M.
Hassell, Christopher. BROOKE, R.
Hayman, Ronald. BRECHT, B.
                KAFKA, F.
Headington, Christopher. BRITTEN, B.
Hemenway, Robert E. HURSTON, Z.
Hemlow, Joyce. BURNEY, F.
Hemmings, F.W.J. BAUDELAIRE, C.
Henderson, Archibald. SHAW, G.
Henderson, Philip. MORRIS, W.
                   SWINBURNE, A.
Hendry, J.F. RILKE, R.
Herrera, Hayden. KAHLO, F.
Hess, Hans. FEININGER, L.
Heyworth, Peter. KLEMPERER, O.
Hibbard, Dominic. OWEN, W.
Higham, Charles. DOYLE, A.
Hildesheimer, Wolfgang. MOZART, W.
Hilles, Frederick Whiley. REYNOLDS, J.
Hingley, Ronald. DOSTOYEVSKY, F.
                 PASTERNAK, B.
Hogwood, Christopher. HANDEL, G.
Holmes, Richard. SHELLEY, P.
Holroyd, Michael. SHAW, G.
Honan, Park. ARNOLD, M.

Hood, Lynley. ASHTON-WARNER, S.
Hoopes, Roy. CAIN, J.
Hopkins, Annette Brown. GASKELL, E.
Howard, Leon. MELVILLE, H.
Huyghe, René. DELACROIX, E.
Hyde, H. Montgomery. WILDE, O.
Indy, Vincent d'. FRANCK, C.
Inskip, Donald Percival. GIRAUDOUX, J.
Irvine, William and Park Honan. BROWNING, R.
Jablonski, Edward. GERSHWIN, G.
Jacobs, Arthur. SULLIVAN, A.
Johnson, Edgar. DICKENS, C.
                SCOTT, W.
Johnson, Thomas Herbert. DICKINSON, E.
Josephson, Matthew. HUGO, V.
Kaplan, Fred. DICKENS, C.
Kaplan, Justin. TWAIN, M.
                WHITMAN, W.
Karl, Frederick R. FAULKNER, W.
                   CONRAD, J.
Keller, Frances Richardson. CHESTNUTT, C.
Kennedy, Michael. ELGAR, E.
Kennedy, Richard S. CUMMINGS, E.
Kent, George E. BROOKS, G.
Kerman, Cynthia Earl and Richard Eldridge. TOOMER, J.
Ketton-Cremer, Robert Wyndham. GRAY, T.
Kiernan, Thomas. STEINBECK, J.
Kilpatrick, Sarah. BURNEY, F.
King, James. COWPER, W.
Kjetsaa, Geir. DOSTOYEVSKY, F.
Klein, Mina C. and H. Arthur Klein. KOLLWITZ, K.
Kossoff, Philip. HEINE, H.
Kripalani, Krishna. TAGORE, R.
Lacouture, Jean. MALRAUX, A.
Lafourcade, Georges. SWINBURNE, A.
Lagercrantz, Olof Gustav Hugo. STRINDBERG, A.
Landau, Ellen G. POLLOCK, J.
Landon, H.C. Robbins. HAYDN, J.
Lane, Margaret. POTTER, B.
Lang, Paul Henry. HANDEL, G.
Langford, Gerald. HENRY, O.
Large, Brian. SMETANA, B.
Larkin, Oliver W. DAUMIER, H.
Lauber, John. TWAIN, M.
Le Vot, André. FITZGERALD, F.
Leppmann, Wolfgang. RILKE, R.
Lesznai, Lajos. BARTOK, B.
Levin, Dan. GORKY, M.
Lewes, George Henry. GOETHE, J.
Lewis, R.W.B. WHARTON, E.

205

Lindsay, Jack. CEZANNE, P.
              TURNER, J.
Lingeman, Richard R. DREISER, T.
Lisle, Laurie. O'KEEFFE, G.
Lockhart, J.G. SCOTT, W.
Lockspeiser, Edward. DEBUSSY, C.
Long, E. Hudson. HENRY, O.
Lord, James. GIACOMETTI, A.
Lottman, Herbert. CAMUS, A.
               FLAUBERT, G.
Ludington, Townsend. DOS PASSOS, J.
Ludwig, Emil. GOETHE, J.
Maass, Joachim. KLEIST, H.
Mack, Gerstle. COURBET, G.
Mack, Maynard. POPE, A.
Mackail, J.W. MORRIS, W.
Mackenzie, Norman and Jeanne Mackenzie. WELLS, H.
                                    DICKENS, C.
Magarshack, David. GOGOL, N.
                    TURGENEV, I.
Mailloux, Peter Alden. KAFKA, F.
Maisel, Edward. GRIFFES, C.
Mallac, Guy de. PASTERNAK, B.
Marchand, Leslie Alexis. BYRON, G.
Marek, George Richard and Maria Gordon-Smith. CHOPIN, F.
Marek, George Richard. BEETHOVEN, L.
                    SCHUBERT, F.
                    STRAUSS, R.
Marquis, Alice Goldfarb. DUCHAMP, M.
Martin, Jay. WEST, N.
Martin, Robert Bernard. TENNYSON, A.
Massie, Allan. COLETTE
Masson, David. MILTON, J.
Matthews, James H. O'CONNOR, F.
Maurois, André. DICKENS, C.
                  DUMAS, A.
                  HUGO, V.
                  BALZAC, H.
                  SAND, G.
McCarthy, Patrick. CAMUS, A.
McKay, Nellie Y. TOOMER, J.
McKendrick, Melveena. CERVANTES SAAVEDRA, M.
McMullen, Roy. DEGAS, E.
McVay, Gordon. ESENIN, S.
Mee, Charles. REMBRANDT HARMENSZOON van RIJN
Mellow, James R. STEIN, G.
Meyer, Michael Leverson. IBSEN, H.
                         STRINDBERG, A.
Meyers, Jeffrey. LEWIS, W.
Miller, Betty Bergson Spiro. BROWNING, R.
Millgate, Michael. HARDY, T.

Milne, Hamish. BARTOK, B.
Minter, David L. FAULKNER, W.
Mitchell, Yvonne. COLETTE
Mochulskii, K. (Konstantin). BLOK, A.
Money, Keith. PAVLOVA, A.
Moore, Jerrold Northrop. ELGAR, E.
Moore, John Robert. DEFOE, D.
Morgan, Charles Hill. BELLOWS, G.
Morgan, Janet P. CHRISTIE, A.
Morgan, Ted. MAUGHAM, W.
Moser, Charlotte. CONNELL, C.
Mossberg, Barbara Antonina Clarke. DICKINSON, E.
Mount, Charles Merrill. STUART, G.
Nadeau, Maurice. FLAUBERT, G.
Najder, Zdzislaw. CONRAD, J.
Nehls, Edward. LAWRENCE, D.H.
Newhall, Nancy. ADAMS, A.
Newman, Ernest. WAGNER, R.
Nordon, Pierre. DOYLE, A.
O'Brien, Justin. GIDE, A.
O'Brien, Sharon. CATHER, W.
O'Connor, Garry. O'CASEY, S.
                 RICHARDSON, R.
O'Connor, Richard. HARTE, B.
Oates, Stephen B. FAULKNER, W.
Olson, Stanley. SARGENT, J.
Osborne, Charles. AUDEN, W.
                  VERDI, G.
Ouelette, Fernand. VARESE, E.
Page, Norman. HOUSMAN, A.
Painter, George Duncan. GIDE, A.
                        PROUST, M.
Palmer, John L. MOLIERE, J.
Parker, William Riley. MILTON, J.
Paulin, Roger. TIECK, L.
Paulson, Ronald. HOGARTH, W.
Pawel, Ernst. KAFKA, F.
Payne, Robert. MALRAUX, A.
Peacock, Carlos. BONINGTON, R.
Pearson, Hesketh. GILBERT, W.
                  WILDE, O.
Penrose, Roland. PICASSO, P.
Percival, John. CRANKO, J.
Petitfils, Pierre. RIMBAUD, A.
Peyser, Joan. BERNSTEIN, L.
Pope-Hennessy, James. STEVENSON, R.
                      TROLLOPE, A.
Pope-Hennessy, John Wyndham. CELLINI, B.
Pound, Reginald. BENNETT, A.
Pritchard, William H. FROST, R.

Pritchett, V.S. BALZAC, H.
            CHEKHOV, A.
            TURGENEV, I.
Proffer, Ellendea. BULGAKOV, M.
Purdie, Edna. HEBBEL, F.
Pyman, Avril. BLOK, A.
Quennell, Peter. POPE, A.
Rader, Dotson. WILLIAMS, T.
Rampersad, Arnold. HUGHES, L.
Ray, Gordon Norton. THACKERAY, W.
Rewald, John. CEZANNE, P.
Rhodes, Anthony Richard Ewart. D'ANNUNZIO, G.
Richardson, Joanna. COLETTE
Riggs, David. JONSON, B.
Robertson, John George. GOETHE, J.
Robinson, Harlow Loomis. PROKOFIEV, S.
Rogers, Pat. FIELDING, H.
Rollyson, Carl E. HELLMAN, L.
Rossiter, Frank R. IVES, C.
Rubin, Louis Decimus. CABLE, G.
Russell, John. ERNST, M.
Sartre, Jean-Paul. FLAUBERT, G.
Saxton, Martha. ALCOTT, L.
Scammell, Michael. SOLZHENITSYN, A.
Schaeffer, Louis. O'NEILL, E.
Schneider, Pierre. MATISSE, H.
Schönzeler, Hans Hubert. BRUCKNER, A.
Schorer, Mark. LEWIS, S.
Secrest, Meryle. DALI, S.
Sewall, Richard Benson. DICKINSON, E.
Seyd, Felizia. SAND, G.
Seyersted, Per. CHOPIN, K.
Seymour-Smith, Martin. GRAVES, R.
Shapiro, Leonard Bertram. TURGENEV, I.
Sherburn, George Wiley. POPE, A.
Sherry, Norman. GREENE, G.
Shivers, Alfred S. ANDERSON, M.
Sichel, Pierre. MODIGLIANI, A.
Simmons, Ernest Joseph. PUSHKIN, A.
                        TOLSTOY, L.
Simpson, Charles Walter. BRONTE, E.
Skelton, Geoffrey. HINDEMITH, P.
Smith, C. Alphonso. HENRY, O.
Snyder, Franklyn Bliss. BURNS, R.
Solomon, Deborah. POLLOCK, J.
Solomon, Maynard. BEETHOVEN, L.
Spaulding, Frances. BELL, V.
Speaight, Robert. BELLOC, H.
                   BERNANOS, G.
Spoto, Donald. WILLIAMS, T.
Sprigge, Elizabeth and Jean-Jacques Kihm. COCTEAU, J.

Spurling, Hilary. COMPTON-BURNETT, I.
Squires, Radcliffe. TATE, A.
Stallman, R.W. CRANE, S.
Stallworthy, Jon. OWEN, W.
Stannard, Martin. WAUGH, E.
Stansky, Peter and William Abrahams. ORWELL, G.
Starkie, Enid. BAUDELAIRE, C.
                FLAUBERT, G.
Steegmuller, Francis. APOLLINAIRE, G.
                      COCTEAU, J.
                      MAUPASSANT, G.
Stevenson, Anne. PLATH, S.
Stevenson, Lionel. MEREDITH, G.
                   THACKERAY, W.
Stewart, George Rippey. HARTE, B.
Stewart, Randall. HAWTHORNE, N.
Stillman, Clara Gruening. BUTLER, S.
Stirling, Nora B. BUCK, P.
Stodelle, Ernestine. GRAHAM, M.
Storey, Edward. CLARE, J.
Stuckenschmidt, Hans Heinz. RAVEL, M.
                            SCHOENBERG, A.
Sunstein, Emily W. SHELLEY, M.
Super, R.H. TROLLOPE, A.
Sutherland, James Runcieman. DEFOE, D.
Sutton, Denys. DEGAS, E.
Sweet, Frederick Arnold. CASSATT, M.
Sykes, Christopher. WAUGH, E.
Symons, Julian. POE, E.
Taper, Bernard. BALANCHINE, G.
Taplin, Gardner B. BROWNING, E.
Taylor, Judy. POTTER, B.
Taylor, Ronald. LISZT, F.
                SCHUMANN, R.
Tennant, Roger. CONRAD, J.
Tennyson, Charles. TENNYSON, A.
Terry, Charles Stanford. BACH, J.
Thayer, Alexander Wheelock. BEETHOVEN, L.
Thomas, Donald Serrell. BROWNING, R.
Thompson, Lawrence. FROST, R.
Thurman, Judith. DINESEN, I.
Tischler, Nancy Marie Patterson. WILLIAMS, T.
Tomalin, Claire. MANSFIELD, K.
Townsend, Kim. ANDERSON, S.
Toye, Francis. VERDI, G.
Troyat, Henri. CHEKHOV, A.
               GORKY, M.
               TOLSTOY, L.
               TURGENEV, I.